POWER DENIED

BY

ROBERT BALL

Power Denied

Copyright © Robert Ball 2025

First published in Great Britain in 2025 by London Book Publishing

Copyright © 2025 Robert Ball

Robert Ball has asserted his moral rights to be identified as the author

A CIP Catalogue of this book is available from the British Library

ISBN

All rights reserved; no part of this publication may be reproduced, stored in a retrieval system, or transmitted, in any form or by any means, electronic, mechanical, photocopying, recording or otherwise, without the prior written permission of the publisher. Nor be circulated in any form of binding or cover other than that in which it is published and a similar condition including this condition being imposed on the subsequent purchaser.

Robert Ball

Table Of Contents

Dedication viii
List of Characters ix
Part One Envisioning – From June 1
Chapter One 2
Chapter Two 4
Chapter Three 8
Chapter Four 11
Chapter Five 15
Chapter Six 17
Chapter Seven 23
Chapter Eight 25
Chapter Nine 32
Chapter Ten 44
Chapter Eleven 46
Chapter Twelve 54
Chapter Thirteen 56
Chapter Fourteen 58
Chapter Fifteen 61
Chapter Sixteen 70
Chapter Seventeen 75
Chapter Eighteen 77
Chapter Nineteen 80

Chapter Twenty.. 82

Chapter Twenty-One 84

Chapter Twenty-Two 93

Chapter Twenty-Three 94

Chapter Twenty-Four.. 96

Chapter Twenty-Five... 101

Chapter Twenty-Six 103

Chapter Twenty-Seven 106

Chapter Twenty-Eight... 109

Part Two Executing – December 111

Chapter Twenty-Nine 112

Chapter Thirty 115

Chapter Thirty-One 117

Chapter Thirty-Two 121

Chapter Thirty-Three 124

Chapter Thirty-Four.. 126

Chapter Thirty-Five... 128

Chapter Thirty-Six 130

Chapter Thirty-Seven 133

Chapter Thirty-Eight... 137

Chapter Thirty-Nine.. 139

Chapter Forty 142

Chapter Forty-One 144

Chapter Forty-Two.. 147

Chapter Forty-Three 157

Chapter Forty-Four 159

Chapter Forty-Five 164

Chapter Forty-Six 171

Chapter Forty-Seven 173

Chapter Forty-Eight 177

Chapter Forty-Nine 180

Chapter Fifty 186

Chapter Fifty-One 190

Chapter Fifty-Two 193

Chapter Fifty-Three 199

Chapter Fifty-Four 201

Part Three Embedding - From January 1st 204

Chapter Fifty-Five 205

Chapter Fifty-Six 212

Chapter Fifty-Seven 215

Chapter Fifty-Eight 218

Chapter Fifty-Nine 223

Chapter Sixty 226

Chapter Sixty-One 228

Chapter Sixty-Two 231

Chapter Sixty-Three 235

Chapter Sixty-Four 238

Chapter Sixty-Five 242

Chapter Sixty-Six 245

Chapter Sixty-Seven 249

Chapter Sixty-Eight 258
Chapter Sixty-Nine 261
Chapter Seventy 263
Chapter Seventy-One 266
Chapter Seventy-Two 271
Chapter Seventy-Three 274
Chapter Seventy-Four 276
Chapter Seventy-Five 283
Chapter Seventy-Six 285
Chapter Seventy-Seven 288
Chapter Seventy-Eight 291
Chapter Seventy-Nine 295
Chapter Eighty 297
Chapter Eighty-One 301
Chapter Eighty-Two 304
Chapter Eighty-Three 308
Chapter Eighty-Four 311
Chapter Eighty-Five 316
Chapter Eighty-Six 319
Chapter Eighty-Seven 321
Chapter Eighty-Eight 323
Chapter Eighty-Nine 328
Chapter Ninety 331
Chapter Ninety-One 332
Chapter Ninety-Two 335

Chapter Ninety-Three 338

Chapter Ninety-Four 340

Chapter Ninety-Five 342

Chapter Ninety-Six 346

Chapter Ninety-Seven 349

Chapter Ninety-Eight 351

Chapter Ninety-Nine 353

Chapter One Hundred 355

Chapter One Hundred & One 359

Chapter One Hundred & Two 362

Chapter One Hundred & Three 364

Chapter One Hundred & Four 366

Dedication

For the love and support:
Natalie and her family
Francisca
Why, my dog

List of Characters

Russia

Mikhail Sokolov	Politburo member responsible for expansion
Dmitriy Morazov	Special Projects Executive
Boris Gusev	Deputy to Sokolov
Vladimir Vasiliev	President of Russia
Aleksandr Bychkov	Foreign Minister
General Ivan Asimov	Chief of the General Staff
Natalia Agapov Morazov	Wife of Dmitriy
Leonid Popov	Minister of Armaments
Lev Novikov	Minister of Health

United Kingdom

Sir Reginald Crosby	Minister and MP for Peterborough West
Stuart Graham	Journalist
Antonia Hyams	Special Advisor
Julia Jones	Prime Minister
Gemma Newman	Foreign Secretary
John Jones	Husband of Julie Jones
Raymond Burke	Leader of the Nostalgia Party
Dick Dickenson	Chairman of the Nostalgia Party

Alex Nolan	British citizen
Isabella Nolan	Alex' mother
Phil Nolan	Alex' father
Jamie Goodwin	Alex' friend
King Philip	Monarch of the United Kingdom
Youcef Mustafa	Valet to King Philip
Andrea Evans	Journalist
Robert Harper	Lecturer
Queen Priscilla	Wife of King Philip
Gordon Godfrey	Government Official

United States of America

Bob Cartwright	Director of the CIA
Eleanor Cartwright	Wife of Bob Cartwright
Chuck Keaton	President of the USA
Sally Keaton	Wife of Chuck Keaton
Dorothy Harkins	Executive Secretary to the President
Chip Weaver	Chief of Staff
Brett Armstrong	Secretary of Defense
Ronald Malone	Former President
Bart Boulter	Billionaire
General Hank Maloney	Chief-of-Staff, US Army
Brett Taylor Malone	Advisor to Ronald
Bill Banks	Head of Security

Cheryl Simpson-Walters for Bart Boulter	Communications lead
Herb Andrews	Oklahoma resident
Cheryl Simpson-Walters for Bart Boulter	Communications lead
Dolly Andrews	Herb's wife
Dana Heaton	Herb's daughter
Cinnamon Heaton	Herb's granddaughter
James 'Griff' Griffin	Texas Senator
Jed Heaton	Dana's husband
Kerry Smith	Executive Aide
Doctor Joanne Fraser	Medical Researcher
Michael Wayne	Sheriff, Chickasaw
Hank Wayne	Michael's Brother
Holly Marchant	Government Official
Gloria Frost	Housewife
Grace Williams	Journalist
Yvonne Long	US Senator

China

Huang Peng	President
Xiu Feng Wang	Deputy President
Zhou Chen	Minister for Defence
Duan Bai Bolin	Minister of Health
Chang Wei Lei	Minister for Coordination

Canada

Brian Quick	Prime Minister
Sylvia Anderson	Deputy Prime Minister
Geraldine Quick	Finance Minister
Frank O'Farrell	Business Minister

North Korea

Paik Han-Jae	President

South Korea

Yun Dong-woo	President

Turkey

Mehmet Akbas	President

Germany

Uwe Haller	President

Estonia

Sofia Hommik	President

Iran

Ayatollah Ahmad Shirvani	Supreme Leader

Ireland

Padraig Kelly	Taoiseach
Portia Green	Cabinet Member
Sinead O'Meara	Cabinet Member

Egypt

Babu Hussain	President

Robert Ball

Morocco
Yousef Chakir — President

Nigeria
Happy Imeh — President

Mozambique
Angelino Pinto — President

Saudi Arabia
Prince Omar Abbas — Prime Minister

India
Raaz Subramanian — Prime Minister

Nepal
Ram Tapadia — Prime Minister
Yousef Chakir — President

Singapore
Lee Michael — Prime Minister

Indonesia
Bimo Agung — President

Australia
Graham Lee — Prime Minister

Fiji
Rupeni Ratu — Prime Minister

Brazil
Paulo Oliveira — President

Venezuela

Victor Leon — President
Lee Michael — Prime Minister

Democratic Republic of the Congo

Charles Ekoku — President

Japan

Akio Hitachi — Emperor

Vatican City

Pope Leonardo — Head of the Catholic Church

Robert Ball

Part One
Envisioning – From June

Chapter One

Sir Reginald Crosby was, as always, brimming with confidence and self-importance.

"This proves, as I have always said, the Russians are no match for our boffins."

Sir Reginald, and it was *Sir Reginald* to everyone except his family, and from whom he would have preferred more respect, was standing in the Lobby of the Houses of Parliament in London. The day before, UK security services had detected and thwarted an attempt to hack into the IT systems of *The Times* newspaper.

"Our democracy demands the Fourth Estate remains free to express opinions, reveal facts, and never be cowed by foreigners."

This sweeping statement conveniently overlooked his own recent criticism of the paper. Just two weeks earlier, *The Times* had published an article which exposed an allocation of government funds to a 'close associate' of Sir Reginald. At that time, anyone within earshot would have gathered that this organ of the media was, in his view, a leaderless and useless rag.

The assembled journalists made notes with little intention of ever referring to them again. This was merely the latest in a long line of supposed victories against the might of Russia.

A newly appointed political reporter, Stuart Graham, from one of the red tops, and therefore not yet as cynical or blasé as his peers, asked, "We hear a great deal about our successes in stopping damage to our institutions. Is it reasonable for us to assume that Britain's enemies never succeed?"

"Of course, they never do. Impossible, as the security of Britain is in the hands of the finest brains in the world."

The Member of Parliament for Peterborough West was not a man to care about mixed metaphors, yet saw every situation as a time for hyperbole.

"To slightly misquote a former Head of MI5, terrorists only have to be lucky once, whereas the authorities need to be lucky all of the time. Is national security certain to enjoy perpetual good fortune?" Graham persisted.

"Good grief, yes!" Sir Reginald almost shouted.

None of the assembled journalists laughed at the pomposity, and his vehemence was largely dismissed. Nobody truly believed this 69-year-old junior minister, whose background was in public relations, was a true authority on cyber security. He was a mouthpiece or perhaps, more accurately, a foghorn.

As people drifted away, Sir Reginald turned to his Special Advisor, usually known as a SPAD, and uttered, "Well, I think that went well. Let me buy you lunch, Antonia."

Antonia Hyams smiled in a way that seemed genuine but belied her real thoughts. Lunch would be fine, at least it wasn't dinner with its accompanying wandering hands. Her most prominent thought, however, was that Sir Reginald's tie would look better without egg stains.

Chapter Two

Russia in winter was a bleak place, or at least 98% of the country was. Since the retreat from the days of President Gorbachev and Perestroika, the atmosphere had become equally gloomy. The Kremlin's message was clear: the whole world sought to obliterate Russia, and only strong nationalism could prevent disaster. The prevailing attitude from everyone, from government officials to street cleaners, was one of defensiveness. There was an underlying sense of negativity, punctuated by brief flashes of hope for reclaiming the Russian Empire, its lands and peoples, as many believed, rightfully theirs.

Dmitriy Morazov entered the headquarters of the Federal Security Service of the Russian Federation, better known as the FSB. The FSB was the latest incarnation of the feared organisation once known as the Committee for State Security, the KGB. In the West, people still ignorantly referred to it as the KGB, despite the name having changed in 1991.

As Morazov reached the desk in reception a perky young woman approached him.

"Comrade Morazov?"

Dmitriy knew that she knew him, or he wouldn't have made it two yards into the building without being forcibly restrained, and his photo was undoubtedly in the 'system'. Still, he was naturally polite.

"I am. How may I help you?"

"Comrade Sokolov has asked you to meet him at 63 Putin Place. You are to go there immediately. I will inform his office I have passed on the message and that you are on your way."

He smiled. Not only was he clear this was an order, but he also noted the woman had proven her worth. A small step forward, but every journey begins with the first step. Was he allowed to think of the thoughts of Chairman Mao? Presumably he was, as his state-funded education had taken him across the world, including to China, the United States of America, and the United Kingdom.

With a swift about turn Morazov stepped back onto the freezing street. Putin Place was only a five-minute walk away, but in the sub-zero temperatures of the day, he scurried along. The streets were quiet as nobody wanted to venture outside. Of course, he could have been driven everywhere but he was naturally active. His time in the army had reinforced this habit, and walking gave him a little more time to think. As per his boss Mikhail Sokolov's edict, he never carried papers. There could be no risk, however remote the chance, of classified information being seen by unauthorised eyes.

The revised venue for the meeting at Putin Place was grey. Even the doors were painted grey, with not even the usual relief of 'shit brown'. Having recognised the dowdy façade, he also acknowledged his own attire was equally understated. To amuse himself, Morazov always wore colourful socks. Whilst he imagined this went unnoticed, there was a line in his personal file but there was no comment, just an observation for others to consider. Nothing went unnoticed, and deep down, he knew this really.

In 53 Putin Place there was no reception, as there were never outside visitors and there was no need to maintain any illusion of normality, as perceived by the rest of the world. Morazov approached the first door and stepped through. Above the portal a sign which read: 'One person at a time.'

Inside was a small, enclosed space. The door created, in effect, a cubicle. It closed almost immediately behind him. Facial recognition software scanned his features. Only after confirming his identity did the second door open.

The FSB used this building for meetings. Amongst the general public it was rumoured that there was a basement room supposedly impenetrable to prying eyes and ears. Only the most senior officials could book it. Morazov always met Sokolov there.

Mikhail Sokolov was waiting, not impatiently, but passively. There would be no meeting today more critical to Russia's future than this one.

Morazov pressed his hand against the pad beside the door and entered. The door closed behind him with a very gentle hiss. He was unaware that both his facial and eye recognition had also been verified.

This was the latest meeting of Operation No Tanks. There were only the two of them there.

"Comrade Sokolov."

"Comrade Morazov."

They shook hands, a highly unusual gesture from the older and more senior man. Whilst he very much liked his subordinate, the handshake symbolised the nature of their work in which they were both involved, work which could literally mean death or lead to spectacular glory. There was nothing spectacular about death.

"Let's be brief. Progress?"

"Excellent, sir," replied Morazov.

"Great but, and this is crucial, we are expected to report to the President. When can we be confident enough to reveal our plans?"

"If it is just an interim update, it could be next week. However, to be sure of success, we need another six months before pressing the button."

Sokolov paused. This would be his final role given he was seventy-three years old and there was no further promotion available. If this went wrong, it wouldn't just be the end of a distinguished career, it would be the end of his life. Every move they would make could be fatal.

This was to be a discussion, not a decision-making meeting. Still, they had to update the President at some point. Sokolov made up his mind.

"I will set up the meeting with the President. Do you need anything from me at this point?"

"Guidance on the relationship with China. How do we position it when we speak to the President?"

"Well, it is the big one. Let me think about it, and we will agree our approach."

They left the room together. Morazov walked out of the building and returned to his office.

Chapter Three

In Washington, the Director of the Central Intelligence Agency (CIA), Bob Cartwright, was waiting to meet with the President, Chuck Keaton.

The two men had worked together on and off for nearly thirty years and were very comfortable in each other's presence.

Dorothy Harkins, the President's Executive Secretary, had also been with Keaton for many years. She was always in the office before him and rarely left until he had retired to the residence. One of the changes she had introduced at the White House was to have a dedicated closet created for extra clothes for herself and a supply of clean shirts for Keaton. She was always immaculately attired.

"How are you, Mr Cartwright?"

"Dorothy, how long have we known each other? Please call me Bob."

"Not whilst we are in this place."

"How far behind schedule is he?"

Harkins glanced at her computer screen and smiled.

"Only forty-five minutes. I will delay his next meeting with one of his personal staff, so you will be in before you know it."

The door to the Oval Office opened and the leader of the Free World stepped out.

"Dorothy, could you put Tim off, and I'll see Bob now?"

"Already done, Mr President." She was hyper-efficient and liked people to know it. Her colleagues often described her as precise and precious.

Keaton and Cartwright stepped into the Oval Office. As the door closed, Keaton turned and smiled at his friend.

"Bob, how is Eleanor?"

"Very well, thank you, Sir."

"You know when we're alone you can call me Chuck," Keaton said with a grin.

"I do, and I'm humbled, but if I allow myself to slip, I might do it in front of others. I need the discipline of always calling you Mr President."

Again, Keaton smiled. That was the nature of the man: a good man.

The President then switched to work mode.

"My early morning briefing implied increased activity in North Korea and Iran. Why now?"

Cartwright was usually unflustered. However, his own detailed reports had offered little insight into why these two countries were adopting more aggressive postures.

"Beyond the usual machismo, internal power struggles, and citizen suppression, we don't know. None of our intercepted communications indicated any coordination between them. One small but interesting detail is that both have sent concurrent messages to Turkey, as well as Russia, of course."

"Turkey!" Keaton whispered.

"One of our key allies talking to our most dangerous opponents. Not a first, but certainly unusual. It may be of no consequence."

"And Russia?"

Cartwright was on firmer ground.

"A persistent itch. They deny everything while stirring up trouble across the globe. We have nothing substantial to report beyond their usual behaviour."

"Isn't that unsettling in itself? That mini dictator won't like a lack of expansionist movement."

"As you know, we hear all of their communications, and we have an operative in a significant position."

Keaton grunted and Cartwright recognised the meeting was over. He hadn't alarmed the President, but he hadn't assuaged his nervousness about Russia and its acolytes either.

Chapter Four

In Moscow, Mikhail Sokolov returned to his office. The room was spacious, befitting his seniority, but the furniture was old. He liked it that way. Brown wooden chairs, a sturdy table, and a sofa into which everyone sank as they sat down. It was an intentional psychological ploy that left visitors subconsciously vulnerable.

His desk was clear except for a phone, a notebook, and a pen. Sokolov wasn't just security crazy; he operated on a different level. He even had a paper shredder next to his desk, ready to destroy anything he wrote before the remnants were transported in a sealed bag to the incinerator.

The door opened and Boris Gusev entered.

"My little goose, how are you?"

"Very well, thank you," Gusev replied. He continued, "And how are the Politburo's machinations?"

Gusev was the only person from whom Sokolov would have accepted this level of familiarity. Short and balding, Gusev had served as Sokolov's aide for twenty-six years and, as the saying went, knew where the skeletons were buried. Indeed, some of which he had buried himself on his boss' behalf.

"What's your honest opinion of Dmitriy Morazov?"

"I trust him as much as any man."

"So, not much then," Sokolov quipped, and they both laughed.

Gusev elaborated, "I actually like him. My trust is as strong as I would ever allow it to be. And, of course, it helps that my niece is married to him, and she tells me everything. Not that there's much to tell. He is never indiscreet, and there's no pillow talk. She knows enough about our work to recognise even the smallest misstep."

Sokolov considered this.

With admirable timing, Dmitriy Morazov joined them.

"Morazov, you and I are going to brief the President next week about Operation No Tanks. Please clear your diary from now until next Tuesday. We'll be living in Putin Place to make sure we get this absolutely right."

It was nearly 9 p.m. when Dmitriy Morazov arrived home, early by his standards.

"Dearest, I'm home."

Natalia Agapov Morazov was the most wonderful person he had ever known and, as a bonus, she was stunning looking; tall, slim, and perfectly proportioned. Better still, Natalia was intelligent and kind.

She, in turn, adored him. Their love had grown long before he had become a powerful rising star in the Kremlin. He was openly talked about as a superstar, though she just wished she could persuade him to stop wearing fluorescent, vividly coloured socks.

Natalia knew better than to ask about the details of his day but was always attentive to Dmitriy's need to relax, unwind, and escape the stresses of his job.

"Hello. You do know I'd love you even if you ran a corner shop with, almost inevitably, empty shelves. Why put yourself through 15-hour days and God knows what worries and pressures?"

"I can't take that chance. Please give me a head massage."

Natalia smiled. "We both know where that ends, don't we?"

"Okay, let's skip the massage!"

"Eat first, then we have all the time we want."

"Darling, I have to sleep at the office for the next five nights. Sokolov wants me to work with him on something. Can we please forget dinner? I need to be back at work by 5 o'clock tomorrow morning and I can eat then. You, on the other hand, won't be."

"Good grief, what is it you are doing?"

"I don't know, but when the boss speaks, I listen."

The next morning Morazov arrived in Putin Place's basement at 4.55 a.m., but he wasn't the first there. Gusev greeted him warmly. The sincerity he felt was reinforced by his niece's text confirming Dmitriy had given no clues about his current task. He was the very essence of discretion.

Gusev had already brought into the room the food and coffee which had been left outside in the corridor. Even staff with the highest security clearance were not permitted inside this room, not even to provide sustenance.

Sokolov entered. The door made a sharp buzzing noise, making them glance up instinctively. This was the biggest thing with which they had ever been involved or ever would be again. Their caution was beyond security conscious; it bordered on paranoia.

"Gentlemen, let's eat first so we can focus. I suggest we work in two-hour bursts. Focus and concentration only lasts so long. Then we eat and urinate, but not simultaneously."

They all laughed, a little too loudly. It was a moment of release, breaking the tension that had them all 'by the balls'.

The room was set up for work. Flipcharts, pens, an overhead projector, stacks of paper but everything was deliberately low-tech. Nothing would be committed to a laptop until the last possible moment. Even then, the laptop would be a brand-new, air-gapped device, having never been connected to the internet.

Chapter Five

In London, the Prime Minister was discussing diplomacy with her Foreign Secretary.

"Did you see that fat prat Reggie Crosby the other day pontificating on the TV news?"

"I did. Thank God, we never let him into any meetings, even low-level ones. He couldn't keep his mouth shut."

Julia Jones had been Prime Minister for three years and was reasonably well respected both in the UK and overseas. She knew when to opine and when to listen. Gemma Newman was her closest political ally and had been at the Foreign Office for most of Julia's tenure.

Gemma's greatest strength was her deep understanding of languages and cultures. In meetings with German and French officials, she never needed a translator. This was particularly useful when her counterparts assumed she couldn't understand their asides, as she had gleaned many valuable insights this way. Few people knew she was also fluent in Russian and Mandarin, and that was precisely how she wanted it.

Gemma asked, "Has MI6 been briefing you about Russia?" MI6 being the UK's Secret Intelligence Service.

"Only to say things are very quiet. Do you know something?"

"Not exactly. I just don't like the sense of inactivity. Are they up to something?"

"What is the Director of GCHQ saying?" GCHQ - the Government Communications Headquarters - based in

Gloucestershire towards the west of England. It is populated by the brightest spooks.

"Nothing, as he is convinced their surveillance abilities are so advanced that the Russians can't fart without us being able to smell it. Perhaps we should consult Reggie Crosby, as he knows everything."

Neither of them chuckled but the levity helped manage the stress.

Chapter Six

Mikhail Sokolov, Boris Gusev, and Dmitriy Morazov stood in the outer office of the President of Russia. The first two were familiar with him, but for Dmitriy this was his first experience of the man face-to-face.

All meetings with the President began late, but it would not have been wise to be tardy. He was aware of everything and not overly forgiving. However, at exactly the agreed time the door was pulled back and the President walked out to greet them. This was beyond unexpected, it was unprecedented.

"Come in, my friends. Take coffee, take pastries."

Sokolov, especially, was taken aback. Why is this happening? he wondered. Given the gravity of the presentation which they were about to deliver, why was President Vasiliev being so warmly welcoming?

The President walked into his office and the others followed. Already seated was the Foreign Minister, Aleksandr Bychkov, also known as "the Bull." It was said that his head was bigger than any man in Asia. Upon hearing this, Bychkov had played along, claiming it needed to be to accommodate a brain the size of his.

President Vladimir Vasiliev was below medium height but muscular. He was proud of his physical condition and revealed it as often as possible. He believed it brought him success with women and the respect of men. Of course, it was also possible that his influence stemmed from his position as one of the most powerful people in the world.

They sat around a large circular table. Morazov plugged in his laptop and connected it to the projector.

The President began.

"Gentlemen, we are, without doubt the five most powerful people in the world. I say this not to boast or boost your egos, though we all know we have big ones."

There was a gentle murmur of self-deprecating laughter.

Vasiliev continued.

"We all know this is a plan which, if executed properly, will change the world and bestow upon us control of the it. Since the first meeting, to which I know you weren't invited, Dmitriy, I have been more than excited about its potential for us."

Vasiliev paused for effect.

"Everyone speaks very, very highly of you, Morazov. Tell me, what colour are your socks?"

"Red, sir. Unfortunately, the same colour as my face, now that you ask the question."

They all laughed naturally, and the ice was broken. The President knew how to handle a room full of men. He was only truly comfortable in conversations with women when they were one-to-one.

"My first topic is security. Could that computer have been accessed?"

"No, Mr President. It is air-gapped and has never been connected to the internet."

This was a significant moment for Morazov the first direct contribution to the leader of his country, a man he held in awe.

Vasiliev looked around the room.

"In the interests of progress, for today only, in this meeting only, and in this office only, you may refer to me as VV. You are, after all, four of the five most powerful people in the world."

Even Bychkov had never called his boss VV. He recognised this was an expression of deep trust.

"Now tell me, how we can have thousands of people working on this and yet there have been no leaks?"

Now Dmitriy Morazov was in his area of expertise, "Firstly, everyone is involved in only one aspect of the project. Their supervisors will see several aspects but cannot know the real, true objective. They are being very well rewarded, mainly because they are spending months away from home and with no means of communicating with the outside world. They are housed, held if you like, in highly restricted buildings in remote parts of the country.

"Finally, they understand the consequences of even asking to leave. They will be held in total solitary confinement. This has already been the case for three junior operatives. I am sad to say one attempted to escape and was shot dead. We have made sure that everyone involved in this work knows what happened."

VV, as he was temporarily known, nodded.

"How does it all come together?"

"That is my job. I do have senior staff, but they all believe we are going to indulge in large scale terrorism and interference."

"If I'm honest, I was certain that by now my security chief would have been pestering me to understand what's going on and why he isn't included in the discussion. So, I am confident that your admirable caution and meticulous attention to detail are paying off."

The other men nodded. The early tension gradually lifted, as the focus shifted to the work rather than avoiding behavioural gaffes.

"Moving on," said the President. "Before we delve into detail, and detail we will delve into, give me the current overview."

Sokolov began, "A single technological breakthrough has allowed us to access every website, every domain, every online system in the whole world. There is no defence against our keyboard wizards.

"At a single moment in time, we will metaphorically flick a switch, and the globe will black out. There will be no communications, except face-to-face; there will be no internet, no phone systems, and all weaponry connected to the web will be useless. We could, if we wished, conquer every nation except China and its connected territories, which we have assumed will remain sovereign, unless you wish to encompass them as well."

President Vasiliev was adamant.

"China is protected. President Huang is a friend and, whilst he has no idea of this breakthrough, we have always committed to maintaining our respective national integrity. So, that is the first major decision. Dmitriy, are you taking notes?"

"No, sir. I won't leave anything for others to find."

"Thank you. Good."

Morazov then described the technical processes in detail. The President nodded dutifully but was itching to move on to the practical and political aspects of the plan.

"It sounds compelling, Dmitriy. But it will only succeed if, and it's a big if, it all happens simultaneously. Can it?"

"I agree. It can and it will. The 'how' has been certain for months. The time has been spent synchronising it all together."

Morazov took a breath. He had just staked his career on that statement. He thought of Natalia and how she would react if he failed. Then he realised she would never even know his fate. It would be terminal.

"One more time, please. There is no defence. The Pentagon in the USA, GCHQ in Britain, none of our enemies know our plans, nor can they defend themselves. Is that correct?"

"Correct," said Sokolov and Gusev in unison.

"You agree as well, Dmitriy?"

"I know every word I utter today confirms my faith in the plan, recognising as I do, the personal ramifications. This is more than a plan or strategy; it is my life."

Vasiliev was impressed and said so. They moved on.

"When we switch everything off at the same time there will be consequences. We are working to isolate communications between aircraft and the ground to allow them to land at the nearest airport. This is proving difficult and may be too much for us. It would result in crashes. Life support machines in hospitals will stop, trains will grind to a halt, lifts will be stuck between floors and there will be many other local problems. My personal fear is centred on nuclear establishments. In fact, when local governments are being informed of our hold over them, the biggest lever to gain compliance will be the potential for nuclear explosions."

"So, back-up systems are also compromised?"

"Everything is, sir," Morazov emphasised.

The President checked his watch.

"Gentlemen, we have been talking for two hours, and I need a comfort break and, ironically, more coffee. Let's pause for ten minutes, then reconvene. What is the next topic, Dmitriy?"

"Thank you, Mr President, sorry, VV. That still feels wrong," Dmitriy burbled. "Next, we will discuss the messages for national leaders, the coordination, and the people responsible."

"Very good. It's fortunate we have set aside the day. If necessary, we can use the whole day. Let's break."

President Vasiliev disappeared into his private rooms, and the others took the opportunity to use the facilities.

Sokolov turned to Bychkov, "How do you think it's going?"

"I'm glad you made good use of the days leading up to this. But he will ask us questions for which we don't yet have answers. My advice is, do not guess. Either ask for his guidance or be honest and say this is the kind of fine detail we are still refining before 'Detonation Date', or whatever we decide to call it."

Chapter Seven

In Washington D.C. as the meeting began in Moscow, it was 1 a.m. In London it was 6 a.m. In both capitals the most senior politicians were awake. And, of course, if they were awake, so were members of their staff.

President Keaton requested to speak with Prime Minister Jones of the UK. The senior night secretary hesitated, asking if he meant immediately, given that it was 6 a.m. in England? Politely, despite his frustration, Keaton confirmed yes, now.

As if sensing the urgency, Keaton's Chief of Staff, Chip Weaver entered the room.

"Chip, this is concerning. Activity levels from our worst enemies are, except from Russia, escalating. Is that a coincidence, or is Russia orchestrating it? I'm trying to reach Julia Jones in Britain, to see if she has any intelligence we don't or has, at least, a better guess than me."

The phone buzzed. The secretary informed the President that the Prime Minister would be on the line in one minute. As he knew she would be, the PM came on the line exactly 60 seconds later.

"Good morning, Mr President. Are you as worried as I am?"

"Madam Prime Minister, welcome to my world. What are you hearing?"

"Nothing, which is worse than hearing a lot."

"Julia, I'm confident our intelligence agencies are fully coordinating, but we need to figure out why the world feels like a tinderbox."

Julia Jones wasn't as convinced about the level of cooperation, but she kept that to herself.

"As you know, we have a man at the very heart of the Russian government. He is giving us nothing, whereas he always provides good insights."

"That's exactly why I called. Your guy, code name Rasputin, is great. Maybe we're overreacting," Keaton mused.

"You will know anything as soon as we do."

"Thank you, Julia. Have a good day."

"It's Wednesday, which means Prime Minister's Question Time, PMQs. In Russia the equivalent is bear baiting. Goodbye, Mr President."

Keaton grinned but Weaver wasn't convinced.

"I like her," he said. "But she's holding something back. Rasputin has been incredible, so why would he stop now?"

Chapter Eight

It took the President twenty minutes to return. He apologised saying, "I assure you this is the most critical conversation but there are other issues at play. If we don't continue making mischief in Eastern Europe, Africa, and South America there will be suspicions. We must appear to be acting as normal. Do you concur, Boris?"

Gusev, the master of interference in Western nations, nodded.

"We need North Korea to be firing rockets, Iran to be antagonising Israel, and our experts to be influencing elections. The more noise the better, but not too much from us."

"Agreed. Now, what is the message for our soon-to-be best friends, like the President in Washington?"

"VV, we have a draft," Sokolov replied. "Once finalised, it will be translated into approximately seventy-five languages, covering ninety-eight per cent of the world's leaders."

Dmitriy took over.

"In essence, the message states:

We now control all aspects of your country, and you cannot resist.

We have seized control of communications, banking, social media, retail, transport, all websites, utilities, and government apparatus. You have three hours to acknowledge our authority and agree to inform your people that Russia is in control. It is in your best interests. You must cooperate. If you resist, everything remains shut down and you and your people will suffer personal consequences. If you accept the situation, you remain in office to assist with the transition. There will be a role for you."

Vasiliev studied the others. Sokolov and Gusev supported the approach and signalled their support.

"What are you not telling me, Dmitriy?" the President asked.

"Our additional advantage is," Morazov explained, "by controlling all technology, we will have complete access to all phones, cameras, and smart devices. This means we can eliminate dissent at every level of society. Any plotting, resistance, or subversion will be dealt with swiftly and clinically."

"This is good, very good," Vasiliev said. "Who will handle the translations?"

"My team," Dmitriy replied. "Only people who are at least bi-lingual are involved. It does mean some will gain a partial understanding of the plan, but only just before it is actioned."

Vasiliev fell silent, deep in thought for thirty seconds.

"Let's take a step back. We can literally monitor every form of communication worldwide, and, if we wanted, that could include our own country?"

"Yes, sir."

"This is remarkable progress. Who will oversee it?"

"As you know, and we will address this later," Morazov continued, "the world will be divided into ten or eleven mega-countries, each led by a designated Supremo. Whilst existing politicians will remain to manage minor domestic matters, we will appoint security forces. Initially, this will be the reward for my teams which are developing the project. They will report to the FSB."

"That the FSB will be in charge was our agreement from months ago, so it remains intact," Vasiliev said, nodding approvingly. "I'm pleased nothing has changed. And if, or should I say when people defy us, what will happen?"

"We have prepared an outline universal law to govern the entire world," Morazov explained. "It demands absolute compliance and criminalises collusion and disloyalty. In the early stages the penalty will be either death or exile. Siberia remains the most feared place for banishment."

Vasiliev's expression hardened. His eyes glazed over, and his lips seemed to shrink.

"Be firm, even harsh. People must understand there is no alternative. Now, what happens if someone has a weapon?"

"On Day One there will be an amnesty. Anyone still in possession of a gun after that will be imprisoned, along with their spouse or another family member."

"This is good," Vasiliev approved. "Make these early statements loud and clear, ensuring they are enforced in every corner of the globe. Should we set some targets?"

Sokolov interjected, "The only target is zero weapons, except for security forces, of course. Remember, any suspicion and we can monitor every conversation. If necessary, we can even direct microphones at their homes."

It was evident that the President was pleased with the progress and the levels of thought that had gone into the planning. The real challenge would be implementation.

"What about their armed forces?" he asked.

"We won't need them," Morazov replied. "In a world controlled by a single authority, national armies, navies, and air forces have become obsolete. With national security a thing of the past, military personnel will be discharged, and their arsenals dismantled and scrapped. The best equipment, naturally, will be kept for us."

Gusev noted, "Some of their technology is highly sophisticated. We'll need local operatives to train our personnel on select systems as we seize control."

Bychkov looked up. "Naturally, Russia's armaments are the best in the world. But there's a vast territory to cover."

"Some rogue factions may attempt resistance," Sokolov acknowledged. "But without communications they will be swiftly eliminated. This does mean that we must involve the head of our armed forces soon. Do you trust him, VV?"

Vasiliev smirked. "He will understand that his life depends on it."

"We'll need ground troops on China's borders, just as a precaution," Sokolov continued. "More importantly, we need both ground and air superiority along our western front. Our orders should be clear: destroy any aggressor. Shoot first, say sorry second policy."

The President leaned forward, clearly more engaged in this aspect of the plan.

"General Asimov will handle this efficiently. I'll brief him personally."

The discussion turned to the specifics of military deployment.

Morazov hesitated before asking, "Will General Asimov be offended that he was excluded from these discussions? Might he be sensitive about it?"

Vasiliev chuckled. "The General will revel in being a national hero."

He looked around the room. "Unfortunately, gentlemen, he and I will be the public faces of this movement. You, the real stars, the masterminds, will have to find satisfaction in knowing the indispensable role you have played."

Bringing the conversation back to international strategy, Vasiliev asked, "Regarding the heads of state of the two hundred plus nations across the globe. What are we assuming?"

Dmitriy resumed, "VV, I imagine you will personally address President Keaton in the USA and President Huang in China. Anyone else?"

"King Philip of the UK and his Prime Minister, Julia Jones. Those two just for the satisfaction of watching them acknowledge Russian dominance."

Vasiliev grinned. "Aleksandr will brief our key allies, the men who will govern the mega-nations that we will create under our rule. Let's discuss those. Which territories do we expect China to claim?"

Dmitriy didn't need to check his notes.

"Taiwan, Mongolia, North and South Korea, Vietnam, and the Philippines. Huang may also demand Laos, Myanmar, and Bhutan. They will be your call."

"A very small price to pay for China keeping out of our way," Vasiliev mused. "And the other blocs?"

"Naturally, all former Soviet states will return to their traditional home of Greater Russia."

This caused the warmest reaction from the President. A quiet, satisfied "Yes" escaped his lips.

Dmitriy picked up again, "Europe will extend to Poland, including the Balkan states. The German Chancellor will oversee this region, especially as our two countries have covertly become very close recently."

Vasiliev nodded. "I like your thinking, but let's place Turkey within Europe and President Akbaş will lead it with a strong hand. We reward our true and long-standing friends. I am sure Akbaş and Herr Haller will work well together."

Dmitriy resumed, "Angloland comprising the USA, Canada, the UK, and Ireland. There is some geographical sense, but that logic is secondary; the real advantage is the use of one shared language for us to monitor, making surveillance significantly easier. The President of the USA will act as the Head of Administration."

"For now," Vasiliev interjected. "I want him to be the first example of what happens to those who fail to align with our vision. Then, our very good friend, the former President of the USA, will take over. This has been his destiny for many years, and he knows our enemies and will deal with them."

Dmitriy elaborated, "North Africa will include all nations north of the Sahara Desert. As ever with Africa, some borders may need to be redrawn.

"Sub-Saharan Africa, including the islands of Madagascar, Mauritius and the Seychelles, will be known as Africana."

Vasiliev leaned back, "Apologies Dmitriy, but I believe I'll need a holiday home in the Seychelles. Make a mental note, please, and arrange for me to visit it during our first year of rule."

Dmitriy smirked. "Noted. Given your close working relationship with the President of Nigeria, we propose he becomes the de facto leader of Africana.

"The Ayatollah will be President of Greater Iran. He will love overseeing Iraq, Saudi Arabia, Israel, and Lebanon, as every country in the Middle East falls under his rule. We can be confident that the Kalashnikov will maintain order.

"India will absorb Pakistan, Bangladesh, Afghanistan, and Nepal. The current Prime Minister of India is already aligned, so he will remain in place.

"The remainder of the region will be West Asia including Malaysia, Thailand, Indonesia, and Singapore in that new mega-country. Perhaps you'd like to select the leader, VV."

Vasiliev considered this. "I'm tempted to appoint the President of the smallest nation, Singapore, just to make a point to the others. Carry on."

"South America will be renamed Brasilia and our close ally in Brazil will lead as a well-earned reward for his years of undermining the West.

"Finally, there is Australasia, comprising New Zealand and the Pacific Islands. Their remoteness ensures compliance. If not, they'll gradually starve."

Dmitriy Morazov paused, scanning the room.

Vasiliev exhaled. "Gentlemen let's eat. Food is outside, so I think we can grab a plate and eat in here. There is much more to discuss."

Chapter Nine

Thirty minutes later, the self-appointed most important people in the world reconvened their discussion. The President held up his hand to halt Morazov's next point.

"Gentlemen, may I ask you, what does Russia stand for, and what kind of new world shall we strive to create?"

Nobody spoke. It was clear that this wasn't a question anyone had truly considered. Until now, the focus had been solely on Russian domination and then worry about the future. However, Vasiliev refused to accept such an approach.

"As you, you know I am an avid student of our history. This morning, I too became engrossed in the project, its potential and its imminence. However, let's begin this afternoon a little more philosophically. Here are some perspectives I have prepared, some of my thoughts and to allow you to consider them further, I am circulating a paper I wrote, with a little help from AI, two years ago. Until today, I have never shared it with anyone. You will find it in your email inbox. I have no concerns about anyone else seeing it because it was created long before I became aware of your technological breakthrough."

He handed each of them a printed copy of his document. Sokolov, Gusev, and Morazov were somewhat startled. Could this delay the implementation of their plan, with all the inherent risks of their secrecy being compromised?

Vasiliev continued, "I want you to read this carefully, so I am returning to my other office to deal with some domestic matters. I will be back in less than an hour. Please use this time well. Comrade Bychkov, come with me, please."

He rose and left them to their task.

The document was printed on exceptionally high-quality paper, immediately imparting a compelling sense of its significance.

At the top of the first page, it read:

Part One: Russian Culture and Values – to be protected:

It is essential to recognise and explicitly state that Russian culture boasts a rich tapestry woven from centuries of history, diverse ethnic influences, and a profound bond with art, literature, music, and traditions. Spanning a vast geographical expanse from Eastern Europe to Northern Asia, our culture embodies the complexity and diversity of our people.

It is undeniable, therefore, that we possess both the breadth and depth of culture necessary to shape the rest of the world. Our strength lies in our differences, which are further enriched when we reclaim our rightful lands snatched away on the promise of independence, and yet they are still totally dependent on Russia.

Other nations and cultures may have their own wonders, but they remain mere players when compared to the magnificence of Russia.

There are numerous defining aspects of our culture but let me begin by reflecting on some of the most profound:

1. ***Literature:*** *Russian literature holds a distinguished place in world literature, with celebrated authors such as Leo Tolstoy, Fyodor Dostoevsky, Anton Chekhov, and Alexander Pushkin. Their works explore profound themes of human nature, society, and spirituality. Russian literature often delves into existential questions, societal issues, and the human condition*

with depth and intensity. This ought to serve as a standard for the entire world.

2. **Art:** Russian art possesses a rich history, from the religious icons of the Byzantine era to the avant-garde movements of the twentieth century. Iconography, symbolism, and realism are prominent characteristics in Russian art. Icon painters like Andrei Rublev are revered for their spiritual profundity and mastery of the craft. The Russian avant-garde movement, featuring artists like Wassily Kandinsky and Kazimir Malevich, made substantial contributions to modern art through their innovative styles and bold experimentation. No other nation matches this depth. Of course, many artistic geniuses exist worldwide, but the West must understand theirs are not the only ones.

3. **Music:** Russian music is diverse, ranging from the classical compositions of Tchaikovsky and Rachmaninoff to traditional folk music and contemporary pop. Classical music holds a special place in Russian culture, with composers such as Pyotr Ilyich Tchaikovsky producing iconic works such as 'Swan Lake' and 'The Nutcracker.' Russian folk music, characterised by its melodies, rhythms, and lyrical themes, reflects the country's cultural heritage and regional diversity. There is a decadence in the music popular across the world which preaches love and lust. We produce work of a philosophical nature for the benefit of everyone.

4. **Dance:** Russian ballet is renowned internationally for its elegance, precision, and technical prowess. The Bolshoi Ballet and the Mariinsky Ballet are among the oldest and most prestigious ballet companies, showcasing legendary performances of classic works like 'Swan Lake', 'The Nutcracker' and 'The Sleeping Beauty'. Russian folk dances, including the lively 'Kalinka' and the graceful 'Troika' are also fundamental to the nation's cultural identity. Even in the West, these are acclaimed as world-class.

5. ***Cuisine:*** *Russian cuisine reflects the country's diverse climate and agricultural traditions. Staple ingredients include potatoes, cabbage, beetroot, and grains like buckwheat and rye. Borscht, a hearty beet soup, and pelmeni, dumplings filled with meat or vegetables, are popular dishes. Blini, thin pancakes often served with caviar or sour cream, are a traditional favourite. Vodka is the quintessential Russian spirit, enjoyed universally. Of all the elements, cuisine will undoubtedly spark the most debate.*

6. ***Religion:*** *Orthodox Christianity has played a pivotal role in shaping Russian culture and identity. The Russian Orthodox Church has a rich tradition of religious art, architecture, and liturgical music. Religious festivals and rituals are deeply ingrained in Russian life, with Easter and Christmas celebrated with fervour and elaborate ceremonies. To quote Marx, "Religion is the opium of the people." It is fortunate they have distractions from the issues of the day and a conviction that the true focus should be on the hereafter.*

7. ***Sport:*** *In international competitions like the Olympics, Russia has been a major force. That we have used technological advancements attests to our superiority. That Western authorities have banned our athletes only demonstrates they cannot compete with us. Like religion, sport serves as a genuine distraction. The more people are encouraged to identify with teams, the less they focus on the realities of their lives.*

Overall, Russian culture is a multifaceted mosaic reflecting the country's turbulent history, diverse ethnic heritage, and enduring spirit of creativity and resilience. From its rich literary heritage to its vibrant arts scene and cherished customs, Russian culture continues to captivate and inspire people around the world. The rest of the world might benefit from following our example, perhaps with the exception of food and drink.

Part Two: Expansion

Prelude to Domination

The current state of international relations is imbalanced, with Russia's dominant position consistently underestimated. However, if we are realistic, our economy faces significant pressure as the West attempts to strangle us.

There are geopolitical tensions brewing across the globe, which are escalating worldwide, with Russia and China cast as the villains. We have instigated many of these tensions and will persist in denying any responsibility.

Our Next Move

Russia's strategy will commence with manoeuvres aimed at asserting dominance in Eastern Europe. Ukraine is ours, Georgia is under our influence, and the 'Stans' are compliant. To date, NATO, the EU and the USA have been vociferous but ultimately ineffective. This is our moment to act.

A New Cold War

Ironically, our intelligence indicates that the West perceives a new Cold War, while our ambitions are far more expansionist and 'physical'.

The current approach of diplomatic confrontations, cyber warfare, and proxy conflicts in various regions across the world appear to bewilder them. They are far more interested in our expertise in manipulating their elections than the territorial advances we are making. This type of operation must continue.

The Asian Front

Our focus on Asia, particularly in Central Asia and the Far East must intensify. While there are informal pacts with China, vast amounts of natural resources are at stake if we control the region and can lift the ludicrous restrictions imposed by the obsession with climate change!

Nonetheless, potential alliances with regional powers could prove extremely helpful.

China: Which territories do they want? How can we tweak trade agreements to our advantage?

North Korea: Let them play their reckless games which distract America, but we must remain cautious of the crazy man's unpredictable antics.

India: The Prime Minister seeks to cement his hold on power. We must do everything we can to support him in this endeavour. Despite, or perhaps because of the rejection of colonialism, the influence of the UK and the so-called 'Liberal Democracies' is not only waning but being rigorously resisted. Talks of UK/Indian trade deals are nothing more than talk, mere rhetoric. India knows where its interests lie and will increasingly align with Russia.

Economic Conquest

Russia's most critical economic leverage is energy, especially fossil fuels. The USA and its allies have painted themselves into a corner by shifting to renewables while still relying heavily on oil and gas. Germany is now in a position where we can dictate prices, delivery, and access. Germany remains highly vulnerable to our influence.

Our membership in OPEC+ amplifies our ability to determine the use of oil and gas. This coalition is focussed on hard business rather than sentimentality and operates on a global scale. We don't need to do much, just vote alongside Saudi Arabia.

The Technological Arms Race

Russia is making significant advancements in military technology, cyber capabilities, and space exploration. It may even be the case that the USA now ranks in third place, behind both us and China.

The impact of technological innovation on global power dynamics has never been more significant.

Good Friends

Russia's diplomatic efforts to forge alliances with rising powers in Asia, Africa, and Latin America are paying off. Perhaps more importantly, the West is alarmed by the emergence of a new bloc that challenges Western hegemony. It almost doesn't matter what we do as the USA and its allies will worry, analyse, and pontificate on the implications of our actions. We must continue to intensify our efforts to keep them looking in all directions at once, distracted and divided.

That said, the benefits of broader markets and stronger bonds are clear. These relationships must be nurtured.

The Final Showdown

Our enemies must understand that we stand ready for the ultimate conflict. It becomes increasingly likely, as we build tension and our expansionist agenda reaches a critical point, that a decisive confrontation with Western powers becomes highly probable. This surpasses mere demonstrations of strength through reclaiming territories or incursions by the Wagner Group and similar forces. This is more than parades of men and equipment in Red Square, it is the unleashing of the colossal force at our disposal.

America must be made to fear testing us!!!

This paper provides an overview of how to set out some of the challenges and, of course, the opportunities we foresee. Our intelligence, military, and strategic teams must have a clear understanding of their roles within this strategy.

Morazov absorbed the contents of the paper and exhaled. His two comrades took a little longer to read it than he had, which gave him a brief moment to consider the implications. There were no surprises, yet the paper was compelling because of its author.

Sokolov and Gusev finished simultaneously, and almost before the papers touched the table the President and Bychkov walked in. Clearly, he had been monitoring them and their reactions.

"So, gentlemen, your thoughts?"

As the most senior Sokolov was expected to answer first.

"Succinct and more than helpful."

"My Goose?"

Gusev allowed a smile to cross his face.

"I assume there is an expectation of controlled aggression in every aspect of this. Given that, I applaud and support it."

"Morazov?"

Dmitriy took a moment before committing himself.

"This is a great strategy, but for yesterday. It's the one we wish to overtly display to the world. It is the one we need the West to believe is our true purpose."

Now it was Vasiliev's turn to smile.

"Exactly. This was written to align all our staffs around one clear approach. Then into my office comes our esteemed colleague, the one and only Mikhail Sokolov, who tells me there is the ultimate technological breakthrough, and world domination can be ours. I wanted you to read this, not because it is elegant prose or innovative thinking, but to show you where we were and how your work will overlay this. We move from thirty kilometres per hour to one hundred at the click of a switch. It is only meant to be practical, not a directive."

There was an almost synchronised nodding of heads. The President continued,

"I agree with you, Dmitriy. This must be our obvious intention. We know America and its allies believe this to be the case and will continue to do so. It will buy us time. I recognise I'm jumping ahead in the agenda, so I apologise. When do you think we can go live with the blackout?"

Sokolov looked at Morazov.

"Technically, we are there. There are still a few wrinkles to iron out. However, the biggest challenges lie in coordination and communication. If we agree on the principles today, we could move ahead in three months. The only real concern is secrecy. I would love it if our enemies could read your paper."

"They will. I intend to leak it deliberately. As we said, there are no surprises, but President Keaton will relish reading the confirmation which indicates that the CIA has been correct all along. We will release the entire document, including the cultural aspects, because it makes the information feel more authentic. We wouldn't deliberately leak this kind of information, but it will appear naturally as part of our thinking," Vasiliev said.

Dmitriy was amazed and showed it.

"How can we be so certain it will be leaked?"

"Because I know a man who is trusted by the British, the superspy known as Rasputin. If he delivers this paper, they will accept it as completely authentic, which it was until this morning! They will then pass it to the Americans."

"Mr President, does this mean we are opening up our plan to someone else?"

"Dmitriy, Rasputin is in this room right now. The ace American undercover agent is Comrade Bychkov."

Whilst Dmitriy Morazov was a highly experienced operative, he was astonished by this news.

"No wonder they believe the intelligence gathered from Rasputin. Don't they ever question the validity of his reports?"

"They don't because we've fed them good stuff but perhaps not in enough time or to its full extent," Bychkov replied.

"And you knew Comrade Gusev?" Morazov asked, as the meeting became more formal.

Gusev shrugged and said, "Don't be upset. Your clearance wasn't high enough that would allow you to know until yesterday. Now you have the highest clearance in the land. The President himself signed the authorisation last night."

Now Morazov's head was spinning.

"Why would things have changed yesterday?"

Vasiliev encouraged Gusev, "You'll have to tell him, Boris."

"Dmitriy, this requires you to be mature and rational. As you well know, your wife is my niece, and we trust each other utterly. She is also one of the very few other people with the highest security clearance. She told me it was okay because you tell her nothing, nothing at all. And I am also very aware of your devotion to her. This is a big surprise for you but take a deep breath before you say anything."

"My wife has spied on me?"

"No. My niece has merely confirmed that you never reveal anything to anyone. As have, by the way, the security services. They have been spying on you, as you would expect."

President Vasiliev raised his hand to stop anyone else from speaking.

"Dmitriy, while you've all been reading my paper, I've been briefing your new second-in-command about this meeting and its content so far. I'm not going to do a dramatic reveal, but she is now joining us, and it's your wife."

Now Morazov's jaw did hit the metaphorical floor.

Vasiliev walked to the door and opened it. He nodded to someone out of sight. Then in walked Natalia Agapov Morazov. The President smiled at her and ushered her to a seat.

"Natalia, you are now one of the most powerful people in the world. Everything said in this room is literally for our ears only. You are, as I have told you, now the second-in-command of this project, working for your husband. As individuals, both of you have risen to high positions very quickly. Our culture respects age above all else, but I respect talent above all else. Perhaps, I respect loyalty most of all."

People exhaled audibly and the ice was broken.

"Mr President, if I may, as I am astonished by how today has progressed. So, Natalia Agapov Morazov is my deputy, confidante, and collaborator?"

"In every aspect of this plan. My only caution to you both is to remember where you are when discussing it. Even your apartment walls may have ears."

Sokolov, in a sotto voce, said, "There will be a bigger house for you as soon as I can manage it without raising suspicions regarding your status and the reasons it has changed."

The President continued, "I know this is an unacceptable thing to say to you both, but Natalia, you cannot become pregnant at this time. Understood?"

Dmitriy and Natalia would have agreed to anything at that point, and procreation was the furthest thing from their minds in that meeting, at that moment, in that building. Neither took offence and totally accepted that this project was bigger than anything anyone had ever done.

"Let us take a five-minute break, and Natalia Morazov can assure her husband she wasn't snitching on him. Afterwards we will be able to focus again on the work."

Chapter Ten

"Mr President, the Director of the CIA insists on seeing you now. I have told him that the Chief of Staff has a meeting scheduled."

"Let them both in, Dorothy, please."

Bob Cartwright entered from the outer office and Chip Weaver, Chief of Staff, came into the Oval Office through the connecting door to his own office.

"Bob, what's the matter?"

Cartwright was slightly out of breath, his pale blue shirt slightly darkened in places by the sweat emanating from his armpits.

"Rasputin has come through. Read this document. Everything we 'knew' has been confirmed. It's high-level intelligence, but we can continue to apply our resources as predicted."

Weaver was aware of Rasputin. However, he held his excitement in check due to his natural cynicism.

"Why do we trust him?"

Cartwright was taken aback. "He, and we do assume it's a man, has given us and the British information for years. It's always been reliable, and this aligns perfectly with our assumptions. We had been mildly concerned that they had gone quiet, but there is nothing understated about this approach."

"Bob, please accept that I'm not trying to throw all of our current ideas away. It's just that we're very well stretched at the moment. It would be better if we could focus our people on fewer targets," Weaver assured him. "Do we know Rasputin's identity?"

"No, but he's certainly very senior in the Kremlin," replied the man from the CIA.

President Keaton mused, "This marries with the intelligence from the Five Eyes." (The Five Eyes is an alliance of the intelligence agencies of the USA, UK, Canada, Australia, and New Zealand). He continued, "We're already spending billions of dollars on defence. Do we need to do more? Can we manipulate the current budget and commitments, or must we need to go through the charade of getting Congress's approval?"

"To answer that we need the Secretary of Defense in the meeting," Cartwright suggested.

"Mrs Harkins, please invite Brett Armstrong to a meeting at 6 pm with these gentlemen. I know he's in the country, as he returned from Poland yesterday."

The others left Keaton alone to contemplate the ramifications of the information they had received, but after fifteen seconds his next meeting arrived to discuss refurbishing the Oval Office. For a fleeting moment, he wondered which one would spark more debate—world peace or the colour of the carpets.

Chapter Eleven

Natalia needed the few moments available to her to reassure her husband that she had never been duplicitous, and that their marriage was the most important thing in her life. Perhaps strangely, Dmitriy felt confident in their bond and tried to dismiss her concerns.

"The one thing that surprises me is your seniority in your own career," he said.

"My presence here astonishes me," she replied. "I have been underselling my role in the state machinery but this…" she wafted her arms signalling her perplexion.

"Can we work together? Can we bear the responsibilities?" Natalia asked.

"I suspect that discussion passed us by some time ago. The fact that we are in this together is already decided. This is the greatest thing we will ever be involved in, perhaps the greatest thing any group of people has ever done. I'm reminded of the quote by a woman named Margaret Mead who said, 'Never doubt that a small group of thoughtful, committed individuals can change the world. In fact, it's the only thing that ever has.' She was right, and we are those people."

The entire meeting reconvened.

"What is next on the agenda, Dmitriy?" enquired the President.

"VV, the next point," Dmitriy Morazov began but stopped as his wife gasped at his use of the President's nickname.

Vasiliev laughed. "Natalia, I failed to tell you that, for today only, as a commitment to our joint efforts, we are all on first name terms or in my case, a different moniker."

It was counterintuitive that Vasiliev had laughed more this day, a time of such heightened seriousness than anyone had seen. Natalia blushed, slightly embarrassed that her first contribution had stemmed the flow of the session.

Dmitriy continued, "We believe most leaders, on behalf of their nations, will accept the inevitability of the situation. For the few who continue to demur, their phones will be reactivated, and they'll have thirty minutes to change their position, or they will be removed from office. When our people are on the ground they will be taken away."

"And shot," stated Vasiliev.

"And shot," Morazov agreed, somewhat surprised.

Vasiliev continued, "As I mentioned earlier, our first actions must show there can be no debate. The best way to show that is to be extremely harsh in the way we deal with dissenters. The general populations will not be pleased, but that will be their bad luck. Gradually, we can impose a lighter touch and create a different society. What will be the simple message to the people?"

"The message, indeed, the basis of our approach has to be captured in a clear, concise phrase. The ones which we are considering are 'Change for the better', 'Here to help', 'Fair and just', and 'Clean and useful'. What are your opinions, VV?"

The strapline felt a little less important than the other issues, but it could make a huge difference to the acceptance of the situation and limiting bloodshed.

"You must have a favourite, Dmitriy."

"I do. My thoughts are based on two aspects: the basic needs of the citizenry and a clear set of principles by which our leaders can govern."

"Excellent. Go on, what do the people want?" Vasiliev asked, genuinely fascinated.

Dmitriy inhaled deeply. "The work of American psychologist Abraham Harold Maslow shows us there is a hierarchy of needs. We are about to throw the world as they know it into the air, and they won't know how the pieces will land. So, we must begin with the base of Maslow's pyramid with security. Are they safe? Are they fed? Are they warm? Are they healthy? From that level we can move to, do they have jobs? Is their income secure? Are they being treated fairly and equitably?"

Morazov took a sip of water, and his wife gave a hint of a smile to encourage him.

He continued, "There will be people who reject the status, such as radicals, criminals, and chancers. They have to be removed. My personal concern lies with organised crime. If we are to stabilise society, there can be nobody abusing the system. We will be clear about their identities, and they will be expunged. Radicals will be imprisoned, and opportunists 're-educated'. Society will be cleansed."

Everyone in the room murmured in agreement.

"I see we are being guided to 'clean and useful'. What about 'useful'?" asked the intensely focused leader.

"People will work. We will create jobs, including cleaning the cities, the roads, and communal areas. Most people in employment will continue to work as they currently do. The caveats and conditions are numerous. Business profits will be redirected to the State. Salaries and wages will be standardised."

Bychkov, who had been very quiet and studious, now he wanted more detail. "Who will pay for full employment? What will the wage levels be? What about pensioners? What about people who physically cannot work? And I'm sure there are thousands of other questions."

Dmitriy concurred, "Probably millions of questions. We will set the principles, and the local leaders will implement them. But let me give you some thoughts on those specific topics. Firstly, the entire economy will be different, with only one currency: the Rouble. There will be no international trading on variable exchange rates. We will define all parameters and, critically, we can print money because there will be no inflation. Therefore, we will create jobs regardless of need. It is more important that people have a job to give them a sense of purpose.

"There will be a base salary rate of three million roubles per annum, and above that four further salary tiers. The highest tier will be limited to just five times larger than the base. Given the absence of inflation, this will be more than enough for anyone to thrive."

"Pensioners will receive two million roubles but only once they reach seventy-five years of age. The family will be expected to support them if they are unable to work until then. People who cannot work will be assessed and, if necessary, relocated to collective accommodation offering very basic care. Naturally, native Russians will be assessed very generously."

The President summarised, "It seems to me we could tweak the slogan to 'Safe, Clean, and Useful' and clarify its applications to the Presidents of the new mega-countries. In essence, if people are capable, their lives will be comfortable, as there will be zero crime, the environment will be pristine, and they will be making a worthwhile contribution. However, society will not bear the burden of excessive care for non-contributors. The vast majority will soon accept the new order and if they don't, the alternative is their removal. We will not be mollycoddling anyone and soon they won't expect anything else."

Sokolov had been very thoughtful. "I believe that if we test various scenarios, we'll find that 'Safe, Clean, and Useful' are highly appropriate values."

Natalia reacted, "There's an old adage, 'The devil makes work for idle hands.' I understand that everyone who can work will have a job, but what about when they aren't working?"

"Great question," Dmitriy over-enthused as it was his beloved who had asked the question. "Firstly, they'll be tired from work. We are proposing a normal fifty-hour work week. We'll set standards for home and garden maintenance which will give people further focus. Then, there are the distractions. We will strongly encourage religion, local customs, soap operas, and especially sport. Naturally, they will be closely monitored."

Bychkov spoke, and the room listened intently. "Let the world know that we'll review progress annually, and if people are adapting, we'll ease the rules. Whether or not we do so is entirely our decision. We could also place the onus on them to ensure their fellow citizens comply."

"I like that," said the President. "We can blame them for the stringent limits never being relaxed."

The President wanted to return to the topic of the jobs that would be created.

Morazov elaborated, "Online shopping will be banned, which will lead to more retail jobs, greater need for transportation, and some deliveries to remote areas. Whilst there will be fewer people needing care, there will be more carers. No manager in manufacturing has ever complained about having too many people. We could impose staffing ratios to compel employers to take on more employees. After all, the State is funding it."

Bychkov raised another point. "We are all adopting the benefits of Artificial Intelligence which is eliminating jobs. How do we balance that?"

"My recommendation is that AI is banned except for us," Morazov opined. "We're envisioning a world of work dominated by the employment of human beings, with less reliance on technology." He continued, "Perhaps I should have made another point earlier when discussing crime. We now have a ninety-five per cent confidence that AI can predict who will become a criminal. This gives us choices about who to monitor, who to educate regarding their responsibilities to society, and, in certain cases, who to pre-emptively imprison, just in case."

"This is *1984* on speed," mused Gusev, and nobody disagreed.

"Next subject, please, Dmitriy," said the President as he didn't want the meeting to delve too philosophically.

"Healthcare. To provide equitable worldwide distribution of medical care, there will be enforced migration of some clinicians. This will mainly be from the wealthier countries to the horribly named 'Third World.' To offset this, people over seventy-five years of age will receive pain management but no remedial treatments. Those undergoing treatment for psychoses will be eliminated, releasing more doctors and other staff for redeployment. Simultaneously, we must invest in the training of doctors, nurses, pharmacists, and other healthcare professionals. Of course, people who have served the Russian State will be eligible for the finest medical attention. How does this sound?"

"Harsh but fair, and it aligns with the 'Safe, Clean, and Useful' principle," replied Vasiliev.

Sokolov spoke, "One of the things mankind desires is control. Are we leaving the individual any sense of control over their lives?"

"Great question," replied Morazov. "In truth, there can be the promise of control. If we return to the suggestion of a one or three-year review, there's an implication that if everyone behaves, if they exercise self-control if you like, then society will regain some self-determination. Until then, Uncle Vladimir Vasiliev will protect them, except for those who don't deserve it. It's all for the greater good, and control comes within the limits we describe."

VV spoke, "Let me summarise. Firstly, thank you all for the incredible work and the success already attained. Continue with the very detailed considerations, and we will reconvene next week. At least, Dmitriy and Natalia, you won't need to explain to each other why you're spending so much time at work. Anything else?"

"So much to consider, but after ten hours today, I suspect we will be even more productive next week," said Bychkov. "I look forward to the update, and next time I would like to hear a projected D for Detonation Date."

The President stood, and the others followed suit. The day of Vasiliev being 'VV' was over. He left the room alongside Bychkov.

"My advice now is to go home, rest and come into Putin Place tomorrow first thing. Bring changes of clothes," directed Sokolov. "I'm sure you want to get back to your teams, Dmitriy, but I want to unpick everything agreed upon today before you do."

With that, they left the Kremlin.

Natalia and Dmitriy travelled home together, discussing the weather, food, and family, afraid to speak about their extraordinary day. One misplaced word could have been disastrous. The next nine hours were theirs, even if some of it would be spent ironing and packing whatever they might need for the week ahead. Notwithstanding, they made the most of the time available.

Chapter Twelve

Secretary of Defense, Brett Armstrong, entered the Oval Office alongside Bob Cartwright and Chip Weaver. The President stood and walked over to the armchair he preferred to use, whilst the others took seats on sofas strategically placed and with the seats at a slightly lower level than the President's. Even in the company of colleagues, there were psychological signals of dominance being subtly conveyed.

Without any of the customary pleasantries usually exchanged between Keaton and his senior aides, the President jumped right into the point.

"Brett, you have seen the leaked document. What are your thoughts?"

"Mr President, it's completely authentic. The source has been first rate before now and this is a document with wide-ranging thoughts. If we were being fed false information, it wouldn't look like this. These are the ideas of Vasiliev. Of course, it's worrying because it confirms our worst fears. That said, these are the foundations upon which we've based our planning. The good news is there are no major surprises."

"My thoughts exactly. But the Chief of Staff has concerns, don't you, Chip?"

"My only nervousness is caused by the fact that we've received it at all."

"Okay, let me ask this question, should we do anything differently or taking any additional steps?"

Keaton glanced around the room and saw three heads shaking their heads. Silence meant acceptance of the current approach.

"Alright, let's continue to be vigilant, but there's no need to change our strategy or objectives. Anything else, gentlemen? Thank you for coming in. I know this was a brief discussion, but I trust you all to express your opinions and then deliver everything we have agreed."

The three executives exited the room and Dorothy Harkins entered with a wedge of papers requiring the President's signature.

Chapter Thirteen

If most members of the public were to be asked, they would likely assume that any conversation between the President of the USA and the Prime Minister of the United Kingdom of Great Britain and Northern Ireland would be conducted privately, with only the leaders present and then kept hyper-confidential. The reality, however, is quite different. Numerous people are listening in; some on an adjoining phone to hear both parties, and official records are taken. If anyone, other than the two leaders, wants to communicate, they do so via hastily scribbled notes or gestures that resemble those of a semi-demented monkey.

Today's conversation, however, was a calm, though crucial discussion.

The President opened straight away on the key issue.

"Madam Prime Minister, can we be truly confident in this intelligence?"

Whilst her staff could see the raised eyebrows of disdain, her voice remained serene.

"Mr President, why should this time be different? Rasputin has provided us with a great deal of substantial intelligence, and I would remind you it has always been ahead of events and reflected the motivations in the Kremlin. This is the kind of information we simply couldn't obtain without those eyes and ears in the room."

"All valid points, but what if we've been set up? What if this is the ultimate distraction? What if the real game is being played on a different board altogether?"

"Mr President, what are you not telling me?"

"It's a gut feeling, instinct honed over decades of service, reinforced by the behaviour of my predecessor, former President Malone. He is very close to Vasiliev and is walking around, preaching to his cult about his grand solutions for the world. He claims all war would be over in twenty-four hours if he regained the White House. But that could only be achieved by conceding everything to our enemies. What does he know?"

This time Julia Jones allowed her emotions to show.

"A disgusting man. As much as I loathe him and know he has a deluded following, surely, he could never reclaim your office? He's a natural strutter and garbler of the lines his acolytes want to hear. Sorry, but I don't think Rasputin's intelligence is diminished by Malone the Bone's narcissism."

"Did he really try to initiate an encounter with you at Chequers?" asked Keaton incredulously.

"He did but he backed off quickly when I asked him if his willy was actually shaped like a parsnip."

Both of them laughed and put down the phone.

In London, Jones relaxed before the next meeting, but in Washington, D.C., Keaton remained pensive. Appropriately, there was beautiful sunshine in England, while it was pouring with rain in the American capital.

Chapter Fourteen

In Beijing, President Huang was having dinner with his deputy, Xiu Feng Wang, a long-term Communist Party member and President of the Beijing Branch, the second most powerful position in China. Amongst the list of roles Xiu held, he was also Head of Security.

"Repeat that, Comrade," Huang asked.

"Our source has confirmed the Russians are ahead of us in the race to develop the mechanisms to block the whole world's devices and online tools. It's a blow because we are only weeks away from declaring our own similar capability."

"And we know this to be accurate?"

"Yes, both regarding their accelerated progress and our imminent development."

Huang considered the situation. The two men had been left alone in the magnificent dining room. Usually, the staff would remain in attendance, as they had all passed extreme security checks. In fact, all the attendants were highly trained security service guards. However, on this occasion, Xiu had used their code phrase to indicate that this evening the topic of discussion was of the highest importance, for their ears only. All Xiu had to do was use the phrase 'Zhongnanhai is beautiful' and, once the food was served, the waiters were dismissed.

"Vasiliev has assured me that we will always be totally independent, and our sovereignty protected. This means he could impose this blackout on us as well. Do we have a sense of his attitude after this breakthrough?"

Xiu was almost gleeful as he replied, "I am fully reassured that he has no ambitions for China. In fact, he is planning to cede territories to the Empire of China."

Huang raised an eyebrow, a rare show of animation by his standards.

"Which countries are we to be granted? It must include Taiwan."

"I believe we can request anywhere, but certainly it is assumed we want Taiwan, North and South Korea, Mongolia, Vietnam, and the Philippines. Where else might we want to request? We could think the unthinkable. What other lands would you truly like to have under our control, after so many years of conflict and pain?"

Huang looked puzzled. He had jet black hair, which was surprising given he was seventy-three years of age. Perhaps it was another state secret Xiu had previously pondered. Then, the 'light bulb' went on in Huang's mind.

"No! You believe Vasiliev would give us Japan. What would he want in return for all of these territories?"

"That is the beauty of the situation. He only wants us to stay out of the way. His agenda will be overflowing. Effectively splitting the world into two, because of the exceptional relations between us, will be perfectly acceptable. China is simply too big to absorb."

Now that Russia was going to surpass them but was giving China a huge second prize, Huang's thoughts began to percolate.

"Imagine we accept the deal and consider our negotiating strategy. We'll then use the next six months to address the issues of integration, whilst at the same time concluding the development of our system to capture the world. In that time, Russia will have choked resistance in America, Europe, Africa, the Middle East, and the rest of the world. We then 'conquer' Russia in the same way they have taken over everywhere we don't control. We can step in looking like the good guys and bring harmony."

Xiu could barely keep his excitement in check. This was their dream; two hundred years of careful military nurturing, economic growth, and suppression of any challenge had led China to this point. This was an unexpected acceleration, but a chance that could not be missed

Huang went on, "We must move forward on three fronts. Firstly, the discussions with Russia. Ask for all the territories you and I have discussed as the ideal scenario. Hopefully, that will go smoothly and not be too distracting. At the same time, we need a plan for the manner we will incorporate Japan, Taiwan, and the other lands we want. Particularly with the first two, we must be uncompromising, even brutal. This is not the time to take too many prisoners. Who will run these other countries? How will Russia hand them over to us after all their technologies have been shut down? The third element is the subsequent domination of Russia and, therefore, the rest of the world. When will we be ready? What will be the nature of our rule? Will it vary by area, and how will we control it?"

"At the risk of sounding flippant, is that all? Three colossal tasks, to be carried out in total secrecy, and within six months."

"At the risk of sounding equally flippant, take a couple of extra days if you really must."

It was a rare day Huang and Xiu laughed out loud together. This was one of those days, probably to relieve the tension.

Chapter Fifteen

After the incredibly intense meeting the day before, Morazov and his deputy, his wife, were scheduled for the review with Sokolov and Gusev. Aleksandr Bychkov had invited himself to the meeting, and everyone accepted that he was there to report back to President Vasiliev.

Mikhail Sokolov brought the meeting to a point where they could make progress.

"Thank you for yesterday. We briefed the President, and we were given the authority to proceed. Please remember, we have the principles agreed, which gives us a mountain of work to achieve it. I am a great believer that a deadline is a lifeline; if we set a date, we will hit it. In a semi-decisive manner, we floated a six-month timeframe, and I suggest that we make that our concrete target date."

The room was silent for a few moments as the ramifications of the proposal were considered. Nobody was reticent, yet this was a massive undertaking, accentuated by the need for complete confidentiality.

Dmitriy Morazov spoke first, "Boss, this is both crazy and inevitable. If we say twelve months, we will finish preparations the day before going live, and I suspect if we now agree six months, we will still finish preparations the day before we go live."

Boris Gusev agreed but added, "We will still be changing details at the instant of detonation."

"So, is it our target, six months from today, which happens to be 25th December, Christmas Day for every one of the Christian faiths, and because of that celebration, many people in other parts of the world will be on vacation? Nicely ironic," affirmed Sokolov.

Natalia asked, "What happens if we miss the date?"

Aleksandr Bychkov answered, "We won't be here for any revised date."

"Enough negativity," said Dmitriy in an overly buoyant tone. "We just have to deliver. Let me suggest the agenda for this session: territory allocation, powers for the new world leaders, arms, communications, and civil standards. Naturally, I am thinking about the priorities for President Vasiliev when we meet next week. When is that set for, by the way?"

Bychkov replied, "I was just with him, and it is 7 a.m. on Monday. He wants to start the week with his utmost priority."

"To it, then, Dmitriy," urged Sokolov.

"Am I correct that you will be discussing, or perhaps negotiating, with President Huang about the countries he wants within the Chinese Empire, Comrade Bychkov?"

"I will, and my orders are to give him a generous allocation. I am meeting Xiu Feng Wang on Thursday. Therefore, we will be able to report to our leader on Monday. I don't foresee any issues, but who knows where the twists will emerge."

Dmitriy considered the running order on his screen.

"Aligned with the lands and new mega-nations, most of which became clear yesterday, will the President nominate the new leaders, or does he want suggestions?"

"Let me ask him. He does have firm favourites, so I don't expect us to worry unduly about this topic."

"Great. As the next issue is troop positions, when do you think General Asimov, as Chief of the General Staff, should be brought into the planning?"

Bychkov weighed up his next reply carefully. He frowned, pondered, and then said, "My view of him is not as warm as the President's. We have already created a bond which I know you will respect, if I am a little indiscreet, but he may be the one whose ego gets the better of him. Again, let me consult upwards."

"The next question is, which powers will remain within the orbit of the new countries? Shall I give you my first cut at it?"

Sokolov nodded and Dmitriy continued, "In no particular order: education, transport, law and order, media, the environment, health, care and welfare, business, banking, surveillance, and morality."

Natalia had worked with Dmitriy until 2 a.m. on this list, and she added, "It is imperative that for each theme we set the limits and the principles. For example, education will have a set of curricula overseen by us, with those guidelines that educationalists will use to prepare the students for the new world. It is the key for the revised long-term society."

Dmitriy was pleased that Natalia had been seen as a key player in this plan. His enthusiasm didn't stop him from taking over from her.

"Laws, and indeed constitutions, will need to be rewritten but checked and guided by Russia. Media outlets will only be permitted to publish and show news we authorise. And so, it goes across all the key themes."

Gusev interjected.

"Describe some of the thinking behind the heading morality"

"As I understand it, at the meeting held with the President before my involvement, the directive was to be 'old-fashioned,' 1950s morality. We need to set the bar at a level for everyone in the world. There will be no drugs, no abortion, no legalised homosexuality, and nothing which challenges the norms of the religious right across all creeds."

"Do you think people will easily accept these standards?" asked Bychkov.

"Firstly, they will have no choice. But secondly, this will bring on board millions of people who hate the manner morals have been liberalised. We may think they are deluded, but it is a great opportunity to get a good chunk of the population on our side. It is a quicker way to move towards the tipping point of mass acquiescence."

Gusev asked, "How does no abortion fit with our desire to only have fit and useful people?"

"The answer is simple but radical. Contraception will be in the water, and only people we deem to be acceptable and healthy will be allowed to have the antidote. Whilst this may sound like a fascist view, the number of people we need to find jobs for will drop, as will the number of people needing care."

"This does neatly marry with the strapline of safe, clean, and useful," added Gusev. "But this might be the most contentious imposition of all."

"If you think about it, so much of our planning is underpinned by only having fit and able people. To add to that, the rule of no abortions doesn't mean that authorities can't enforce it, if necessary, to eradicate the potential drains on society."

Nobody demurred.

Sokolov saw a gap in the conversation.

"May I suggest a couple of extra subjects, please? There could be a local thrust in science and innovation. It goes without saying that all new ideas will be given to Russia to spread everywhere, or not, if it doesn't suit us. The other one is entertainment and sport. Natalia raised the issue of keeping the masses occupied yesterday, and we must invest time and thought into these."

Dmitriy nodded.

Bychkov said, "Few people have travelled and experienced the world like I have. A big issue, linked to religion, is burial rituals. This is a very detailed point but maybe one which causes too much heat. Can we please recommend that local customs will be honoured?"

There was complete unanimity amongst the group.

"These aspects of the new society will have their parameters drawn up before D-Day, and the new leaders will have a very long list of items to implement."

"If I may ask, to reverse the thinking, what won't the new countries be responsible for?" asked Gusev.

Dmitriy consulted the notes on his laptop screen.

"Defence, energy, and treasury will all be managed from Moscow."

Bychkov was, in this meeting, far more active. Whether they were his questions or those of the President didn't matter as they needed answering.

"Tell me, what happens to nuclear weapons?"

Natalia answered, "We need the Chief of the General Staff's input. Because we shut down all systems, there is only a short time before there is a serious problem. This, of course, leverages pressure on Heads of State to accept Russia's position of dominance. The plan is for all nuclear arsenals to be relocated to Russia."

Bychkov nodded and went on, "I will press the President to bring General Asimov into this discussion as soon as possible."

Mikhail Sokolov looked across at Aleksandr Bychkov. The Foreign Minister appeared relaxed, but he was a poker player in the highest stakes games of international politics. This was a man used to keeping an impassive demeanour when under severe pressure from the most powerful people across the globe. Sokolov needed to know if their general direction was in accord with the President's expectations.

"Are you happy for us to move on, or should we re-address any of the topics?"

"This is all very good. The President will be pleased by the progress."

"Will the technical aspects be ready for D-Day?"

This was the area Dmitriy felt most assured in, and his body language showed it. He had risen very quickly because of his technical capabilities and had reached his current very high level because of his personal qualities. People liked and trusted him. In one of the most political environments in the world, the Kremlin, he didn't play games and did honour his commitments to colleagues. Most importantly, Dmitriy didn't try to take credit for other people's ideas and successes. This made him a unique individual.

Natalia had heard about Dmitriy Morazov long before she met him. The only criticism she had ever come across was from someone overlooked for a commission Dmitriy had been given, and then the worst his 'opponent' could come up with was, "Surely, he can't be genuine." From the moment they met, she was totally smitten. A good guy, good looking, very funny, and courteous to everyone he met.

Natalia was certain Dmitriy hadn't noticed her. However, a mutual acquaintance had performed the role of go-between, and as they say, the rest is history.

In the room, the real Dmitriy Morazov was in control.

"Comrade, we are actually ahead of the targets set for each of the Gateways in the project. Please accept I am not being complacent, just reporting the status accurately. The next stage is the crucial one, as we bring together the various strands that have, until now, been operating independently. This begins tomorrow. I will kick off the process but leave it to my team leaders for a few days, as I continue with preparations for meeting the President next week."

Gusev was glowing with pride but kept himself under control.

"What if there are hiccups?"

"My reaction that six-month timescale being very tight wasn't about the system's readiness," Dmitriy said. He continued, "My concerns relate to the complexity of the logistics surrounding D-Day. Communications, troop movements, general unrest amongst the citizens of all the countries of the world, and then the imposition of our regime."

Bychkov understood and was supportive. "You are addressing the biggest logistical challenges anyone has ever faced. Of course, when I say 'you,' I am recognising the exceptional efforts of all of you. What is next?"

Sokolov responded, "Communications. To the 200-plus leaders of the nations as configured now, then to the populations of the mega-countries after the event."

Dmitriy spoke again, "I think if we draft the main text for these two initial communications, we may find they prompt more questions. Notwithstanding, they will need to be translated."

Natalia agreed and volunteered to create the first drafts for the meeting with President Vasiliev on the following Monday.

Sokolov expressed his gratitude and attempted to move on. However, Gusev wanted to consider a connected issue. "What about controlling social media and the messages there?"

"Simple. We have thought about this deeply, and the only conclusion is that all online interactive technologies will cease to function. They will be dead. Full stop. Period."

Bychkov smiled. "Well, that was clear enough. I gather you dislike social media, Morazov."

"I do, but that's irrelevant. That too many people spend too much time looking at screens is unfathomable. However, this is an action to suppress any chance of collusion and conspiracy."

"Natalia, when you draft the missives for the general population, please ensure they reflect the positives," asked Bychkov.

She replied, "Whilst the emphasis will be the ways the world will be better for them, there will also be clarity about their responsibilities for helping to make society great."

"Forgive me, Natalia, for continuing, but there's one aspect I would like you to give particular visibility to, the lack of taxes. Nobody likes paying them and we are giving them a life devoid of payments to the State. It was the American statesman, Benjamin Franklin, who said, 'In this world, nothing can be said to be certain, except death and taxes.' Let them see this new nirvana."

Natalia was genuinely impressed, not just with the quote, but also with the insight. "Consider it included as a key aspect of the changes."

Gusev became agitated. "It occurs to me there is a third communication to prepare, the one to our own people. Maybe that's two extra announcements: one for true Russians and one for the people of the countries being brought into the Russian Empire."

"Very good point, Boris. There will be many of the messages which are the same, but there needs to be something specific for each group," concurred Sokolov. "Sorry, Natalia, but those need to be drafted too."

"Anything else for now?" asked Bychkov. "Because I need to get to President Vasiliev with our request to involve General Asimov."

The meeting wrapped up, and they moved off.

Chapter Sixteen

President Vasiliev was expecting Aleksandr Bychkov.

"How is it going?"

"Exceptionally well. This is a very accomplished group. Irrespective of how we brought them together, they are working as a small but highly cohesive group."

"Will they be ready to meet me on Monday?"

"They will, and you will be asked to make some decisions. As it happens, one request now is for General Asimov to become a member of the team. It has reached the point at which his expertise is vital."

"Do you like him, Aleksandr?"

"Mr President, whether I like him doesn't matter. My reluctance regarding his participation in anything, is due to the size of his ego and my doubts about his ability to maintain complete confidentiality."

"You've told me this before, and I have been observing him. Last week I told him we were considering cutting off oil supplies to India. Totally untrue and he was the only one to whom I mentioned it. Guess what, within one day I was asked by the Ambassador to India if it was true. Untrustworthy."

Bychkov replied, "It doesn't surprise me, but it does sadden me. A life dedicated to service undermined. What will you do?"

Vasiliev paused for a moment before speaking. "It's the end. He is joining us now."

Vasiliev pushed a button under his desk and General Asimov entered. He was a small, podgy man, wearing many medals. Bychkov privately thought there were more every time he saw him. Asimov's appearance was always immaculate, the result of forty years in the Army. Asimov was inevitably very proud to be in the company of the President, and he beamed as he entered. He was less pleased to see the Foreign Minister, whom he considered less worthy than himself.

"My dear General, how are you?"

"My President, I am well. And thank you for asking. In what ways can I assist you?"

"Let me tell you about a secret group which is meeting to progress a plan to take over the world. The thinking is well-developed but now it needs the expertise of the head of the armed forces to help in some lesser ways."

Asimov almost exploded.

"There is a group operating without me, and now I am to be a junior member? I should be running it, not assisting! Who is leading?"

Bychkov replied, "Comrade Sokolov."

"Sokolov? He only did two years in Army intelligence. Not even in the 'trenches', a paper-pusher."

Vasiliev spoke very quietly, "A highly respected colleague."

Asimov was not reading the mood and shot back, "He's a nobody. Not a hero of Russia."

"Before we move on, General, last week I told you about oil to India. Did you tell anyone else?"

"No, Mr President."

"So, why did the Ambassador to India challenge me about this decision?"

"Somebody else must have leaked it to him."

Power Denied

The blood drained from the President's face.

"It was a ruse. There is no such plan, and I only told you, Asimov. You are a walking leak. And now you know we are planning to take over the world. Can you be trusted with the news?"

"I was only trying to help. Everything I do is for Russia."

Asimov believed his career was on the line. He was wrong.

"General Ivan Asimov, I have found you to be guilty of treason. There is no appeal, and you are now going to be taken to a room below here, where you will be executed."

Vasiliev pressed another button, and two armed guards walked through a side door.

"Take him away and carry out my orders immediately."

Asimov said nothing, as he was too stunned to speak. He never spoke another word, perhaps the greatest irony for a man who had never stopped talking throughout his life.

Back in his office, Vasiliev appeared upset.

"Sometimes we have to make these decisions. But Asimov is just an early casualty in our conquest."

"Who will now head the Armed Forces?"

"In a moment, he will walk in and the three of us will discuss the situation."

Once again, Vasiliev pressed the button under his desk and the door opened. This time it was Boris Gusev who entered the room.

"Boris, I understand you have pressed for the head of the Armed Forces to join your working party. I understand the request for that perspective, but given your background, why can't you provide it yourself?" Vasiliev asked.

"Mr President, I have the background, but I am not up to speed with today's numbers, deployments or priorities."

"How long would it take you to be adequately informed?"

"That largely depends on the good offices of General Asimov."

"Ah, sadly, I placed General Ivan Asimov in a precarious position, and he hasn't survived. This hasn't been announced yet, but he will, naturally, be given a hero's funeral."

Gusev was genuinely shocked. "This is a national tragedy."

Vasiliev looked at Gusev with piercing eyes.

"Not such a tragedy. He had an illness. Asimov was terminally indiscreet. Now, I know that is not an affliction from which you suffer, Boris. Therefore, with immediate effect, you are appointed as Chief of the General Staff, head of all of our armed forces. Please take this document of authorisation and go to Asimov's office. I will make the announcement, including informing Mikhail Sokolov. You will need to very rapidly assimilate the data required to return to your second, but simultaneous, position in the Sokolov/Morazov project. Any questions?"

Gusev paused for a moment, "Thousands but I will only ask, am I a member of the Central Executive Committee?"

"You are but that is your third priority after taking over the world and running the military. Of course, attend all its meetings, but limit your time spent reading the associated papers and resist joining any sub-committees."

"Thank you, Mr President. I am greatly honoured."

Gusev pivoted and left.

"I must make those calls, Aleksandr. Anything else?"

"Before Monday we must finalise the appointments to run the mega-nations, at least to begin the process."

"Fix a meeting for tomorrow. And, Comrade, get behind Gusev. He is someone I want to succeed."

Bychkov bowed his head and departed.

Chapter Seventeen

Dmitriy and Natalia were alone in Putin Place, each focused on different aspects of their workload.

She paused and looking up from her papers and asked, "Do you ever ask yourself why we're doing this? What's our purpose?"

Dmitriy swivelled in his chair, confused. "Why? Why what?"

"Why are we taking over the world? Not you and me, but why does Russia need to run the world, excepting China and its territories?"

Dmitriy thought for a moment. "I suppose I'm just doing my job. But if I really think about it, the main reason would be the defence of our country. I have no doubt that America would destroy us or at least try to damage us irreparably, if they weren't afraid of the consequences."

"Are there positive reasons for doing it?" she asked.

"Perhaps I love the Russia described in VV's paper that's been leaked to the West, and I believe in our philosophy. I think it's worth pursuing."

Natalia considered his words for a moment before speaking again.

"I'm glad you believe there's a purpose. For me, I believe this is the only way we can bring true peace to the whole world. With Russia and China as good neighbours there can be lasting harmony. Some people will suffer in the short-term, but for the greater good, it's necessary. This is my great calling."

Dmitriy smiled softly, nodding in agreement. "You're right. That's a perspective I hadn't considered. This makes it even more worthwhile. Thank you."

Then, in that quiet moment, despite their location, they kissed, as true lovers do.

Chapter Eighteen

Federal Prison Camp Pensacola is a minimum-security federal facility for men, located in Florida. It was also the most well-known jail in the United States of America, primarily due to one inmate, former President Ronald Malone.

Malone had been the highest profile politician of his era and had built an almost cult-like following. However, he had also harboured the dangerous belief that he was above the law, and it had been a seismic shock when he was convicted of treason. His friend President Vasiliev had surreptitiously received copies of NATO's national defence plans – a critical document for NATO (The North Atlantic Treaty Organisation), the single body ensuring Russia's good behaviour. Sentenced to five years in prison, Malone had used his time behind bars as a platform to campaign for re-election the following year. His release was now just four weeks away, and if he was looking forward to it, that emotion was several times stronger for his security detail. Not only would they remain at the prison and, for a variety of reasons, many of the other inmates would have eagerly attacked Malone if given the chance. It would be a perfect opportunity to gain some notoriety.

There had been very few visitors for Malone, but he had been granted access to a phone. He was prohibited from contacting certain individuals, from running his businesses, engaging in any campaigning, or communicating with anyone from Russia. Yet, despite these restrictions, Malone carried on as though nothing had changed, and remarkably, there were no consequences. His security team dutifully reported his actions to their superiors, who assured them that it was all within acceptable limits.

Among Malone's few 'friends' was Bart Boulter, a multi-billionaire and funder of his political aspirations. Boulter was a man with extreme views and a fierce defensiveness about his own wealth. Any imposition by the state meant the potential for some of his fortune being spent on the 'undeserving' poor; after all, in his view, if they were truly worth anything, they would be earning it. His philosophy was based on an easy equation that the salary someone took home reflected their true worth, so if teachers were underpaid, it was their own fault. Boulter appreciated the strength of President Vasiliev, the might of his military power, and the Russian loathing of the liberal elite. He saw no irony in spending tens of millions of dollars ensuring he spent a lot less than that in taxation.

Malone always rang Boulter and never the other way around. He had convinced himself that this was because of his imprisonment, but the reality was he needed Boulter more than Boulter needed him. Late June in Florida meant the weather was hot, very hot. Malone, a large man, was sweating like a pig.

"Bart, my old buddy," opened Malone on the phone call he had initiated.

"Mr President," came the reply. Boulter wasn't impressed by the man but respected he had created a persona that had once reached the White House. Boulter was also well aware that for someone like Malone, flattery was everything to any narcissist.

"How can I help you, Sir?" Boulter continued, the words dripping with a feigned deference.

Malone revelled in the subservience of the multi-billionaire. His delusion of grandeur remained persistent.

"Just four weeks until I am released. The campaign begins then," Malone said, his voice thick with anticipation.

"Mr President, I want you to listen carefully and do not interrupt. Leave prison quietly and keep your head down," Boulter advised, his tone firm.

"But my people want to hear from me! I cannot keep my mouth shut," Malone protested, frustration evident in his voice.

Boulter sighed heavily before continuing, "I know things. I can only advise you to please take this seriously."

Malone, a large man, was perched on the edge of his bed with his head bowed. He let out a deep sigh. "I'll consider it, but my people need me," he whined, his voice barely above a whisper.

Chapter Nineteen

Bychkov entered the Presidential office.

President Vasiliev greeted him cordially, "Aleksandr, welcome. I believe this is a meeting regarding the appointments to the role of President in the various mega-nations."

"Correct, Mr President."

"I have prepared a list, including the Deputies. What are your thoughts?"

A sheet of paper was passed across the desk. Bychkov leant back in the chair he had taken opposite his leader, taking a moment to read the proposals.

"The Angloland nominee is Ronald Malone. But isn't he still in prison?"

"He is but will be released in a few weeks' time. And, frankly, it wouldn't matter even if he weren't. We will be in control. Malone is being rewarded for his earlier cooperation in releasing sensitive information to us. Between you and me, this is a temporary appointment. Afterwards, the billionaire Bart Boulter will assume the mantle. Boulter has funded Malone's campaign, allowing him to serve our interests."

"I must admit, I'm surprised that the Irish Taoiseach is being appointed as his deputy."

"Everyone loves the Irish and his appointment will help maintain balance."

The two continued working their way through the list. The only other notable point of discussion was the appointment of the President of Turkey to oversee Europe. However, the President was adamant that this had to be a very strong character in the job. Additionally, the appointment of a Muslim to the position would likely provoke significant backlash in Western Europe.

Bychkov stood up and concluded, "Thank you for this. The team and I will be here early on Monday morning. Unless a crisis arises, I'll see you then."

"And what about the talks with Xiu in China?"

"They're scheduled for tomorrow. Would you like an update before Monday?"

"Monday will be fine."

Chapter Twenty

It was more than fortunate, to say the least, that Aleksandr Bychkov and Xiu Feng Wang both spoke English. Their conversation, conducted over a highly secure line, didn't require translators. However, there was still an obliqueness to references regarding the nations being discussed.

Xiu began, "I believe you know which of our neighbours we feel closest to."

"I can hazard a guess. If you'd like to confirm them, I will tell you if we feel any particular affection towards them."

"Our primary aim, which has been the case for years, is for Taiwan to be recognised as a fully integrated land in the Chinese Republic. Given their proximity, we also believe that Mongolia, the Koreas, Myanmar, Laos, Vietnam and the Philippines should forge closer ties with us."

Being careful not to appear too eager, Bychkov paused before responding.

"The Philippines might not be too far away but there don't seem to be any obvious links."

"We have become close politically over the last few years," Xiu countered. "But that's not a deal breaker. If we could discuss Japan instead?"

Bychkov feigned astonishment. "Really? That's a rather unexpected turn. Is this because of old animosities?"

"We believe it's time to overcome previous difficulties and work towards harmony in the relationship."

"Agreed," Bychkov replied, leaning forward slightly. "For the sake of our friendship, I will support your quest to have better links and strengthen ties with Mongolia, the Koreas, Myanmar, Laos, and Vietnam. In return, as an understanding of our mutual interests, we will develop stronger connections with the Philippines, while you work on Japan. I'll need to justify this back home, but for now, consider our thoughts as a decision."

Xiu's voice softened with approval. "If only every conversation could be as clear and straightforward as this. Thank you."

Chapter Twenty-One

Sokolov, Gusev, the Morazovs, and Bychkov convened on the Friday before their meeting with President Vasiliev which was scheduled for three days later.

Sokolov began, "Dmitriy, Natalia, we firstly need to bring you up to date with some developments from our discussions with the President. We asked for the Chief of the General Staff to join this group. I am not only pleased this will happen, but I am also delighted to inform you that Boris Gusev has assumed that role."

Dmitriy and Natalia smiled broadly and congratulated the older man.

"What has happened to General Asimov?" asked Natalia.

Bychkov replied, "A very short illness. He will be buried with full military honours tomorrow."

Sokolov was amused at the naivety of his colleagues, and added, "It was an ailment brought on by his failure to look after his own health or, more accurately, his failure to look after the President's best interests."

"Oh, now I understand," said Morazov, although his wife still seemed unclear. "I'll explain it later, so that we can proceed this morning."

Bychkov was more blunt. "Natalia, he died from lead poisoning. It was administered through a barrel."

Natalia blushed and blurted out, "Sorry, you must think I am an idiot. In one way, it is very motivational. I mean, if that's the price of failure…"

Gusev, the subject of the conversation, who had remained silent until now, spoke for the first time.

"Thank you for your kind words. Asimov was a fool who couldn't keep his mouth shut. This is a tight-knit group, but our real problems will arise when more people begin to see more of the bigger picture. If you have any doubts about someone, let's isolate them. I've spent the last two days bringing myself up to speed with our armed forces' strengths and current deployments. With a limited amount of tweaking, we can have people and their equipment in position by early December."

Bychkov was pleased. "I will. I'll leak it to the West, using my alter ego, Rasputin, that something big is coming just before the troop movements. They will continue to believe it's typical Russian behaviour."

"And you have more to report, Comrade Bychkov?" asked Sokolov. Though now the third most senior person in the room, he remained in control of the project. It was a very unusual situation in Russia for status to be of little concern.

"Indeed," Bychkov replied. "The President has given me the list of his proposals for the leaders and their deputies of the new countries. If anyone has objections, we can raise them but there must be a strong rationale. Let me read them out:

Angloland

Ronald Malone	USA
Padraig Kelly	Ireland

Europe

Mehmet Akbas	Turkey

Uwe Haller   Germany

North Africa
Babu Hussain   Egypt
Yousef Chakir   Morocco

Africana
Happy Imeh   Nigeria
Angelino Pinto   Mozambique

Greater Iran
Ayatollah Ahmad Shirvani Iran
Prince Omar Abbas   Saudi Arabia

Greater India
Raaz Subramanian   India
Ram Tapadia   Nepal

West Asia
Lee Michael   Singapore
Bimo Agung   Indonesia

Australasia
Graham Lee   Australia
Rupeni Ratu   Fiji

Brasilia

Paulo Oliveira	Brazil
Victor Leon	Venezuela

Russian Empire

Vladimir Vasiliev	Russia
Aleksandr Bychkov	Russia

The President has helpfully added the capital cities. They are: Washington DC, Istanbul, Cairo, Lagos, Tehran, Mumbai, Singapore, Sydney, Rio de Janeiro, and Moscow. You can see that, for many, these are the capital cities today but, in a number of cases, the new capital will be a larger city in that country. This, I think, is for ease of access and to facilitate our monitoring. Any comments?"

The room fell silent, and silence was taken as agreement.

"Comrade, we cannot let that final name pass without comment and congratulations are in order," Sokolov said.

Bychkov merely waved his hand dismissively, urging them to move on.

Dmitriy Morazov asked, "What's the status of the agreement with China?"

Bychkov replied, "China will take lands pretty much in alignment with our expectations: Mongolia, the Koreas, Myanmar, Laos, and Vietnam plus, and this may surprise you, Japan. Note, I've excluded the Philippines. They've been kept for their assets."

Dmitriy knew better than to debate these decisions and simply asked, "Which of us will communicate with the new nations of the Chinese Empire on D Day?"

"China will handle that," Bychkov said. "Remove them from any list of actions you have."

The meeting moved on, an indication of the absorbing nature of their plans and China's absorption of Japan was almost accepted without comment.

"Natalia, you were going to draft the communications. What progress have you made?" Sokolov enquired.

"I'll put them onto the screen. No paper drafts yet.

The first document is the script for the conversation with State Heads. It reads:

Mr President, Prime Minister, Your Highness,

Whilst you are aware that your phone, all electronic devices and those of people near you are no longer working, please let me assure you this is the situation across the whole globe.

Russia has developed technology to suspend all electronic communications. There are no phones, no internet, no electronic signals, no ability to use any weapons except the most basic ones. In short, there is no way to do anything.

In particular, you may be concerned about your nuclear weapons and nuclear power stations which will heat up rapidly.

I will re-connect your phone connection and ring you in one hour to hear how you wish to proceed. You will either communicate to your nation that we are in control and full co-operation is required, or they will face the consequences of your inaction.

I will not answer any questions.

Please be ready with your answer in one hour."

Natalia paused, waiting for comments.

Gusev said, "I will go first. I think there should be a statement about a new world order."

Bychkov agreed, "I concur and just emphasise Russia is in total control."

Natalia nodded and made the adjustments.

Sokolov gave his approval. "Excellent. We can refine this further if necessary, and the President may have additional comments. Next is the communication to the citizens of the whole world, excluding the Chinese Empire."

Natalia changed the document on the screen.

"This one is longer," she proffered.

Friends,

You will know by now that your government has had no choice but to accept that Russia now controls the world.

This marks the beginning of a new order, one which will bring stability and fairness for everyone, and in which lasting peace will be created.

There will be new mega-countries, and you will be told which one you belong to, along with the name of its President.

Our technology means we can monitor everything you do; there can be no criminality, no conspiracy and no collusion.

There will be a job for everyone who is able to work, with a guaranteed income. And nobody will pay taxes.

Our ethos is based on a society which is 'safe, clean and useful.'

There will be a new morality in which there is no abortion, no legalised homosexuality, no acceptance of transgender changes, and no guns. There is an amnesty for all weapons until 5th January. Please take them to your local police station.

There will be no social media, but we will support religion, television and sport. We want people to be happy.

Television will resume on 1st January, and we will let you know a great deal more information then.

We will strictly enforce the law. Anyone who violates these laws will feel the full impact of the new State, which has the autonomy to use force and capital punishment.

Again, Natalia waited for their thoughts.

"I will start again," Gusev said. "Can we substitute rebellion for collusion, please?"

"I like that," Dmitriy supported.

Sokolov had been thinking about its application across all continents, whereas it was tempting to merely wonder about the reception in the West. He added, "There are tribes and sects in Africa that might see this is the time to settle old scores. Should we specifically state that bloodletting will be met with extreme force?"

"Why not? It makes the message more powerful in its own right," agreed Bychkov, the Foreign Minister and de facto Deputy President of three-quarters of the world. "And add the President's name!" he said as an afterthought.

Natalia updated the text.

"So, the proposed changes will be reflected in the revised draft," she affirmed.

Sokolov moved the meeting forward. "Great work. Now, the message for the Russian people."

Natalia revealed the next missive.

Fellow Russians,

Our great nation is now the leader of the entire world. Through the brilliance of our engineers and technicians, we have conquered the world without violence.

There is a new Russian Empire, into which all our cousins from the old Union of Soviet Socialist Republics will rejoin us.

Russians are special people and will be treated as such. You will have guaranteed employment and an excellent wage, pay no taxes and have full healthcare.

A few people may be unhappy, but we will be monitoring anyone who resists. Please accept the new order and enjoy the benefits.

We now have peace, peace based on our victory.

President Vasiliev

"Okay?" asked Natalia.

"It is and I think President Vasiliev should make a TV appearance."

"Try and stop him," mused his deputy.

"Finally, the message for the new 'Russians' brought back into the Empire," Sokolov continued.

Natalia revealed the final slide.

Friends,

Russia has conquered the world peacefully. Your nation has been reintegrated into the Russian Empire.

Russians are special people and will be treated as such. You will have guaranteed employment and good wages, pay no taxes and have full healthcare.

A few people may be unhappy, but we will be monitoring anyone resisting. Please accept the new order and enjoy the benefits.

We now have peace, a peace based on our victory.

President Vasiliev

"Again, the simplicity of the message makes it all the more powerful," Bychkov confirmed.

"Are we ready for the meeting with the President on Monday?" Sokolov asked.

Dmitriy offered, "I am hugely grateful for your support. We will be working on the details over the weekend, but I believe we'll be ready to brief him fully on Monday morning."

Chapter Twenty-Two

In Beijing, Huang and Xiu met in the former's office. Neither wore a suit and tie but instead wore the more informal but more traditional jackets, the style most commonly associated with Mao Tse Tung.

They were alone, this time without the need for a trigger word, as both knew the subject matter.

Huang was very keen to hear about Xiu's meeting with Bychkov. "How did it go?"

"Very well," Xiu replied. "I didn't secure the Philippines, but I was able to negotiate to get the real prizes of Taiwan and Japan. Our agent in the room had indicated this was the way to go."

"Excellent news," Huang said. "We can settle them before we take the final step halfway through next year. Please write the communications and ensure you're very clear about the penalties for resistance."

For a few minutes, the two men relaxed and drank tea together.

Chapter Twenty-Three

At 6.55 a.m. on Monday, the group assembled in the outer office of President Vasiliev. None of them had slept much the night before the meeting.

Natalia and Dmitriy had been working until past midnight, yet they both appeared fresh and focused, despite the underlying tension.

"All good?" Mikhail Sokolov asked, his voice steady but his eyes searching.

They smiled in response, projecting positivity. Inside they were squirming, as it could go badly and then who knew what might happen.

At exactly 7 a.m. the door to his office opened and the President stood there. He beckoned them to join him inside.

Over the next three hours, President Vasiliev challenged, probed, questioned, and occasionally praised the team. There was no further use of the nickname 'VV' as this was a meeting regarding the most critical state matters. Several of the team's assumptions were tweaked and a number of even more hardline policies were introduced.

"This is exceptional, and I can only thank you all."

He paused, then added, "We will meet at least monthly as a team. Aleksandr will brief me weekly, and, of course, I may ask everyone to reconvene at short notice. Finally, I need to discuss how we will brief the people to be appointed as the Presidents and Deputy Presidents of the new mega-countries."

It was Sokolov who responded, "This is one of the most problematic points because there is no guarantee that secrecy will be maintained, no matter how much they are threatened. My observation over the years is that everyone has one person they trust implicitly. But, unfortunately, that one person also has one person in whom they place trust, and very quickly the confidentiality is lost. My recommendation is that we brief them immediately before the switch is hit. By this I mean literally five minutes beforehand. We can still insist they tell nobody, but by that point, it won't matter. The alternative is to synchronise their phones so they're accessible simultaneously, as the existing Heads of State are informed. They are, after all mostly already in those roles, with one exception."

The President considered this carefully before replying, "I prefer the latter option. If we then allow our nominees to be able to speak to the heads of the respective armed forces, we can ensure proper control."

The meeting concluded and the team returned to their secure base in Putin Place.

Chapter Twenty-Four

It was 18th December and Sokolov, Gusev, Bychkov, and the Morazovs were working non-stop. It was incredible that there had been no leaks, although a small number of staff had been lost, those who sought to leave their isolation in remote locations or who had begun to object as the true purpose of the operation became clearer.

"Have we finalised the President's address to the new world leaders?" enquired Bychkov.

Natalia Morazov nodded and began, "Let me run this by you."

My friends, and if we are not friends, there will be profound consequences.

You will be aware that nothing works in your country. There are no phones, no internet, no electricity, nothing.

Your video conferencing facilities have been activated specifically for this meeting.

You are, with the exception of former President Malone, all the leaders of your nations.

If you agree to our proposal, you will become the head of a new mega-nation.

Every other world leader has been given one hour to accede to our domination. In truth they have no choice because we have conquered the world, with the exception of the Chinese Empire, without firing a single bullet.

There is, however, a caveat, about which they will be unhappy, in that we are setting the rules.

For now, let me show you the configuration of the political make-up of the new world order.

Angloland

USA, Canada, Ireland, UK

Europe

Western and Eastern Europe as far as Turkey

North Africa

Lands north of the Sahara Desert

Africana

Lands south of the Sahara Desert

Greater Iran

Iran plus the Middle East, including Iraq, Saudi Arabia and Israel

Greater India

Incorporates India, Pakistan, Afghanistan, Bangladesh and Nepal

Eastern Asia

The Philippines, East Timor, Thailand, Singapore, Indonesia, and Malaysia

Australasia

Australia, New Zealand, and the Pacific Islands

Brasilia

The whole of South America and Central America, as far north as Mexico, up to the border with the USA, plus associated islands

Russian Empire

Our traditional lands, as previously configured in the USSR

The Chinese Empire

China, Taiwan, Laos, Korea, Myanmar, Vietnam, Mongolia, and Japan

It is critical that you understand there will be no debate. We may tweak things in the future but there will be no land grabs or arguments. Your positions of power exist solely because I have chosen you. I can change my mind at any time.

For now, instruct your head of the military to prepare for a smooth transition.

Do not take a soft line. Embedding our vision requires the firmest implementation. I trust you understand my meaning.

With regard to the USA, President Keaton will either surrender or die in the White House. President Malone, your political base, your followers, will love our moral ethos, which will make it easier for you.

Your electronic media are now fully operational, as will be those of the leaders who will now report to you.

Bring them up to speed and make it clear what their future holds if they resist. There may be skirmishes involving conventional weapons but deal with them decisively.

While we cannot predict all of the reactions but against the criteria we have set, you can impose our will.

President Akbas, you may be surprised to find yourself President of Europe. Impose your authority, impose your religion if you wish, but our aim is not to create conflict. It's simply to ensure that everyone understands how life will be structured from now on.

Your briefing packs have been sent to you. Please digest them with the greatest speed but remember, our goal is peace though there will be resistance. The moral foundation is a conservative one, yet everyone who can contribute to society will be well treated.

Safe, clean and useful. These are the guiding principles. In six months' time, there will be a totally new world order.

Do not fail, for any divergence from the described path will be fatal.

Either my deputy, Aleksandr Bychkov, or I will have a one-to-one briefing with each of you within the next 24 hours. I expect to hear of significant progress."

Natalia Morazov stopped and looked at her President.

"I may add a touch of my own style," Vasiliev said, "but this reflects our views exactly."

He continued, "In essence, if the technical solutions are in place, we are ready. Let's be clear, there will, of course, be issues to confront, and it will get messy. But we have the power to impose our will in a manner never before available to any nation. It is our destiny, and it is the destiny for the world."

The room fell silent for a moment as the magnitude of the plan was allowed to sink in. This was the moment it moved from conception to become reality.

"One week from today, in my office," Vasiliev concluded, his voice unyielding, "we will hit the switch."

Chapter Twenty-Five

President Huang sat in his office, visibly impatient as he awaited news regarding Moscow's actions. His usual calm was being tested by the rising tension in the air.

The door opened abruptly, and Xiu Feng Wang hurried in. "I have an update, Mr President."

Huang was expressionless as he suppressed the frustration he felt.

"Why has it taken so long?"

"Mr President," Xiu, slightly out of breath from the rush, responded, "Our agent is literally in the room and has to be exceedingly careful. It's the small price we pay for the quality of the information that we receive."

"I understand, but I am not used to waiting," Huang replied, his voice betraying his frustration for just a moment. "Sorry, my friend. What is the news?"

Xiu took a deep breath and appeared to grow by three inches, "The Russians go active at 9 a.m. Moscow time, on 25th December. This means the American President will be woken at 2 am, disoriented and vulnerable. In the UK it will be 7 a.m. and their administration will be about to crank up for the new day. However, it's Christmas Day, so hardly anyone will be at their desk. Crucially, it will be dark. The Russians are keen to limit any possible resistance."

Huang nodded slowly, a faint glint of admiration in his eyes. "Very sensible thinking by Vasiliev. His only mistake is appeasing China, and for that, he will ultimately suffer."

Power Denied

Huang paused, considering the next step. "Have you moved the troops into place as our part of the ruse?"

Xiu's eyes gleamed with confidence. "One hundred thousand men and women are in position and ready to act, should Vasiliev decide that immediate and total domination is possible."

Over the next sixty minutes, Xiu brought his leader up to speed with China's preparations and their own plans to dominate the world.

Chapter Twenty-Six

Even by Moscow's standards it was cold, very cold at minus 10 degrees Celsius. Temperature is only one dimension; the killing factor was the easterly wind. There was no escape from its penetrative thrusts.

The walk from their car to the office took less than thirty seconds, however, for Dmitriy and Natalia it was literally painful. Being wrapped up in coats, scarves and gloves was inadequate protection. Dmitriy had been a student of Russian history since his childhood. He was astonished that so many people survived the winter when living conditions were primitive. Perhaps it was the deprivations which created the defensive psyche which prevailed. If even the weather is against you, why would you accept the friendship of foreigners? Dmitriy knew of families of eight or ten people living in two rooms with only three beds. No sanitation, little natural light, and infestations of bugs, which were also trying to survive.

The grand project in which they were engaged was about to give the Russian people a new life. They would be wealthy and, most importantly, warm. On the occasional moments he allowed his mind to wander, Dmitriy saw a future in which his wonderful wife and he were heroes of the State and had been rewarded appropriately. Natalia had disturbed this picture when she had asked him if he had a 'Why'? Until that point it was just his next task, albeit the biggest task anyone had ever undertaken. Today was 23rd December and the final stage of preparation.

In the 'war room' in Putin Place the Morazovs were the first to arrive at 6 a.m. They had grabbed six hours for themselves, only two of which were for sleep.

It was a matter of tremendous amazement to Dmitriy that there had been no leaks. The only issue had been a technician from Irkutsk who had told his family of his suspicions and, even though they were pleased he was involved in such a quest, it was a potential problem. The whole family had been eliminated, although it was as humanely as possible; they knew nothing about it until the last second. Pride comes before the fall.

Gusev came in. He had been up all night personally directing the military. Troops were now moving towards the borders, including the one with China. President Huang was fully aware this was a feint and not a threat. Notwithstanding, for the pretence to be accepted as a reality by the West, China had to move their forces into position.

On the western borders Russia deployed masses of its army near to Finland and Norway in Scandinavia, across the frontier with the remainder of Ukraine, the Baltic States of Estonia, Latvia and Lithuania, Mongolia, and all of the connected States of the USSR. The greater numbers were adjacent to Ukraine and the Baltic States, exactly the places which would create the strongest fears the USA, European Union and the UK would have.

"Everything is in place. Not only have we moved the armed forces forward but there are also explicit supply chains in place. Ammunition, fuel, food and everything else we need are clearly seen to be on the move," confirmed Gusev.

Bychkov nodded in his usual considered way.

"Well done, Boris. Let's wait for the reaction."

As he said it, the President of Estonia, Sofia Hommik, rang on his private phone, only available to a few people. It allowed them at times of crisis to circumvent the usual processes involved.

Bychkov answered, "Madam President. How can I help?"

"Mr Foreign Minister, what is going on? Why are my territories being approached by Russian forces?"

"Training exercises, I assure you. There is nothing to worry about. Your intelligence will be telling you we have moved troops towards all our borders."

"Whilst I appreciate your perspectives, I assure you this feels very intimidating."

Bychkov smiled at his colleagues as he smoothly continued, "My dear lady, Estonia is a friend, you, Sofia, are a friend and friends trust one another."

Sofia Hommik was even more worried but recognised this was a pointless call, except letting Bychkov know that she knew and would be reacting.

Mikhail Sokolov had entered the room during the exchange.

"Neatly done. She doesn't believe a word you said and will repeat verbatim to the Americans."

Gusev agreed and went on, "I wish it was D Day. This is killing me. We know that the technology will work, and every hour could be the one it all leaks out. However, I accept that there are two days to go. I wonder how President Keaton is in Washington. I imagine this is spoiling his supper."

Chapter Twenty-Seven

On the east coast of the contiguous United States of America it was 10 p.m., and 7 p.m. in Los Angeles.

Every effort had been made to keep Russia's activities secret, but the news channels were full of it. Rampant speculation regarding the motivation was not helping and the White House was expected to give a public reaction.

In the Oval Office, President Keaton was consulting with his top officials, both civil and military. Nearly forty people were there, most standing. The 'top brass' had migrated there from the Situation Room, which contained all of the latest intelligence from around the globe.

"Ladies and gentlemen, in one hour I am going on television to reassure our people. Should I do this confidently, knowing there is no imminent Armageddon?" asked Keaton.

General Hank Maloney, chief of staff of the Army, spoke, "The Ruskies will not attack, it's a bluff to bolster Vasiliev's popularity in Moscow."

It was typical of Maloney to be dismissive and patronising in equal measure. This time, perhaps for different reasons, nobody disagreed.

"Okay, if we are of an accord, my theme will be the real problem is the sensationalism of the media. We are the dominant force, and Russia is playing games for their own purposes. Before we break up, may I ask how we had no idea these troop movements were a surprise to us?"

The silence meant it was left to the Defence Secretary Brett Armstrong, a political appointee, to reply.

"This is something we will need to investigate thoroughly, Mr President."

"Okay. I won't see many of you again before Christmas, so may I wish you and your families a wonderful time. Please rest and come back prepared to face anything our enemies have for us."

The meeting broke up with an uncoordinated amount of handshaking and backslapping.

Only Chip Weaver, Chief of Staff, remained in the room. Keaton was unamused by the reaction of his people.

"January will be the last time Cartwright heads the CIA. Hundreds of thousands of Russian people are on the road and we only see them when they are in position. Our people saw it and he hasn't put in place the basic process for escalation. And CNN revealed it to our people. I am beyond annoyed."

Weaver said nothing, mainly because Cartwright had informed him the day before and it was Weaver who made the decision to suppress the news, even from the Commander-in-Chief, the President.

"Have the speechwriters done their work? Get them in and we can rehearse," requested the President.

An hour later, the news channels across the USA were interrupted for an address from the White House. Keaton was, as ever, perfectly attired, reflecting his view of the manner a person of his stature should present himself.

"My fellow Americans,

I am speaking to you from the Oval Office in the White House.

You will have seen and heard about Russian troop movements, especially in Europe. My purpose in this very short communication is to reassure you there is nothing for us to worry about.

President Vasiliev has personally confirmed these are planned exercises.

I am, of course, disappointed that our media have chosen to exaggerate the situation.

Have a great Christmas. God bless you all and God bless America."

The light went out over the camera and Keaton relaxed. Weaver nodded his appreciation and left the room. Sally Keaton, his loyal wife, kissed her husband and retired to her rooms.

Keaton sat and smiled at the technicians, all of whom ignored him. A cold seeped through his body, a feeling his grandmother would have described as 'someone walking over my grave.'

Chapter Twenty-Eight

At 7 a.m. Moscow time, everyone working on the project was given an overview of the coming hours. Of the 3,000 people involved only seven objected. They were removed and their silence ensured.

President Vasiliev was dressed in military uniform, prepared for his TV messages to the peoples of the Russian Empire. He was surrounded by his inner circle as 8 a.m. approached.

Even after the months of preparation, this was the moment the full magnitude of their efforts became blisteringly clear.

Aleksandr Bychkov, Mikhail Sokolov, and Boris Gusev were very senior members of the Russian hierarchy, but for Dmitriy and Natalia Morazov this was a level beyond their realistic aspirations, albeit they were very well connected.

The time passed both quickly and slowly. This existential moment in which they wanted to get on but were equally fearful of the consequences of failure.

At 8.55 a.m. the President stood up, and the others joined him.

"I want to say thank you for everything. I know the real breakthrough was technological, but your efforts, creativity and, I will say, brilliance has brought us to this point. If it doesn't work, we are actually able to deny everything, so let's not worry. However, I am totally confident that in less than five minutes' time we will be in control of the whole world. Think about that, in five minutes nothing will be the same. There is a huge responsibility involved, and we must bear it with compassion. Remember, safe, clean and useful."

Vasiliev moved to the phone. He picked it up and pressed a single button. Instantly it was answered by a man with a voice which sounded like it belonged to a very young person.

"Mr President?"

"The password is Domination. Domination Day is here; D Day has come. Press the button."

Robert Ball

Part Two
Executing – December

Chapter Twenty-Nine

At 2.07 a.m. in Washington, Chip Weaver burst into the Presidential bedroom. He didn't care about the niceties of the moment. He was using a large and powerful torch.

President Keaton shouted out, "What's happening?" He was, as predicted, disoriented.

Protocol was lost as Weaver shook Keaton.

"Everything has shut down. Nothing electrical is working."

President Keaton was awake and alert, "Is it just Washington?"

"We don't know. There are no communications. Nothing."

Keaton took a deep breath. "So, we could be under attack, and not only could we not resist, but we also wouldn't know it."

"And the Russians are at the borders of Europe."

Keaton and his wife had separate bedrooms because he was frequently awoken in the dead of night.

"I won't wake my wife. It could just be a major power shutdown."

Spooking both of them, Keaton's private and secret phone rang. Perhaps with hindsight they might have described their reactions as ridiculous as they both stared at the device.

"You may want to answer," suggested Weaver.

Very hesitantly, Keaton picked up the phone and answered. "Who is this?"

"Vladimir Vasiliev. Good morning, Mr President."

"How did you get this number?"

"The whole of your country is shut down and your primary concern is the fact I have your phone number. You are ludicrous. Let me outline the situation for you. The great people of Russia have taken control of everything. At this moment nuclear plants and hospitals have emergency generators which can only last for a short time. There are airplanes flying without contact with the ground and some will soon fall from the sky. Some of your traditional weapons will function but, in reality, they are irrelevant against our sophisticated weaponry. Russia has conquered the whole world and done it peacefully."

Keaton was stupefied; he couldn't move. Here he was, the most powerful man in the free world, and utterly helpless. Weaver began twitching with rage as his normal red complexion rapidly moved to purple.

"What do you want?"

Vasiliev was calmness personified. The hours of discussions and rehearsals meant he was fully prepared for whichever direction this conversation went.

"I am sure you have guessed you are now former President Keaton. I was going to offer you the chance to address the American people to endeavour to ensure a smooth transition to the new order, but I have changed my mind. In thirty minutes, your successor will arrive at the White House. President Malone will later today speak to the people and reassure them of the generosity of the Russian Empire. You will be taken to a secure place and removed from office. You have nothing to worry about in terms of the safety of you, your family and your colleagues."

"You can't do this. We are a democracy; my people have chosen me and rejected Malone."

"Please don't be an innocent. We have won. It is a fait accompli. Kindly do not annoy me."

And the phone went dead again.

Keaton and Weaver looked at each other, confused and uncomprehending.

"Get the Chiefs and my security."

"How?"

"I must tell my wife." And Keaton swept through to the adjacent bedroom.

Chapter Thirty

In London, His Majesty, King Philip, was taking a cold shower when Vasiliev rang. Whilst he was aware there was a power cut, the broader implications had not filtered through.

The phone number was only known to the family, so a strange number showing on the face of the phone unnerved him. Added to his discomfort was his nakedness and the dripping water. The towel wasn't effective, and his valet wasn't there. The man was late, a fact of the blackout created by Russia he would later realise.

Vasiliev wanted this call to be a positive one.

"Your Majesty, this is Vladimir Vasiliev calling. Please accept my apologies for using your private number. You may not be aware that the Russian Empire has peacefully taken over the whole world. We have suspended all systems and, I am afraid, this includes the United Kingdom. Our sole quest is peace, but we will be replacing governments."

The King was dumbstruck.

"What? How? Why?"

Vasiliev moved on, "You will, if you cooperate, remain monarch of the UK. Sadly, any influence you had in the Commonwealth is over. I see you having a significant role in maintaining a balance, keeping your subjects away from dissent and rebellion. They cannot win and nobody wants bloodshed."

"I must talk to the Prime Minister."

"You can't, she is incommunicado. In one hour, I will need your answer. Please think about the welfare of the nation."

The phone went dead, and Philip was a beaten man. There was no alternative, and he even attempted to persuade himself that his capitulation would be for the greater good, and not self-preservation.

In Downing Street, the home and office of the Prime Minister of the United Kingdom of Great Britain and Northern Ireland, after her call from Vasiliev, Julia Jones was mortified. She recognised there was no escape.

"How can this have happened?" she asked nobody. She too was alone and had no means of contacting anyone.

Chapter Thirty-One

Over the next hour, Vasiliev, Bychkov, Sokolov, Gusev and several fully briefed senior statesmen, and they all were men, rang every world leader.

The responses varied from abject fear, through genuine pleasure to outright aggression. The national heads who took the latter view were placed on a 'Soon-to-be-replaced' list, though that would be settled by the new leaders of the mega-countries.

Naturally, there were fundamental questions, most of which related to their own future. More generally, when was the power going to be switched on? How will 'Safe, Clean and Useful' be interpreted? How will dissidents be treated? When will people know the details?

The feedback was collated for a meeting of Vasiliev's inner sanctum which was the original group plus eight Politburo members. It had only been three hours since the button had been pushed but the speed of it all had taken everyone by surprise.

Thirty minutes later they convened.

"This is the Supreme Cabinet of the Russian Empire. We fourteen people rule the world, excepting the Chinese Empire. For the next forty-eight hours we will meet every six hours, not to debate, but to hear updates and decide on our actions," began Vasiliev.

There were no smiles, no expressions of satisfaction, just an absolute determination to fully enforce their victory.

"In the next day, the new rulers of the mega-countries will convene with us to clarify their roles and actions. Remember, we are the decision-makers," continued the President.

"Comrade Morazov, you are coordinating the intelligence. Where are the major points of issue?"

Dmitriy was outwardly composed, but inside his guts were in turmoil. Thankfully he wasn't prone to sweat or show other signs of nerves. Here he was, with his wife, amongst the people with the fate of literally billions of people at their mercy. This time it was the Minister of Armaments, Leonid Popov, who broke the tension, "Purple socks Morazov?" Perhaps it is at times of the greatest tension and seriousness that humour is most important.

Dmitriy exhaled and began, "All of the proposed leaders of the mega-countries have accepted their invitations."

Vasiliev interjected, "I suspect some of them may be too excited about the opportunities for retribution with old enemies. I want very strong action to ensure compliance with the new regime but, and I really mean this, I want to bring harmony in the medium term. Bloodletting for reasons of ego and emotion must be kept in check."

Sokolov supported, "This may be particularly the case in Greater Iran and Africana, and perversely in Angloland, specifically the United States of America."

There was a general murmur of acknowledgement.

"Your address to the Presidents of the mega-countries will be crucial, Mr President," said the Minister of Health, Lev Novikov. "For what time is it scheduled?"

Vasiliev replied, "You are correct Comrade. In one hour, we meet. These appointments can be cancelled as easily as they are made. Morazov, please continue."

"Perhaps I may ask Comrade Gusev to update us about the military situation, please."

Gusev assembled his papers.

"In many countries our diplomatic staff will have to take control because the local authorities have ceded their sovereignty, and Comrade Bychkov has more detail. However, our troops have crossed borders into the ex-NATO nations to support the Ambassadors. There is resistance but mainly, we think, because there are no communications and the forces on the ground don't know what is happening."

"So, the addresses from the new regional Presidents must be clear and unequivocal. That will be on January 1st. The scripts are written, and we must monitor that they are followed. I am especially concerned about President Malone who cannot control his tongue, but he has been a loyal friend," said Vasiliev.

Gusev carried on, "In most cases in which the new Presidents are strong leaders, their armed forces will take over. This does mean that Morazov's team will begin to relax the communications media for the individual leaders."

"The ability to open specific areas and ensure only the authorities can use them was the trickiest technical issue, but we have succeeded, indeed this was the breakthrough which has given us this victory," confirmed Dmitriy. He immediately realised that it sounded like he had conquered the world and continued, "However, the mechanistic aspects are a small contribution to our President's master plan."

"Well recovered, Morazov," said Vasiliev.

Gusev jumped in to move the conversation forward, "Our forces will be landing on every continent during today. Without the local people we couldn't cope, but our ability to identify dissidents will mean strict adherence from the respective peoples being maintained."

Vasiliev nodded, "It all seems too smooth. When will our first big problem arise?"

Bychkov had been absorbing everything. "When we allow any form of communication, the people will want to know how it will affect them, and how they can revert to their 'normal', whatever that is."

"My view is the biggest issues relate to nuclear plants and the currently airborne planes," Natalia said.

Of course, Gusev wanted to support his niece, "This is true, and whilst I fear a few planes will be lost, we cannot afford a nuclear incident."

Bychkov came back in, "We know where all the reactors are. I will contact the key people but Morazov, we need them to have communication in two hours."

"As soon as I am given the nod, it will happen," came the confirmation from Dmitriy Morazov.

"Next point?" asked Vasiliev.

"Our ongoing monitoring is critical as the power is returned, but the next major event is your briefing to the new Supremos, Mr President," said Sokolov.

"Let's adjourn until midday, by which time that meeting will have taken place, and we will have more intelligence from around the world."

Chapter Thirty-Two

In Beijing, President Huang Peng and his Deputy, Xiu Feng Wang, were to put it mildly, keenly interested observers.

"Do we have any information on how it is going across the world?" the President asked, almost breathlessly.

"We don't. Remember, our embassy staffs are also incommunicado. However, our Washington Ambassador has a phone which works separately, and he reports total blackness. Our agent in the room is, well, in the room and, therefore, cannot update us. Our troops are on high alert, just in case, but it is fair to assume Russian forces are being aligned elsewhere. Importantly, the commitment to keep our power and systems operational has been met."

"You must update me as soon as we receive credible intelligence. Of course, we want Vasiliev to be successful, as our time horizon is approximately six months. I will admit to you I am nervous."

Xiu had never heard his boss sound so vulnerable, and his loyalty meant he would never divulge this to anyone else. They were engaged in the most significant game ever and, at that moment, they had no control over the tactics or strategies: it was pure impotence. The Chinese President and his Deputy sat in silence for five minutes contemplating the evolving situation and its ramifications.

It was at this moment that Vasiliev called President Huang via video conference.

"Mr President, you now have control of the extended Chinese Empire. Our Deputies will coordinate the switching on of the technology, but you will then need to deal with the individual nations as you feel appropriate."

Huang paused before responding. He was not a man given to behave emotionally, but this was a pivotal moment in his career. Taking control of Taiwan and Japan cemented his position at the pinnacle of Chinese politics for the rest of his life. That he had also absorbed North and South Korea was beyond the expectations of his compatriots, and the negotiation of the inclusion of Vietnam, Mongolia, Myanmar, Laos and even, at the last moment, an Indian state was the icing on the cake. His place in the history books was assured, even before the desired denouement. However, he was acutely aware that while Vasiliev was currently satisfied with his position, there could come a time when his ambitions grew, and the threat to the Chinese Empire became tangible.

"Mr President, congratulations on the brilliance of your conception and the outstanding implementation. You are a genius," Huang beamed, fully aware of the character of the Russian leader.

"Too kind, Mr President. For once, I will acknowledge the outstanding contribution of my team."

Huang was genuinely interested in the next question, "How did you manage to keep it secret?"

Vasiliev's face lost its smile. "Discipline and compartmentalising, added to a few red herrings, in fact, a huge shoal of red herrings. A few people forgot their place and then their lives. It's a very effective method for focussing the thoughts of others."

Huang nodded in agreement. "I can see that very clearly. A lesson for us all. Thank you, President Vasiliev. In our own ways, we will strive to make this a better world."

"An inspirational thought. Goodbye."

The line went dead. His Deputy sat silently next to the President.

"Talk to Bychkov immediately, please. I want to reach out to the current leaders of our new countries as soon as possible, ideally within the next hour."

Xiu left, leaving Huang to tweak the messages he was about to deliver.

Chapter Thirty-Three

"Ronald, I want you to be firm, I even want you to find reasons to demonstrate to the people of Angloland that our rule will be both firm and fair," Vasiliev said calmly. He felt that his demeanour was going to be crucial in managing the new situation effectively.

"But the first thing I want to do is speak with your predecessor, former President Keaton."

Malone blanched and prevaricated.

"Vladimir, I have everything under control. Leave it with me."

"Ronald, I insist. Bring Keaton to the call or have him ready to talk to me later."

Malone began to sweat. Like all bullies and narcissists, his behaviour was tied to his control of the situation, but if the roles were reversed, there was no strength.

"Unfortunately, Keaton resisted his arrest and there was an accident."

"An accident? Is he injured?"

"Terminally injured."

Malone had the thin smile of a man without lips. He was uncertain whether he had made a grave error, considering that Vasiliev had wanted to order the death of his enemy himself. Or even if Keaton would have been spared under different circumstances. Those options had disappeared because of Malone's desperate desire for revenge, to eliminate the man who had beaten him twice in elections, defeats which seemed impossible for a man who had been given everything he had ever wanted since he was a child. Psychologists had revelled in analysing him publicly from the first day he declared his ambition to become President of the now defunct United States of America.

Now Malone found himself reporting to a greater authority and didn't like it. He did recognise that, at this juncture, there wasn't a healthy alternative and was prepared to play the long game until he could hatch a plan.

It took Malone thirty seconds to realise that Vasiliev hadn't spoken.

"Sorry Vladimir, but these things happen."

"From now on, you will, in both public and private, refer to me as Mr President. For now, send me an image of Keaton's body."

The line went dead. Malone turned to his friend, Brett Taylor, a man he wanted to occupy a key position in the new Administration.

"Brett, we may have made a mistake killing Keaton. Let's not let Vasiliev know we had his family dealt with in a similar manner. We need to be more careful as we move forward, but those who have crossed us will be dealt with."

Taylor nodded but felt a sense of unease. He was deeply concerned that Malone was oblivious to the Russian's omnipotence and was displaying a troubling naivety. He didn't see Vasiliev as someone who would accept bluster as an excuse for anything. Taylor was the intellectual force behind Malone's public persona, the educated and sophisticated half of their partnership.

Chapter Thirty-Four

President Huang Peng sat upright in his chair behind a solid and ancient oak desk. The setup was deliberate, as everything with Huang was, to demonstrate the seriousness of his message.

Five minutes earlier, lights, televisions, and radios had been switched back on in Taiwan, though phones remained silent. A message had been transmitted announcing that a statement of supreme importance was to be made on the hour. It was later estimated that 60% of the population had tuned in. Huang's expression was unsmiling as he began.

"Citizens of Taiwan,

For the past few hours, the Chinese Empire has taken control of a number of territories which are rightfully and historically part of its lands. Most importantly, Taiwan is one of these former nations. You will now be governed from Beijing.

I know many of you will be concerned but I am here to reassure you. You have lost the notional sovereignty to which you have clung, but to a very large degree your daily lives will remain unchanged.

Inevitably, your political leadership will be replaced, and major decisions will be taken by my government. We will be generous to all members of the newly renamed Chinese Empire. After hundreds of years, our Empire will bring unity to the peoples of China, Hong Kong, Taiwan, Mongolia, Laos, Vietnam, Myanmar, North Korea, South Korea, Bhutan, and the Indian State of Jammu. The opportunities for everyone to be richer and happier are immense. However, this does rely on your full commitment to our shared prosperity.

Over the coming few days, we will outline the detailed changes, but until then, we will revert to a blackout. I know you will believe me when I say that we will not tolerate any dissent or rebellion. From the bottom of my heart, I urge you to recognise the situation and make every effort to be successful citizens.

The Chinese Empire is supreme."

Over the next half-hour, Huang delivered the same message to each of the newly subsumed countries, making only minor tweaks. Even in his presentation to the Japanese he managed to suppress any hint of joy at the final victory. One of the oldest conflicts in the world had ended painlessly.

In Moscow, Natalia Morazov had been monitoring the Chinese leader's performance throughout all the broadcasts. Naturally, there had been numerous subtitles for the highly interested observers. She wondered if the Chinese leadership would enforce the compulsory use of Mandarin.

She was able to report to Sokolov that Huang's message had been in line with the agreements made with President Vasiliev, that there were no signs of expansionism, and it had had a very reasonable tone. However, there were clear threats directed at potential troublemakers and dissidents.

Sokolov felt a sense of relief. Only that morning he had expressed a view that the Chinese might still think a more traditional conflict with Russia was possible. Now it appeared they accepted Russia had the capacity to be more than just difficult neighbours.

Chapter Thirty-Five

In Tokyo, crowds of predominantly young people gathered outside the Chinese Embassy, chanting their resistance and demanding a return to their democracy. The demonstrations were uncoordinated, just a spontaneous reaction to an act of aggression by China. No members of the staff in the Embassy building could be seen and the confidence that came from being part of a large crowd grew. Stones were thrown, bins were set alight, and threats were shouted.

They could not know that during the night nearly 20,000 Chinese troops had landed from ships in the Port of Tokyo. The few workmen who witnessed the ships dock and the armed forces disembark quietly drifted off home. With no communications or media coverage available, only their families heard about the invasion.

The noise outside of the Chinese Embassy, in the area of Minato City, was so loud that none of the demonstrators heard the rhythmic footsteps of the approaching soldiers. When the Chinese troops were fifty yards from the edge of the crowd, they halted and, on command, fired tear gas towards the gate and the most vociferous protesters. The mood didn't just change, it turned vicious. Those at the back, closest to the army, raced towards them. The line of soldiers at the front, who had fired the tear gas, dropped to their knees, and the second row opened fire with live rounds into the mass of humanity. In the next three minutes, 411 Japanese citizens were killed, over 600 injured, and a total of 1,220 were captured. None of the injured were given any medical treatment for six hours and a further 236 lost their battle for life.

Two battalions of Chinese forces entered and surrounded the Japanese parliament building without challenge, while another battalion arrested the Prime Minister, his deputy and key ministers.

Chapter Thirty-Six

Thirty minutes after Vasiliev finished his call with Malone, and it would have been sooner had there not been other pressing issues to address, Natalia Morazov was ushered into the office. She was now totally composed and in control, as she had accepted her position within the inner sanctum. However, like her husband, Natalia knew better than to take liberties with regard to her relationship with the President. As always, she was dressed in black, albeit very well cut and enhancing her figure. This choice was not about allure or sexuality; it merely gave her confidence by allowing her to control a variable. It was simply how her mind worked, and it was exceedingly attractive to Dmitriy.

"Mr President, I have the transcript of the conversation between President Malone and his associate, Brett Taylor."

"What does it say?"

"As we suspected, former President Keaton has been eliminated, but so to have eighteen members of his family. It seems Malone hated that they had mocked him in public, a crime against his ego which burned very deeply."

Vasiliev took the paper from Natalia and quickly read it, letting out an audible sigh. "I gave him a chance to govern the most significant mega-country in the world. I wanted him to be tough, but in ways which ensured our success. This is pathetic and demonstrates that he is unfit for the position. Thank you, Comrade Morazov. Would you be kind enough to ask Comrade Gusev to join me, please?"

"He is in the outer office waiting to see you."

"Excellent. Send him in."

Natalia withdrew, nodding to her uncle as he entered for his turn with the boss, now President of the World, or at least most of it.

"Gusev, Malone must be taken out. Are our troops in Washington?"

"They are, Mr President."

"Cut off telecommunications access for Malone and have your people remove him from office. Send him to Siberia for six months to learn his lesson, then execute him. I will ensure that all the other leaders know of his exile. It is up to you to decide who else must also be eliminated, but it must include his confidante, Brett Taylor."

"It will be actioned immediately. May I raise some additional points, please?"

"Go ahead, but are they just for me or should we call together the key team?"

"Good call, sir. Let's bring the group together. What about Malone's replacement?"

Vasiliev took a moment to consider his next move, not that he didn't know the name, but it was more about revealing the answer even to Gusev or to anyone else. However, on balance, there was no reason to delay.

"It will be our good friend, Bart Boulter, a billionaire who has long understood where his true affiliations lie. Without his efforts, our influence in American politics would have been far less significant. The medium-term plan has always been to put him into the role. I will call him the instant you confirm Malone has been removed."

Gusev, fully aware of everything that had transpired and what was planned, remained amazed at the breadth and depth of their actions and that he was a key player in them.

"When do you want us to reconvene as a group?"

"In one hour, I hope you have dealt with the matter of the President of Angloland by then, if you understand me, Boris."

There was no light in Vasiliev's face, and Gusev was only too aware of the instruction and its implied message. His own face remained impassive, but his about-turn and swift exit demonstrated to Vasiliev that he was clear on the priority of his request.

Chapter Thirty-Seven

Across the Chinese Empire, troops moved into position prior to power being reconnected. Huang wasn't perturbed by the reactions of the general populations of Mongolia, North Korea, and Vietnam, but he expected resentment elsewhere.

Huang was acutely aware that the incumbent leadership teams would resist if they were given the chance. The orders to the commanders on the ground were explicit: take no chances and remove all members of national governments. He had nominated his own people for the roles of national heads of government who were waiting to be given their orders to move into their new positions. Again, there were very clear instructions for the immediate behaviour, to bring total control was paramount.

Huang took a few moments alone to think through the progress made thus far and the plan for the next stages. These brief moments of solitude were important for him. The members of the State Council were highly opinionated and had diverse perspectives. This diversity was both the aim of the National People's Congress and a personal goal of Huang's. Different and varied thinking had propelled China to its current status as a global force. However, after the debate came the need for commitment, accountability, and delivery. This meant complete discipline and a united front, both in public and in private. Any deviation or discord was to be swiftly crushed.

The Council was about to convene. Should he disclose the ultimate plan to dominate the world or keep it to the progress of the new Chinese Empire? Huang understood that his power was absolute for the time being, but ambition would inevitably stir in the souls of some of his colleagues. Constant forward momentum was crucial to his grasp of power, as was the occasionally enforced changes in personnel. The Council could not become complacent. Huang was also mindful that becoming leader of the Chinese nation was a colossal prize and leader of the Chinese Empire would be many times more attractive, especially if they knew the potential for global dominance. For some of them it would be too much of a temptation. On balance, an update was necessary. A projection into a glamorous future could wait.

The Council members shuffled into the room for their conference. Huang's office was so large that it featured a table in one corner capable of accommodating twenty people. There was a distinct pecking order among the Council members, which dictated the seating arrangement. Huang remained at his desk until the others had taken their seats, then he walked slowly to the head of the table. As he sat, Huang carefully caressed the magnificent oak table, which had been a gift from the President of Turkey.

"There is a Chinese Empire."

The Council erupted into genuinely delighted applause. This marked the end of the first stage of their collective dream.

Huang continued, "As you are aware, Taiwan is ours, the Koreas are ours, as are other expected countries, but today I can confirm that Japan is ours."

This time there was a collective gasp.

"Our forces have flown in. I have spoken to Emperor Akio Hitachi, and he has recognised that there is no longer a Japanese Empire, but there is a Chinese Empire, and we cannot be beaten. His only request was that we don't take wholesale retribution against the Japanese people. I agreed, and we, gentlemen, must ensure it doesn't happen. Our aim is to consolidate all the nations into one cohesive, functioning Empire. My understanding is that following our conversation and my commitment, Emperor Hitachi did the only honourable thing in his culture and took his own life. It is expected that many of his government ministers will act similarly. Our policy must be 'iron fist in a velvet glove.' Does anyone disagree?"

The Minister for Defence, Zhou Chen, who was taken aback by the rapid changes and feeling a little bemused, sought guidance.

"Do we stop them from committing hara-kiri?"

"Technically, it isn't hara-kiri, as that is a ritualistic disembowelment, but no, don't stop the suicides if that is their decision."

"How do we prevent rioting?"

Huang now twitched, almost imperceptibly. Most in the room noticed it but not Zhou Chen, who continued, "My fundamental question is, why do we want to control Japan?"

"Gentlemen, we have control of all communications channels, we manage all power, we can hear every conversation, we can eliminate all resistance, and we are answerable to nobody. Japan has sought conflict with us for centuries. Of all nations, even more than America, Japan has been our greatest foe. Now it will, and I emphasise will, be a key part of the glory of the Chinese Empire. Each of you will have increased responsibilities because of the geographical spread and the complex cultures that must be integrated. Does anyone need to debate their role?"

Naturally, nobody spoke or moved. The message was blatant, the alternatives beyond unacceptable.

Huang concluded, "My Deputy will distribute a full briefing pack for each of you. Remember, for now, we must maintain a level of secrecy. Tomorrow, when our control is secured, I will make an announcement to our people, in which I will call for unity and even greater efforts towards our success."

As they accepted their order documents the Council broke up.

As they left, the Minister of Defence, who had poor hearing and because of that could not speak quietly, began to grumble about the fait accompli and how he would have done it better. Later that afternoon, his office was visited by the Secret Police and Zhou Chen was no longer in a position of power. He was quickly removed to a relatively comfortable prison in Qinghai Province, near the provincial capital, Xining. His reward for years of service was his escape from execution. If the others needed to learn a lesson, this would be it. The difficulties and challenges facing them across the new Empire were so vast that everyone had to be aligned, unity and focus were imperative.

Chapter Thirty-Eight

Vasiliev began, "Comrades Bychkov, Gusev, Sokolov and my Morazovs, what an unbelievable success this has been. We have only reached a certain point, but to recap: every country in the world, with the exception of those of the Chinese Empire, is now under our auspices. China has behaved impeccably. All our nominated Presidents of the mega-countries have accepted their roles and have started, except for Ronald Malone, who is en route to Siberia. Bart Boulter has been spoken to and will be in Washington imminently."

Vasiliev took a deep breath, then continued.

"All of the world leaders have acknowledged the circumstances, and our troops have entered the key cities. My address to the peoples of the world is being translated with subtitles for simultaneous transmission to every corner of the globe. Our task is to monitor the leaders, to ensure compliance, and to impose our culture along with our interpretation of the laws we have described.

"Ongoing communication will be crucial. At a minimum, either I, Comrade Bychkov, or the respective President must make an address every week. The narrative must unfold with a balance of restrictions and freedoms in equal measure. What issues need to be discussed here?"

Sokolov spoke, "Mr President, we propose that we 'mentor' each President. I imagine you would want personal responsibility for Angloland, while each of us will take two or three of the others. Our guidance will also benefit from feedback from our people on the ground."

"I like it. You are correct, I will guide Boulter. He is our man, but he is accustomed to being his own man. The change will require him to compromise."

Bychkov grunted in agreement and continued, "Twenty or so planes have run out of fuel and been lost. Given that our forces are now on the ground, I suggest we reinstate air traffic control to allow landings, but nothing can take off, not even private jets."

They all nodded their acquiescence.

"Let it be so," said Vasiliev, who appeared to be growing increasingly grandiose.

"Just for your information, the President of Liberia took off with his family in a government plane this morning. There was no flight plan, but it didn't matter as the plane was never seen again. Perhaps that serves as another message for our friends," Bychkov added.

"Natalia, let's refine my message to the world. I say 'to the world' because I know China will be listening for any indication we might renege on the agreement."

The meeting broke up, and all except Natalia left.

Chapter Thirty-Nine

In London, Prime Minister Julie Jones was aghast. "This is worse than I thought. I am a puppet of the American President, who, in turn, only farts if Vasiliev agrees to it. We will discover the areas in which we have some autonomy, but it is relatively insignificant. Why carry on?"

In the room with Jones were Gemma Newman, the Foreign Secretary, and John Jones, her husband. Gemma had been tempted to point out that John didn't have high-level security clearance, but she quickly realised that it would be nonsensical in their current situation. They all looked haggard and none of them had had much sleep. It was perhaps ironic that they had all made the effort to dress 'properly'. Serious times called for serious behaviour.

Gemma Newman responded to what may have been a rhetorical question. "You, we, carry on trying to act as a buffer and moderator against the excesses of Vasiliev. If we aren't here, God alone knows who will be appointed."

John Jones's only concern was for his wife's welfare. "If you are useful to them, whilst serving the people of Britain as best you can, we may get through this. A former Prime Minister may be entirely disposable."

"Thank you, Darling. But my only interest is how to make life bearable for our citizens, our people. I think Gemma is right; we should stay in position, accept the limited responsibilities, and make the best of an exceedingly bad job."

The Foreign Secretary considered the next steps. "What happens now?"

"The US President will call me at 10 a.m. our time. It's convenient for him as he doesn't sleep it seems, and I have no say in the matter. Perhaps we will have more clarity then. My first priority is to talk to our people. If resistance is impossible, I don't want futile deaths."

"Will I have a job?" asked Newman.

"No idea. I can't imagine foreign affairs will be any business of ours, but there will be a great deal to do. Even Moscow and Washington, D.C. cannot micro-manage all aspects of life. There will be a key position for you when I establish the boundaries. I already feel impotent. If I am to sit at home knitting in Oxfordshire, I will go crazy. If this is inevitable, let's swing with it rather than against it."

"How will the economy work?" John, her husband asked. He was CEO of a multinational food distributor and importer.

"My instinct is you will be required to run the business as you do now, but for the greater good rather than profit. There must be recognition of knowledge and skill, but the rewards will be nominal. We will maintain an adequate lifestyle. You heard the address: basic wages, no taxes, employment for everyone."

Gemma Newman interrupted her boss, if that was still her status, "Safe, clean and useful were the words used. How will that affect those who cannot be useful?"

"Like which people?"

"I'm not sure, just speculating. Maybe older people, sick individuals, or those with special needs. I don't know, but there could be ramifications we haven't considered."

Jones pouted and said, "I haven't even begun to consider the effects. God, this is going to be hell."

The Prime Minister continued, "I walked to the Palace this morning. It felt right and I was accompanied by my protection team. The King has acquiesced to Vasiliev. Knowing him as I do, it is for the safety of the people. Of course, it also protects him and the Royal Family, but he has read the runes as we have."

"Weren't you a bit nervous about the people on the streets, not the King?" asked Newman.

"Not at all. There was a blanket of confusion but no aggression. As Vasiliev hasn't yet spoken to the world, I was able to remain similarly ill-informed, and nobody challenged it. One man told me I should know if I was running the country; little did he know!"

Chapter Forty

President Vladimir Vasiliev was making his final preparations for his first global pronouncement. The television company had sent in the usual team of makeup artists, hairstylists, and general helpers. One of them was brushing off any remaining, though invisible, detritus from the shoulders of his jacket.

Five minutes before the broadcast, various communication devices flashed a message around the world to say that power to their devices would be restored temporarily, allowing viewers to see and hear the President as he explained why they were living without any form of energy.

In nearly every corner of the world, beyond the Chinese Empire, people scurried to ensure everyone near to them knew Vasiliev was about to speak. At least now they would move from wild speculation and projected Doomsday scenarios to concrete facts. The more rational among them understood that the prospect of bad news is frequently worse than the reality when it finally becomes known.

The President's intention was to appear grave and unforgiving. He could later reveal a more compassionate side to his character, but for now, he wanted his people to be fearful. The dresser had adjusted his tie, ensuring it was symmetrical and neatly held at the top of his shirt. The dresser often wondered why so many people, typically men, struggled to knot a tie properly; many were oddly shaped, an inch below the collar or skewed to one side. His unforgiving view was that people are idiots.

Vasiliev sat bolt upright behind his desk. The black jacket starkly contrasted against the off-white background. The messages were unsubtle; he meant business and would tolerate no resistance.

The production assistant used his fingers to count down from five. As he clenched his fist, the red light at the top of the camera came on.

"Good day to you, citizens of the world.

This is a brief message to inform you that the Russian Empire has conquered the world without the use of excessive force. We have total control of all power and have accessed all systems within your country. Further, we are able to listen to, read, and intercept all of your communications.

There will continue to be a total blackout for one week. During this time, the experience will teach you what life could be like if our dominion is not accepted. Conversely, if you recognise Russia's control, I will make life much better for you. Your governments have failed you, and we have walked through online security.

Over the next few days, you may see Russian troops. Do not be alarmed; simply follow their instructions.

You will be hearing a great deal more from me in the coming weeks, particularly regarding the importance of traditional values and the elimination of unnecessary liberal policies.

I wish you a peaceful existence."

The red light went off, and across the world all devices shut down.

It felt as though the world had fallen silent.

Chapter Forty-One

In Strood, Kent, in the south-east of England, the Nolan family sat together in the darkness, only slightly alleviated by a single candle. Having assumed that the power might be off for nearly a week, they were conserving their dwindling supply of candles. They were also almost out of matches. As a basic measure to help, the candle was placed in front of a mirror which nearly doubled its effectiveness.

Strood was traditionally a conservative area, prone even to far-right sympathies. Alex Nolan was an outspoken follower of the Nostalgia Party, which was anti-immigration, didn't believe in trying to achieve net-zero emissions for the planet's survival, and advocated for less bureaucracy. To quote its leader, "It was a commonsense way forward." Privately, this was a politician who had Russian sympathies. As a follower, Alex was already pleased with Vasiliev's address.

"We will get back the country we want. You heard him, traditional values and no liberal policies."

His mother, Isabella, by profession a schoolteacher, was less inclined to expect simple solutions to highly complex problems.

"Don't you want to vote? Don't you want to make your own decisions?"

"Not if the liberals can spoil our country, I don't. For too long, we've been hurtling downhill."

His mother tried to suppress her angst, "The truth seems to be that we are to be told what we want. Today you may like the things you hear, but if tomorrow you hate the next policies, you won't be able to change anything."

"I trust Vladimir."

Isabella was mortified. "You call him Vladimir? The man who has invaded our country for the first time in a thousand years? He doesn't care about you or anyone else. We are dispensable, the equivalent of amoebae. This is for the good of Russia and its President. Let the first few days pass, and then we will start to see reality."

Her son stormed out of the house to meet his best friend, Jamie Goodwin.

Leaving the house in a huff would have been more satisfying if he could have seen where he was going. Without streetlights and with cloud cover obscuring the moonlight, Nolan floundered in the dark. At the end of the road a single car passed, which for a second gave him a glimpse of the contours of his surroundings. Very few people were using their cars as they endeavoured to conserve energy. Who knew when the ability to move around might be critical?

Having gained a better sense of direction, Nolan moved to the middle of the street, where he wouldn't risk falling into the gutter or tread in a puddle, or worse. He had agreed to meet Jamie at the corner of the road. There was nowhere to go but at least they were out of the house. Home might mean security but without electricity it meant utter tedium. Nolan and Goodwin were nineteen years old and felt they should be living exciting lives. They had an agreed greeting of high fiving, accompanied by a strident "Yo!"

"Are you scared?" Nolan asked.

"I'm more angry," his friend replied. "What gives Russia the right to rule the world, to dictate which laws we must follow and who our leaders should be?"

"There is nothing we can do about it. You know the old saying, 'If rape is inevitable, lie back and enjoy it.' Perhaps we just have to accept it. Everything changes back eventually."

Jamie Goodwin was appalled and, whilst his mate couldn't see his face, he sensed the disdain.

"Only a man would say that. It goes beyond misogyny to outright brutality. Have you read *The Handmaid's Tale*? Do you understand what we are facing? How will women be treated in this new frightening world? How will men be treated?"

"All I meant was we have no options; we need to avoid any more trouble than we're already in."

Goodwin relaxed a little. He was conscious that he was looking down at his feet, even though he couldn't see them. It was his default body language when he felt beaten.

"I just can't believe there's nothing we can do. I refuse to lie down and let the Ruskies run over us. It occurs to me that our new rulers in this country will also be Brits, but Brits who have always sympathised with the fascist regime in Russia and around the world. We'll know more when Vasiliev deigns to tell us. Got any fags?"

Chapter Forty-Two

"Right, run me through the situation across the world, please, Comrade Bychkov," Vasiliev began the meeting. Small talk had evaporated, leaving only a total focus on the operation. Bychkov was present alongside Sokolov, Gusev and the Morazovs.

"Mr President, I am naturally grateful to my colleagues for much of the information I am able to give you."

He waved a hand in a circular motion as the team sat around Vasiliev's desk. There were some very tired people in the room, as troops were deployed, speeches prepared, and technology fine-tuned. That nothing major had gone wrong felt like a miracle. Inevitably, the one person who appeared refreshed was the President, who had actually slept well for three hours, confident that his team had everything under control.

"I recognise the invaluable contributions of the team. What are the reports, please?" asked Vasiliev, though with a hint of frustration.

"Apologies," Bychkov continued. "The worst situation is in the eastern Democratic Republic of the Congo and the adjoining countries. We cannot be surprised that old scores are being settled, and it is all occurring under the cover of darkness. We are monitoring the situation via satellite. Our soldiers will be there in a few hours, and it will stop. I expect a full-throttle battle in which we will suffer a few casualties, while the locals will have many. We won't be taking prisoners for Siberia."

Gusev chimed in, "My guys have been instructed to take the firmest action, preferably from distance to avoid any losses. I believe the President of the DRC, Charles Ekoko, is very willing to show his allegiance to the new order. I have asked our new President of Africana, Happy Imeh of Nigeria, to coordinate. Of course, I suspect Ekoko will be playing both sides. But the violence will cease after a burst of severe aggression."

"Disappointing but expected. Where next, Comrade?" Vasiliev enquired.

"In Greater Iran, there are extreme reactions, especially from Israel. They fully anticipate the destruction of their country. The Ayatollah has made it his mission to exterminate the members of the Israeli Government. They are literally fighting for their lives, and we all know how skilled they are. Unfortunately for them, they only have access to mechanical weaponry, which is no match for our affiliates. The question for us is, do we countenance genocide and, to a large degree, the end of Judaism?"

Vasiliev remained unimpressed, "When we constructed the mega-countries, we knew that there would be issues. Indeed, I recall a specific conversation about Israel, and we all agreed Iran would be harsh, and that was the message we wanted to deliver. In my address to the world on January 1st this will be a key theme: behave, accept the situation or face the consequences. However, I will speak personally to the Ayatollah and counsel him to make examples but not indulge in total obliteration."

Bychkov added, "The Ayatollah also needs to maintain discipline with Hamas in Gaza and Hezbollah in Jordan. My view is that Gaza has to be a separate nation, albeit as a member of Greater Iran. With independence comes responsibilities."

Vasiliev concurred, "I will ensure that happens. All the leaders of the mega-countries need to know that they are vulnerable. The story of Ronald Malone will resonate with them. What about South America?"

"So far, it's relatively quiet, although it may change when power is restored. Even after your address, Mr President, we must acknowledge there will be many people in South America and Africana who won't be aware that anything has changed. There are many people who have little contact with civilisation."

"And America?" Vasiliev pressed.

"We know the vast majority of Americans have guns. I suspect large numbers won't accept the amnesty. There will be standoffs like they had at Waco in Texas, which ended in 80 deaths. Regrettably, our attitude has to be, 'so be it.' Their military has hunkered down, to use an American phrase. Boulter will need to get a grip quickly. Our forces are in Washington, New York, Los Angeles, and Houston to enforce discipline."

"What about the United Kingdom?" Vasiliev asked.

"Full capitulation from the government. Julia Jones will seek to keep everything in order and manage her areas of responsibility as we define them. The King only wants to protect his people and will do whatever we ask. I think we should consider making him King of Angloland. The Americans crave a monarchy, although it may irritate the Irish."

Vasiliev nodded vigorously. "I love it. It will show we are sensitive to the needs for levels of independence within our rules. Great idea, Alexander. Where are the other hotspots?"

Bychkov didn't need to refer to his notes. "There is nowhere else to overly concern us yet. However, as we have already discussed some of the problems which will emerge when power is returned, and people can communicate widely. Our priority must be our messages and the enforced discipline."

Sokolov had been quiet, deferring to the President and his deputy. He was respected for only speaking when it mattered. "A very useful tool would be for the respective governments to identify key opinion formers. For example, in the USA as was, Grace Williams, a talk show host, has always been a reactionary and will love the 1950s morality. In the UK, the leader of the now defunct Nostalgia Party, Raymond Burke, has spent many days in Moscow. Whilst he is a polarising figure, he is impactful."

There were some blank looks around the room.

"If we are the only ones telling people how good the new ways are, they will stop believing us. However, if there are commentators respected by at least some of the population in each country, it will add different voices espousing the benefits of compliance. I know we want to make examples of some dissidents and criminals, but the overall aim is a harmonious civilisation."

President Vasiliev grasped the point with fervour, "Exactly. What percentage of the population do we need to accept the new order for us to achieve a tipping point?"

Dmitriy Morazov had learned when to participate in these highest-level meetings. He was seen as the font of knowledge, "Studies have shown that any change only needs twenty-five percent of people to accept it, in order to influence and convert the rest. Of course, there will always be laggards who claim to be on board while doing everything they can to resist. Ironically, those people, who are the last to change, then are often the strongest advocates resisting any further alterations."

Gusev was amazed, "Twenty-five percent is all it takes? This is incredible and exceedingly helpful."

Dmitriy continued, "There are even studies which suggest it might be as low as ten percent."

"This gives us more than a fighting chance of a relatively quick move to the new equilibrium," interjected the President. "My address to the citizens must emphasise that this was bloodless, highlighting the benefits and the freedoms they will enjoy. Where are we with the draft, Natalia, please?"

"I have it with me, so if you want, we can review it now," Natalia said.

Over the next twenty minutes the group poured over the first iteration of the speech the President was to deliver to the Russian dominated world. Whilst speech editing might have been seen as an act of administration that people of their seniority didn't need to consider, they all recognised that a peaceful transition would be highly influenced by the fifteen minutes during which the President spoke. In fact, Natalia's first draft was exceptionally close to their requirements; indeed, for some of them, it even touched on aspects they hadn't considered.

The major discussion revolved around the nature of freedom. Is freedom our ability to avoid the negative and awful things imposed on us or whether freedom is scope to openly create, innovate, and express oneself?

Sokolov, the deeper thinker amongst the group when it came to more philosophical matters, spoke up. "Truthfully, it is both. All societies have rules to curb the excesses of others and to ensure equity and fairness. It is the context which sets the boundaries. We will be imposing new laws and morality which may be resisted, but not by everyone. This is where the tipping point is relevant. This draft from Natalia does a good job at describing the protection we are providing and the many ways life will improve. Of course, we must not be explicit about the ways those who cannot be useful will be eased out of the way, but when we do, hopefully enough people will already be aligned with our approach."

Dmitriy Morazov looked agitated, almost physically twitching, as he added, "Comrade Sokolov is absolutely right. The great philosophers, including him, know this to be true. Freedom isn't unfettered space to do anything you want; that is anarchy and lawlessness. Those who think of themselves as nihilists, believing nothing actually exists, would allow murder and mayhem. The vast majority of people want structure and certainty. They will progressively come to accept and live normally within the constraints we are applying."

As ever, Vasiliev absorbed the conversation, "I want us to reconvene at the end of the day to review the updated draft. That I leave to you, Natalia. Please circulate the amended version and we will finalise it at 9 p.m. Questions?"

The room emptied and Vasiliev made a call to the new President of Angloland, Bart Boulter. Replacing Malone with Boulter was inevitable as the former wanted to be a star, not a member of a star team. It also gave Vasiliev the opportunity to send the most profound message to all the newly appointed leaders and their senior teams. He needed them to know that he was literally listening and watching.

On this occasion the medium was a video conference. Vasiliev preferred to see faces and for his demeanour to be apparent to the recipient, "President Boulter, how are you settling in?"

Boulter was a big man, both in stature and personality; he wasn't accustomed to not being the biggest fish in the pond. Behaving in a subservient manner was not his usual style. As a billionaire, Boulter wasn't prone to taking orders, but he was also aware his survival meant there was a role to perform.

"Mr President, being given this position is the greatest honour of my life. There has been no settling-in period. I am appointing my key advisors, but at this point, they are without portfolio, pending definition of the breadth of their responsibilities. The exception to this is Head of Security, Bill Banks. As you may be aware, Bill has been Governor of Texas where he has been implementing an array of firm measures against immigrants and liberals. There will be no slackening off on your decrees."

"Great. He will need your guidance from our strategy meetings for all the Presidents. This call is to ask you two questions. Firstly, have you planned your initial speech to the people of Angloland and its contents? Secondly, have you thought about the role the King of England can play? For your information, I have decided to appoint him into a titular role as King of Angloland. This isn't an executive position but, in terms of selling the new order, he will be very helpful."

Boulter came very close to making a mistake, "Are you crazy? I mean, the idea is perfect. But could having a King and a President be confusing? Is the decision final?"

"If it wasn't before, it is now. Surely your ego can accommodate the former King of the United Kingdom and Head of the Commonwealth as a member of the team under you. In effect, he will be a voice of sanity and reason. Use him wisely."

Boulter quickly thought of a way out of his gaffe, "Mr President, please understand, I was merely concerned for the King. It must be close to humiliation."

"The King wants to keep his subjects safe and recognises that we have won. I think that tone in all communications is crucial, Bart."

The use of his forename was designed to indicate Vasiliev was in a forgiving mood. His face said something else, and Boulter received the message very loudly and clearly. It had been a long time since Boulter had felt dominated, but he was second best in this discussion. A single bead of sweat formed, the first he had shed in twenty years; he didn't exercise very often, as in never.

Vasiliev persisted, "What about your speech?"

"Nearly ready, Mr President," Boulter affirmed, adopting a more obsequious manner.

"Please let Natalia Morazov have it. We must coordinate with my speech and those of all the leaders of the mega-countries. Also, have a draft speech prepared for His Majesty the King of Angloland to address the new amalgamated country of which he is now monarch, again dovetailing with ours."

"It will be with her in the next few minutes and the King's speech by the end of the day."

"Excellent. I am sure we will communicate more effectively as time goes on."

The line went dead before Boulter could express his admiration for Vasiliev's wisdom.

Boulter shouted for his communications guru. The irony that he bellowed for his communications woman was lost on nobody except Boulter, who felt his humiliation should be passed down the line, presumably ending with the White House cat being pushed out into the garden.

Boulter's secretary was still Dorothy Harkins, who had also served Keaton. Boulter had taken the sensible view that having some people with in-house knowledge would be advantageous. Harkins herself had grasped the situation far more quickly than senior staff. She had little else to do and wanted to witness history being made from the inside, so she had stayed. Hearing her new boss' voice, Harkins summoned Cheryl Simpson-Walters, the de facto communications supremo.

Cheryl Simpson-Walters was typically known as Chez or CSW. She gracefully entered the Oval Office. She knew she shopped on a budget, but everyone thought she was so stylish that a small fortune must have been spent on clothes and accessories. A few people referred to her as Mrs Accessorise, but not within earshot.

"Chez, I have just spoken to Vasiliev. Do you want my opinion of the guy?"

"No, Mr President. The walls have ears, and I suspect from your tone that it wasn't going to be overly complimentary."

"You are correct. I just fouled up, so I need to get back onside. Do we have a draft of my speech to Angloland? By the way, I will be angling to revert the name to the United States of America."

"As we just discussed, now that you have said it, President Vasiliev will know about it very shortly. Yes, the draft is in your inbox."

"Shit. I need to get used to the whole monitoring thing quickly. Do you think he can listen in every room?"

CSW smiled at the innocence, "Rooms, cars, street corners…" She let it hang there.

Boulter flushed red as he realised that his personal moments with CSW must be known to Vasiliev. She, on the other hand, was relaxed about it. After all, it was an open secret, but maybe not to Mrs Boulter, who was more of a trophy wife than an intellectual equal.

"Moving on. Can you send the draft to Natalia Morazov, who is pulling it all together, please?"

Simpson-Walters turned and left the room doing a comic and exaggerated twerk.

"Very funny," Boulter said, his tone devoid of laughter. It hadn't been a good last fifteen minutes.

Chapter Forty-Three

Five minutes after the Angloland draft of the speech landed in Natalia Morazov's inbox, she had read through it and placed a call to Cheryl Simpson-Walters.

"Cheryl, this is Natalia Morazov. Please accept my apologies for ringing you directly rather than going through your secretary."

CSW was taken aback.

"Nobody has this number."

"I would have thought by now you might have caught on to the reality; we know everything we need to know. Anyway, just to say I'll send over a few tweaks, so the two speeches are in sync."

Having regained her composure, CSW was genuinely pleased to be in the loop.

"Thank you, and please do let me know if I can be of any assistance to you or President Vasiliev."

"Oh, I will, thanks. And just as an aside, I very much liked your advice to Boulter a few minutes ago in the Oval Office. Please be discreet."

The line went dead. Simpson-Walters looked as though she had seen a ghost. She rushed to see her boss to confirm the things she had counselled earlier.

Meanwhile, Natalia Morazov was smiling to herself. She hadn't received any transcript of the conversation between Boulter and Simpson-Walters, but she had guessed. Very obviously, the arrow had hit its mark, and perhaps that would help keep Boulter under control.

Natalia neither liked nor trusted the President of Angloland. In her opinion, the King would make for a much more cohesive figure.

She returned to the task of melding all the speeches together, for consistency and to avoid any potential gaffes.

At this stage, Natalia's only concern was just how smoothly it had all gone so far. She also knew, as she had discussed with Dmitriy, that the truly vulnerable time would be after the power was restored and people could begin to collude. The security forces could only monitor a small percentage of conversations, and they would have to focus on people for whom there was already adverse intelligence.

After reading through all the speeches, which generally were fine, Natalia gave herself a break. As a contrast to the speeches, she read through the reports regarding the newly appointed Presidents. Not surprisingly, the real outlier was Boulter. It seemed the Americans really did see themselves as God's chosen people, and the pattern emerging was an unsettling one. There might need to be micro-rule from Moscow until the right balance is found.

Chapter Forty-Four

"So, has our 'eyes in the room' reported to us yet?"

President Huang Peng was pacing around his ornately decorated office. There was plenty of space to move without coming near to the elaborate furniture.

His deputy, Xiu Feng Wang, looked relaxed.

"I have rushed here from our communications room on the second floor. Only our most trusted operative was with me, and he couldn't hear our agent speak. Things continue to go very well throughout the Russian Empire. Yes, there is fighting in some areas, but it's far less than expected. Technically, the Russians have done a perfect job. Critically, not only are there no voices calling for the conquest of the Chinese Empire as the next step, but also, they are also still unsure about us. Our agent continues to operate at the very highest level. If there were any issues, we would know by now."

Huang nodded in approval. This was the time to consolidate his grip over the Chinese Empire. At least he could release troops from the Russian border without worrying.

"Talk me through the situation in each of our territories."

Xiu began on a sombre note.

"It appears as if some dissidents within our own country have seen this as a chance to make trouble. Some Muslims in Xinjiang Province are attempting some sort of coup. They want an independent Islamic State."

Huang snorted in derision.

"Has a group ever misread the political situation less well than these people? Hit them hard. We cannot allow anywhere else to hear about this and think it is a good idea worth pursuing."

Xiu agreed and was about to continue on to the situation in the next country, but Huang had another thought.

"A better idea! Use armed forces from other nations. We don't put our people in danger, and the messages will filter back through the troops from Mongolia, Japan or wherever to their fellow nationals. It's a win-win. I like it, and this should be a principle for any uprising we encounter."

"Will this send a message that Chinese citizens are being given preferential treatment, which might, in their minds, mean slower integration?" asked Xiu.

"It might," Huang conceded. "But it could also mean that whilst it is slower, it's more deeply embedded. They will want to be seen to be well behaved, to be accepted as true patriots of the Chinese Empire. We may end with only one country resisting, and their soldiers being sacrificed."

Xiu understood and was merely ensuring the thought was fully explored.

"If we get to a point where only one nation is not being totally immersed, then we've done a good job."

Huang persisted.

"Think longer-term. In six months' time, how this approach might prove invaluable."

"Ah, you are correct. We will potentially have bigger issues to deal with and reactions to suppress."

They moved on. Over the next hour, their conversation touched on the behaviours across the empire.

"Mr President, the biggest reactions are in Taiwan and Japan."

"Talk to me about Taiwan, please."

The Deputy President took a deep breath but spoke evenly, "There are sporadic outbreaks of resistance which have been dealt with by our people. They can't organise properly because there are no phones, so it is sporadic and minimal for now. The real concern is for the days after power is restored. My suggestion is that we delay restoration for an extra week. Let's make the point strongly. A few will die, but we might crush the fight before it gains any momentum."

"Agreed. Now, what about Japan?"

"I suspect the same applies, albeit there are youths protesting in the streets. There have already been some fatalities, and this will increase. My expectation is that the number of deaths will eventually become very large. I am grateful we have our notional six months to deal with the first wave of problems before we attempt to address those of the whole world."

Huang rocked backwards and forwards.

"You aren't wrong. The more I reflect on this, the more incredulous I am. Even just a year ago this would have been unthinkable, or at least it was without nuclear conflict. Our technicians are doing a great job. Whilst I may ask why and how the Russians got there first, I can't help but think that this has worked out even better for us. I almost feel sorry for Vasiliev. By the way, the most important word in that sentence is almost!"

They both laughed, an unusual occurrence. Perhaps not surprisingly, they then both felt a bit awkward.

"Next?"

"South Korea is my only other major concern. Not only is it becoming part of our empire, but its people are also inevitably worried about the little fat controller of North Korea. I have asked the Head of the Army to send ten battalions to the area traditionally known as the DMZ, effectively the border between the two Koreas. To be less rude about the President, Paik Han-jae, he has always told us that his greatest wish is a unified Korea. However, a burst of genocidal mania is not what we want."

Huang delved more deeply, "Have there been North Korean troop movements?"

"Not yet," Xiu replied. "But I am certain that is just because of the lack of phone connections."

"I will personally talk to Paik and Yun Dong-woo, the South Korean President. At least Paik cannot use his nuclear and ballistic missiles. If we play this well, the ordinary people of both Koreas will be delighted, as they can move freely and meet friends and relatives who have been across the border. Paik has been too defensive for too long. We can turn this into a triumph. Perhaps we could take a leaf out of the book of Western businesses and promote Paik to a level beyond his competence but without any actual authority."

Xiu was perplexed. Seeing the blank look on his face, Huang explained.

"Let's create a new role for him, Assistant Deputy Controller of Cultural Affairs, reporting directly to you. Base him in Beijing and keep him out of Korea. You can define the role, but his entire family must be removed from Phnom Penh."

"Does he have to report to me?" Xiu asked.

"I am sorry, but yes. If he becomes a problem, we will think again. Flatter him and build up the importance of the position. In fact, it could turn into a valuable role as we continue to spread our ethos."

Xiu Feng Wang was not a man to complain, so he gave a mental shrug and accepted the idea.

"Will you tell him yourself?"

President Huang gave the impression that it was a conversation he would enjoy.

"I will. Believe me, Paik will be pleased."

The two men continued their discussion of the other nations now within the new Chinese Empire and agreed it was time to bring a very small number of senior colleagues into the loop. There was a great deal to organise and the planning was just beginning.

Chapter Forty-Five

At 9:00 p.m. Moscow time, deliberately chosen for maximum daytime coverage across the world, President Vasiliev addressed nearly six billion people within his dominion. There had been a flashed message an hour before. For sixty seconds communications media had been restored. People heard it, and word spread quickly among neighbours, but there was no time to call anyone, as phone networks had not been fully restored. Vasiliev was confident that people would be eager to hear about their future, so his address was going to be their sole focus of attention.

The light flashed in front of him, and Vasiliev knew all eyes were on him. This was his moment; this was his destiny.

It was December 27th and only two days since Russia had launched Operation No Tanks, yet nothing would, or could, ever be the same. In all countries outside of the Russian and Chinese Empires, all power would remain off until at least January 1st.

This might have been the time for rebellion, but there was no way for people to collude, and a week of 'nothing' would ensure they understood the terrible prospects if they didn't comply with the edicts of Moscow. Families and immediate neighbours could chat, but agents could listen.

President Vasiliev stood before the cameras in a sharply tailored suit, shirt and tie, carefully chosen colours to emphasise his power.

He began, clearly and strongly. Whilst the words were translated in subtitles, he knew his tone was crucial; firm and sincere, with a hint of menace.

"Citizens of the World, I greet you from the centre of Government in the Kremlin.

I fully understand that you may be concerned and disconcerted by Russia's move to take control of the entire globe, except for China. But remember, this was achieved without bombs, and it was bloodless; we called it Operation No Tanks. There can never again be the threat of war, and in particular, nuclear war.

It is a point of more than a little significance that the Chinese Empire exists separately, encompassing China, Taiwan, the Koreas, Vietnam, Mongolia, Japan, together with a number of other nations in the area. I tell you this because I want you to see this is not megalomania.

So, why have we done this?

Our world was stuck in a cycle of conflict and in a downward spiral. As long as there were millions of competing agendas, there was no chance of peace and harmony.

Now, there will be new mega-countries, and you will be informed which one you belong to and the name of your President.

Thanks to our advanced technology, we can monitor everything you do. There will be no criminality, no conspiracy, and no rebellion.

This marks the start of a new world order, one which will bring stability and fairness for everyone, and in which there is world peace.

When we consider the best time to be alive, most people talk about the 1950s, although they love the advances in media, healthcare, communications, transport and so many other aspects of life. We have now brought you to a point in which we can achieve the best of both worlds.

There is no longer the threat of major warfare. We will eliminate crime. Everyone will receive a fair wage, and you will not pay any taxes. This will all be aligned to a morality which is based on earlier times. Each mega-country will have its own laws and ethics described, but I can tell you now there will be no legalised homosexuality, no acceptance of transgender changes, no abortion except in some very specific circumstances, no public demonstrations, no social media, and no instant credit to buy things.

Private companies will still exist to ensure a constant food supply and the basics of life. However, profits will be re-absorbed for the benefit of the community. Professionals and executives will be rewarded with a salary of two or three times the average wage. Offshore bank accounts and other financial mechanisms will be irrelevant, as there will be no way of generating excess income. We will be citizens of the world, not cogs in a capitalist machine. This isn't communism; it is a third way, utilising all our talents.

For the first time, you will be beholden only to society and your fellow citizens, not to a boss who can dismiss you at any moment. Naturally, you will need assurance that this will apply to everyone, and here is one of the things to which may take you some time to get accustomed; we can monitor everything you do and say. This means we can eliminate crime which could undermine our balanced society from working. Initially, as people get used to all of this, the penalties will be severe, very much in keeping with the morality of yesteryear. The death penalty will exist everywhere; new prisons are being built in Siberia and in the jungles of Africa and South America. In certain cases, immediate family members of felons will also be punished.

I can already hear people crying out that their freedom is being stripped away. Let me explain that this is, for the first time, the true freedom for which you have been longing.

The bases of all our decisions will be simple: to make the community, the lands and its people SAFE, CLEAN, AND USEFUL.

Every society has rules and laws, and I have just explained ours. They are easy to understand and really do apply to every person equally, even the King of England, who incidentally has graciously accepted the invitation to become King of Angloland. Tradition matters when linked to progress. You will be able to live freely within these common-sense parameters.

You are free to make suggestions for improving society.

You will be free to work and make a real contribution without the obscene practice of taxation penalising you for your hard work.

You may be wondering how we will guarantee employment. The use of Artificial Intelligence will be banned for non-governmental business. There will be no online shopping, and retail will return to traditional shops. We will have a massive focus on infrastructure projects to make life efficient and address climate change.

You will be liberated from worrying about money as income is guaranteed and everyone will work unless they are unfit to do so. There will be no early retirement age. People will work until at least the age of 75, as they will want to contribute. Pensions will be paid from that age.

You will be free from concerns about immigration, as there will be work and income available globally. Jobs in your country will be reserved for you and your family.

You will be free from harassment by misfits on the streets. Homelessness will not exist, beggars and other societal parasites will be removed, and drug addicts will be taken into care. People with issues of mental strife will be absorbed by the state.

Without crime, you will be able to go about your daily duties without threat.

More of your time will be free, as trains and buses will run on time, and our processes will work efficiently.

You are free to love someone of the same gender.

You are free from the threat of guns because we are all safe. There is an amnesty until January 5th, by which time all firearms must be handed in. Anyone found retaining a firearm will be imprisoned. The argument that you need a gun to keep safe has been removed, as nobody will have one. Similarly, the claim that you need a weapon to defend yourself from the government has now been categorically shown to be irrelevant. The government has total power.

You are free from worries about the effects of climate change because there will be less travel, less waste, less consumerism, and many jobs will be created to improve the state of the world. This is a cause we can all agree on.

Education will be provided free of charge. It will focus on themes which support society, encouraging people to commit to making it better, whether those relate to science, medicine, engineering, or the arts.

Medical treatment will be free, regardless of nationality. This will mean a major training and recruitment campaign. Anyone qualified will be required to return to the medical profession.

Religion will be allowed, but the persecution of others because of their beliefs will categorically not be tolerated. We have established the structures for peace, but it means people's behaviour must reflect it. We will make sure actions align with these principles and that behaviour remains in harmony with these values.

People will be free to wear whatever clothes they choose, as long as they are clean and do not obscure identification.

Freedom of expression through the arts is encouraged, but it cannot conflict with the world's new values.

You have freedom to have a family if you can look after the children and there are no defects in your DNA. In the future, we can only have people who will be useful.

We will achieve solidarity, in which everyone who is useful will be kept safe, in a world which is clean, and rewards will be universal.

To be young means you are free to look forward to a life of fulfilment and contribution.

There will be no social media, but we will support religion, television and sport. We want people to be happy.

Television will resume on January 1st, and we will let you know a great deal more then.

We will be strictly enforcing the laws. If anyone takes actions against them, they will feel the full power of the new state, which has full autonomy to use force and capital punishment. A lesser penalty will be exile to Siberia for those directly involved, possibly including their families.

In the short term, you will see changes, but ultimately, you will realise the benefits which will come from our benevolence.

Every group has its rules, and ours is no different. By monitoring everyone, we are making everyone free. We are all living by the same standards and laws.

I am giving you freedom, you are liberated. We have a government that exists for the greater good, and which is predictable.

Do your best for yourself, your family, and society. This is not our duty; it is our honour.

SAFE, CLEAN, AND USEFUL."

The address concluded with the screens going blank. The world returned to darkness, which also reflected the sombre mood of many of the people.

Chapter Forty-Six

In London, the Nolan family were stunned.

"We're now part of a mega-country. What does that even mean? We're going back to the 1950s. What the hell has happened?" spluttered Isabella.

Her son had heard bits he liked.

"Guaranteed work with no taxes. What's not to like?!"

"I wish we could see it all written down because there was so much to hear and I haven't taken it all in," said Phil, Isabella's husband.

"No social media seems terrible," Alex mused. "How will I find out what my friends are doing and how will I get the news?"

"More pressing is Vasiliev telling us there'll be no power until the New Year, and that's still four days away. No shops open, hardly any food left, not even for the dog," said Phil Nolan.

Isabella had been making the best of the situation but had only a very small amount of food left. They had been sensible and filled pans and buckets with water in anticipation of shortages. It was inevitable that there would be a shortage, as the water infrastructure was bound to falter.

"The thing that worries me most is that we have no certainty the Russians won't just deprive us of power at any moment. This could be our life now. It may well happen if we don't just accept everything and don't object or protest. We can't afford to be anything but well-behaved and loyal subjects."

Her husband thought there must still be some scope to live some kind of normal life. "They'll let us vote, surely."

"Vote for what? Vote for which party? God only knows if there'll be politics of any sort," Isabella replied.

Their son, Alex, was pensive.

"If there can't be war, if we have a job and we will be safe, why do we need to vote? If Vasiliev can guarantee a better society, why would we want to vote?"

"I guess it is what we expect to do. Voting is the essence of democracy, and democracy means we can change the government," Phil reacted.

"But if we can't do better than this, why change it?" Alex asked.

"But how do we get rich if everyone is paid the same?" asked his father.

"Which do you want; to be rich or happy?"

"I want both."

"And how's that going for you at the moment?"

Phil became defensive, "But I might be able to do both, but not, it seems, under the Russians."

The family fell silent. There was too much to absorb, and even then, there were millions of other questions left unanswered.

Chapter Forty-Seven

President Bart Boulter of Angloland was preparing his speech for his new mega-country, to be delivered on January 1st.

Cheryl Simpson-Walters entered the Oval Office.

"CSW, have a look at the speech I would like to give, though I know it won't be possible."

Cheryl picked up a handwritten note from the desk. Crafted from solid oak, the desk symbolised continuity and permanence. It was known as the Trump Desk, after the 45th and 47th President. Some people thought the desk was as intelligent. Unfortunately for those who sat behind it, there was no such certainty. They were all vulnerable, some because of their own faults and failings.

"Mr President, I strongly urge you not to write things like this. You are being watched, and you know cameras have a zoom facility. Someone could read this."

Boulter was defensive and sulky.

"You keep saying that, but I'm the President of Angloland, soon to be the United States of America again."

"Again, Mr President, please limit your thinking out loud. This paper is dynamite. Would you really want the society you've described?"

"I would, and it's time we found a way to get to a fundamental rethink."

CSW reread the list silently:

Freedoms:

To pay the lowest wages to those desperate for work; they should be grateful

To avoid funding the poor (Blacks)

To use slaves

To ban Trade Unions

To own multiple guns

To dominate the weak

To make women stay at home

To take what we need

To be extremely wealthy

To suppress governments we don't like

To interpret the truth

"Mr President, do you think this list would be acceptable to President Vasiliev?"

"I don't care. Gradually, this will be the country I run."

"I think this list should stay with me. I will burn it."

Boulter was about to object, but there were other pressing issues with which to deal. He placed his hands on the desk signalling he was ready to listen.

"We've had clearance for the King to fly over. Naturally, it must be a daytime flight, so he's leaving London at 10 a.m. their time, arriving in Washington at 11 a.m. our time. He will be driven here for a meeting with you before being taken to his hotel. Ordinarily, the King would stay here, but he has acceded to your request that he uses other accommodation."

"I don't want that English elitist anywhere near me unless I have to see him."

"Mr President, the orders from the Kremlin have made it very clear that King Philip is seen as a very, very important person in the quest for a peaceful transition to the new order."

"I don't care. You do as I say. Your insolence is only accepted because of your horizontal talents. Remember that."

"How could I forget? Before I go, do you want to discuss the actual speech you're giving tomorrow?"

"Yes, please. Have we heard back from Natalia Morazov? Although why we have to take guidance from another woman, I don't know."

"We have. She has made some minor suggestions, but my version is close to being good to go." CSW made the point very clearly it was her work and Boulter should be thankful, but there was no chance of that happening.

Boulter took the script and asked for some peace to rehearse.

CSW left and returned to her office. She began another task whilst waiting for the inevitable phone call from Moscow. Her secret mobile phone rang within five minutes.

Natalia Morazov got straight to the point.

"Send that paper to me immediately, please. I heard the disappointment in your voice."

CSW took a photograph of the handwritten list and sent it over to Moscow while Natalia was still on the line.

There was a protracted silence, then CSW heard another voice came through.

"Comrade Simpson-Walters, this is President Vasiliev. Let me assure you that you are a highly valued asset for the new Russian Empire. I want you to leave your office immediately and return to your apartment. After one hour, return to the White House. You will receive new orders. I emphasise, go now."

The line went dead.

Cheryl grabbed her bag and ran from the building, flashing her pass but ignoring the request to sign out. She had no idea what was happening, but she had a strong suspicion, and she did not want to be around the White House if she was correct.

Her apartment was only two hundred yards from her office. As she reached the front door of the block there was a rumble of armed vehicles in the near distance. CSW rushed inside and locked the door, an act she later realised was pretty irrelevant, as soldiers in combat don't ring the bell and wait to be given access.

Chapter Forty-Eight

Vasiliev had been waiting for confirmation that his decision to appoint Boulter had, indeed, been a hasty one. Natalia had warned Gusev, Gusev had warned Vasiliev and they had all waited for CSW to send the document.

As the President was speaking to CSW, Gusev spoke briefly to the Colonel commanding forces in Washington D.C. All he said was: "Peregrine Falcon."

A chain of actions began instantly.

The convoy of people carriers rolled into motion, soldiers readied their weapons, and visors were pulled down to obscure the identities of the men and women involved. It would be a story to tell the grandchildren one day, but for now, it was clinical, calculated, and impersonal.

Inside the Oval Office, Boulter whistled to himself as he read his speech. He wasn't happy as it was too soft for his liking. He would tweak it, he thought to himself. He was oblivious to the adverse impression he'd already made with Vasiliev. There are none so blind as those who will not see.

Boulter was aware of some movement within the building, but it didn't concern him. The security at the front entrance didn't try to stop the soldiers rushing in. The FBI operatives quickly dropped their weapons and stood back. The leader knew his route by heart, having studied the building's blueprints.

Dorothy Harkins was taken aback, her mouth opened, then closed again, and she sat down. Nobody went into the Oval Office without her authorising it, but not this time.

Boulter looked up just as eight soldiers in full camouflage stormed the room.

He managed to say, "This is my…" when the first of twenty bullets struck him in the head and chest. Remarkably, those outside of the office heard little due to the silencers being used.

The initial eight soldiers left and four more, clad head-to-toe in white overalls, entered with a stretcher. The residue of the man who had been Bart Boulter was scooped up onto the stretcher and they were gone. Four more appeared, and the office was cleaned, albeit there were bullet holes in the chair and the eastern wall of the Oval Office, behind where Boulter had been sitting. From start to finish, it had taken under five minutes.

White House staff were in a state of literal shock. 'Stunned' and 'amazed' were words used later, but at that moment, they were simply paralysed.

Dorothy Harkins saw herself as a woman of the world, but this belonged to a world far beyond her comprehension. She prided herself on being unflappable, but her quiet demeanour was down to her lack of control, not her grip on the situation.

The phone rang, startling her as it was the first call in several days. In a very amateurish way, Harkins just said, "Hello."

"Ms Harkins, this is Natalia Morazov. I am an aide to President Vasiliev. I don't know if you've heard of me?"

Harkins pulled herself together quickly.

"Mrs Morazov, I am aware of you. Cheryl Simpson-Walters has spoken very highly of you."

"Good, that means I don't need to explain to you that I have the authority to tell you what to do. In a few minutes, CSW will return to the office. The President himself ordered her to leave earlier, in case she was in the Oval Office when our people entered and she was accidentally caught up in the operation. She will now organise to receive the King tomorrow. Please ensure that all staff on duty know that anything CSW says or asks is done so with the absolute authority of President Vasiliev."

"Please don't worry. We will give Cheryl all the support she needs. I, personally, am very much looking forward to receiving His Majesty."

"Thank you, Dorothy. You may well become a key player for us too. Goodbye."

Being addressed by her forename had an effect on her. Dorothy was an early convert to the Russian view of the world.

When Cheryl Simpson-Walters returned twenty minutes later, Dorothy immediately launched into a graphic account of what she had witnessed and, as with many eyewitnesses to dramatic events, that which she thought she had seen. Cheryl had already been briefed by Natalia, but she wanted Harkins to be able to function and believed that letting it all out would help her psychologically.

"Let's get ready for the King," CSW urged.

"I am ready," Harkins proclaimed.

It was only some hours later that Dorothy considered CSW's reaction, given she had been Boulter's lover. Dorothy wasn't sure whether to be impressed by her stoicism or afraid of it.

Chapter Forty-Nine

King Philip was being flown at 35,000 feet aboard the aircraft once known as Air Force One. It was a flying fortress, a mobile command centre, a high-security workplace, and a marvel of design. The King had never experienced anything quite like it. It wasn't just that it was luxurious, it was the scale and technical detail that impressed him. Under different circumstances, Philip would have been excited and fascinated. On this journey, the flight plan out of London took the plane over Ireland, then swept down along the east coast of Canada and the United States of America. He was already King of the United Kingdom of Great Britain and Northern Ireland, and of Canada. Now, he had now added Éire (Southern Ireland) and the USA to his Kingdom. He didn't know what it meant yet.

President Vasiliev had asked him to serve, to help ensure a smooth transition to Russian rule, and, most crucially, to save lives. Even knowing they couldn't succeed, some people would try to resist the inevitable, Philip was assured by the President that his sincerest wish was to avoid bloodshed, and Philip believed him. So, here he was, flying to Washington D.C. to meet his new boss, the President of Angloland, Bart Boulter.

King Philip was nervous, but not because of the meeting itself. He had met Boulter before and found him obnoxious, a bully and a braggart, an unpleasant combination. He suspected Boulter was also a psychopath, as four per cent of CEOs were. Philip often wondered how these executives would cope without their own little 'empires'?

The King's Valet and Private Secretary were accompanying him. They were midway over the Atlantic Ocean when the phone beside him rang. The King had occupied the desk in the office from which the former President of the United States had run the so-called free world until three days ago.

"Philip," he answered without ceremony.

"Your Majesty, this is Vladimir Vasiliev. How is your flight?"

"Remarkable, thank you. I'm looking forward to meeting President Boulter."

"Now, there is the thing! The reason for my call is to inform you of some… changes that have been forced upon me. We knew there would be many issues which we couldn't foresee. However, the behaviour of my American appointees has been a major distraction.

"As you know, Ronald Malone's ego instantly got the better of him, and he has been sent to Siberia. That is a shame, as he had been a useful silent friend to Russia for years. Notwithstanding, he had to be replaced, and I appointed Bart Boulter into the position of President of Angloland. He too has been a massive supporter of Russia and of me. Well, to cut to the chase, as Brits like to say, he turned out to be even worse than Malone.

"He was warned that we could see and hear everything, but he plotted to make wholesale changes to our edicts, for his personal glory, and to achieve his own agenda."

"Is he in Siberia now?" asked the King.

"No. He is dead."

"Good grief. Was he tried for treason?"

"Your Majesty, I do admire your innocence. There was no trial, he was simply removed. When you reach the Oval Office, you will see the bullet holes. Now, whilst I trust you implicitly, leaving them on display may remind everyone that we do not play games."

"You had him shot?!"

"He was in his chair, contemplating ways to brutalise minority groups. We don't want persecution, we want equity and fairness, which, I believe, is also your aspiration."

"It is," Philip said. "It was my desire for the British people, and now that my role has been expanded to the whole of Angloland, it is my strongest wish for all of my subjects. I must say, I do not like random executions."

Vasiliev took a moment.

"I completely understand your position, but please try to understand mine. We've conquered the world, and we've done it painlessly and bloodlessly. There will be many reactionary forces, very many people looking to exploit opportunities, and many who will take time to adjust to the revised normal. I must act, and act quickly. Bart Boulter and Ronald Malone will be used as examples to ensure discipline among others in the new administration."

King Philip was processing the news and wondering if Vasiliev had rung him just to inform him of his own fate. The King had never been a politician, though he was prone to give advice to his Ministers, whether they sought it or not. This, however, was politics on steroids, and he needed to learn quickly.

Vasiliev continued, "So, Your Majesty, let me come to the point. You are highly respected across the globe. You have a simple perspective which is to minimise harm and avoid violence wherever possible."

"Correct."

"So, rather than appoint an avaricious political operator, I've decided to make you the head of Angloland. You will retain the title of King and serve as monarch of the USA, UK, Canada, Ireland, and all associated territories. You will be given all the support you need, as this role is so far beyond anything you have ever done before. It will be a powerful message to the general population, and not just to your mega-country. The especially good thing is you didn't seek this position."

King Philip was stunned. He just sat, staring at the phone as if it was the inanimate object responsible for this dramatic turn of events. In its most literal sense, the King was speechless. Vasiliev broke the silence.

"What are your thoughts, Philip?"

The King would tell his staff that it was the use of his first name which brought him back to the present.

"Mr President… I truly don't know what to say, or even if I have any thoughts. This is so far removed from my expectations. Do I have a choice?"

"Naturally, I want you to embrace the role with enthusiasm, as it will give you much more scope to achieve your ideals for your people. Having said that, no, you don't have a choice."

"I will, of course, do my best, but whether my best is good enough, I truly don't know. I suppose… we'll find out."

"Thank you, Your Majesty. I'm very pleased, and I mean that. We may have arrived here in an unfortunate way, but I am convinced this is a wonderful outcome. Now I must move on. Natalia Morazov will call you very shortly to talk through some of the detail. Goodbye."

As the call ended, King Philip remained seated in what had been the President's office, his first thought was, this is now the King's office. He was deeply conflicted; perhaps he could make a significant contribution, but he was also afraid.

Simultaneously, Natalia Morazov was on a secure line with Cheryl Simpson-Walters.

"Are you alone, Cheryl?"

"I am. Nobody can hear me, except your agents, of course."

Natalia let out a rare, genuine laugh, something which had been scarce over the last six months.

"I'm glad you are aware and on board. For your ears only, at least for a short time, His Majesty King Philip is Bart Boulter's replacement. As a non-political but highly respected figure, President Vasiliev believes he will succeed in pulling things together, to minimise any overt reactions and to embed the new culture."

"Wow. I was not expecting this. But what an inspired choice. What do you want me to do?"

"For the moment, just continue preparing for his arrival. Now he will take up residence in the White House's private quarters. So, clear all traces of Malone and Boulter. You have full authority to get it done. Use anyone and make the most of the talents at your disposal. I suspect Dorothy Harkins will be very helpful."

"Leave it with me."

Cheryl was about to end the call when Morazov spoke again.

"Cheryl, President Vasiliev is extremely impressed by your loyalty and comprehension of reality. He will be recommending to the King that you become his closest advisor. This will be an unrelenting job, at least for the first few months, but aligned with great satisfaction. Are you ready for such responsibilities?"

Cheryl paused only briefly before replying.

"It's a daunting prospect. I could not have imagined the events of the last few days. And yet, it feels like I have been preparing for this my entire life. The King will have his most ardent supporter."

"By the way, our President has decided Philip will retain his title as King, the King of Angloland."

"Excellent decision. I will rewrite his address to the people of Angloland and send it to you for approval."

"Thank you, Cheryl."

Chapter Fifty

President Huang Peng sat at the head of the long conference table, flanked by his Deputy President, Xiu Feng Wang. They had been joined by Duan Bai Bolin, newly appointed Minister of Defence following the enforced departure of Zhou Chen, and Chang Wei Lei, recently elevated to the newly created position of Minister for Coordination.

Duan had been Minister of Health and was an absolute loyalist. Chang had only been a minister for eleven years, which in China meant he was still virtually a tyro, a new boy.

The President shook each of them by the hand. This unsolicited acknowledgement signalled that his colleagues were special, and they all knew it. The level of warmth and camaraderie rocketed upwards.

"Gentlemen," Huang began, "thank you for accepting my invitation to this informal meeting for the consolidation of the Chinese Empire."

He looked at Duan and Chang, seated opposite him at the conference table. Xiu sat next to Huang.

"Tell me, how has the news of our expanded global reach been received by our senior colleagues?"

There was the slightest flicker of hesitation from Chang, almost imperceptible. But Huang noticed it and fixed his gaze on him.

"In this room we are all friends. I know others may have an alternative view of our direction, which is, to a degree, healthy. Once it is known you are meeting with me, you will be treated differently, perhaps with more respect and, certainly, in a more guarded way. This means your current intelligence is key. What is being said?"

Chang Wei Lei decided he had nothing to lose and everything to gain.

"Mr President, I can assure you everyone is thrilled and delighted by your personal achievements."

Huang raised an eyebrow. "I hear an implied 'but'…"

"Not a reservation as such. Senior people have egos, and if they know no more than others, it diminishes them, or at least it does in their own eyes."

Huang accepted the point, "I know but my Deputy and I were engaged in delicate negotiations with Russia, and its success might have been undermined by a leak out of China. That could have meant nuclear conflict. I hope you will accept our need for total secrecy. What else is being said?"

"Only the usual jockeying for position within the hierarchy. I imagine my own elevation is causin conversation."

The President smiled, acknowledging the politics at play. He knew that there were intense ambitions swirling just outside the walls of the room and that factions existed. In normal circumstances, half of his job was managing relationships and egos.

"Which does take me to my role as Minister for Coordination. What is its scope?"

He leaned back slightly, weighing his words.

"You're right to ask what it entails. With all these additional territories under our influence, I need a central figure to ensure all communications are consistent, all laws are compatible with ours and, if I was to give it a simplistic, crude title, it would be Minister of Propaganda. You will be the face of this Government within the Chinese Empire and facing outwardly to the many elements of the

Russian Empire. In some ways, having the world divided between the two largest entities there has ever been makes it easier. You will also have a team reviewing the manner of the implementation by the Russian Empire, across its vast array of cultures, noting difficulties and successes. We can learn from their losses and victories. This is a huge role which will make you very powerful if you do it well. To help, and nobody outside of this room knows, we have an agent operating at the highest level in the Russia's Kremlin itself. Literally, our agent is in the room with President Vasiliev himself."

Both Chang and Duan gasped audibly. Neither could imagine how this had been achieved or how it could be that it had been kept such a secret. They also understood the weight of responsibility that came with this knowledge. If it became more widely known, they would be suspected of indiscretion or worse.

Huang noted their expressions, then asked calmly, "What are your initial thoughts about the role?"

"I am excited and a bit nervous. The scope is complex. I have the skills, but will it be too unwieldy?"

"I'm glad to hear you admit to an element of nervousness. Too often, people refuse to accept that I am asking for the extraordinary and make rash commitments. Let me assure you, you will have all the resources you need. Again, I remind you this is a highly political role, and you will need to draw on your connections and diplomacy to make it work."

He paused, satisfied that the weight of responsibility was sinking in.

The President was pleased that the group had a grip on the size of their task. Huang and Xiu then fully briefed their colleagues without any reference to their thoughts for the next phase of their strategy, not yet revealing the entire vision for what lay ahead.

Chapter Fifty-One

Dmitriy and Natalia Morazov had been instructed to have a good night's sleep and then to take a morning away from their workplace. The supervisors in Dmitriy's team had been ordered not to contact him. If there was an emergency, either Boris Gusev or Mikhail Sokolov would handle it. Both of them accepted that, ultimately, they might need to contact Dmitriy Morazov, as he was the man who held all the knowledge in his head.

Natalia had prepared in draft President Vasiliev's next speech for January 1st and coordinated the addresses that the respective new leaders of the mega-countries would deliver to their citizens.

Dmitriy had an outstanding team who could more than adequately cope for a few hours. He did, however, feel very guilty about not being in the office. In forty-eight hours, the power would be reinstated everywhere. The timing was to be at 9 p.m. Moscow time, which had been chosen to accommodate everyone, as the new leaders would speak to their people for the first time, immediately after President Vasiliev.

Despite his subconscious negative feelings, Dmitriy was determined to make the most of his free time. Thankfully, Natalia felt the same way, and the hours were very fruitfully used. Dmitriy behaved like a new man, and Natalia smiled a lot as they returned to work.

The preparatory work on the technical aspects of the project meant there was little for Dmitriy to do aside from monitoring and testing. Natalia, on the other hand, had to brief all the Presidents and the King, and the President of the Russian Empire. She served as the ears and eyes of the most powerful people the world had ever known.

Both she and Dmitriy also had to attend the daily meeting of the inner sanctum, which occurred at 7 p.m.

The main topic at that day's meeting was the video conference Vasiliev would be having the following day with the Presidents and the King.

"Natalia, are they ready for the meeting?" Vasiliev began.

She replied, "They are, Mr President. The timing is awkward for a few, but they will be there. I have assured them they will be invited to Moscow for a subsequent event. It appears there is an enthusiasm for meeting you and ensuring you are confident in their loyalty."

"Good idea, and there's no better way than looking someone in the eye to know that messages are received and understood. Let's arrange it for the third week of January. By then, we'll have a clearer picture of the issues, and which leaders aren't in control. We can then outline our next steps."

There was, inevitably, a general murmuring of agreement from the rest of the members of the meeting. They already knew which side their bread was buttered on, the President thought, amused by the fact he was using an old British phrase. It was a product of a year's service in London when he was a young agent.

Natalia continued, "Would you like to discuss the agenda for tomorrow?"

Vasiliev declined. "There's no need, as everyone here is busy, and you'll all be on the call."

The next fifteen minutes were spent touching on various hotspots, but it was relatively quiet, and any signs of insurrection had been swiftly dealt with by Russian or local forces. It was noted which nations had been keen to show they were integrating, even at the cost of their compatriots' lives.

As they were leaving the room Alexandr Bychkov asked Natalia to join him in his own office.

"Tell me about Cheryl Simpson-Walters."

"Loyal to herself, but that translates to commitment to the President and the King. Why do you ask?"

"I have come to the conclusion that if Angloland remains orderly, it will send a strong message to the others. Having a most persuasive influence in the White House, and wherever the King decides to reside, is critical. Is she that person?"

"I've listened to the recordings from the Oval Office with the ex-presidents, and believe me, she has a crystal-clear understanding of the way we want to run our administration. She is no shrinking violet."

Bychkov delved deeper.

"Is it true she was in a relationship with one of them?"

"It is, and possibly with both, but that hasn't affected her. I suspect she was always the dominant force. I have suggested she uses me as a sounding board, which would allow me to mentor her."

"That I do like. Thanks for reassuring me."

Chapter Fifty-Two

King Philip arrived in the White House earlier than expected. Some had imagined there would be formalities at the airport. Instead, the King was on the freeway within five minutes of the airplane stopping.

This fazed neither CSW nor Dorothy Harkins.

"Your Majesty, welcome to America and Washington DC, capital of Angloland," enthused Harkins.

"Thank you."

"I am Dorothy Harkins, your Executive Assistant, and this is Cheryl Simpson-Walters."

CSW almost curtsied, having never met the King before and, as yet, wasn't sure the ways the niceties of rank would develop.

King Philip was keen to put them at ease.

"After I spoke to President Vasiliev, Natalia Morazov rang me. She was very complimentary about you both. I am sure we'll work well together. Now could one of you tell me what is happening and what I am doing?"

The fact that he said this with a broad grin on his face meant the two women relaxed immediately. If, even in the new world, first impressions still mattered, then the King had made an excellent start. As they discreetly assessed him, CSW and Dorothy Harkins recognised the quality of his clothes, definitely a Savile Row suit.

"Come into the Oval Office, Sir. How would you like us to address you?"

"It's a new order, so I suspect things need to be more informal without losing the authority. So, perhaps 'Sir', unless we have visitors, then it might have to be 'Your Majesty'. What do you think?"

"Great. Would you like to be taken to the residence first? You may like to freshen up."

"Could we talk first, please?"

"Of course."

"Are you aware that President Vasiliev has appointed me Leader of Angloland?"

Cheryl and Dorothy nodded, perhaps a little too vigorously.

CSW spoke, "Natalia Morazov rang me a short while ago and informed us. Congratulations."

The King wasn't sure it was a cause for euphoria.

"You know better than anyone the fate of my two predecessors. This all happened within a few days; it could be the poisoned chalice."

CSW was the rational voice.

"Sir, if you are, as we believe you are, a force for peace, you'll be in post for decades. You have lived your life knowing that being monarch is not a role from which one can be promoted, so you'll be able to suppress any latent ambition. You will have frustrations, you won't like everything, but if your goal is the preservation of lives and a smooth existence for your people, then it will go well.

"My one piece of advice is, when you feel thwarted or you are sad, don't express those thoughts. Literally, every word you say is recorded and monitored, including in your private quarters. And in case you're surprised I'm saying this aloud, let me assure you I've been encouraged to keep you safe and useful, as per our ethos. I am sure cleanliness isn't an issue!"

His Majesty laughed. "Mustafa, my valet, would be mortified if I was anything other than immaculately turned out."

"Shall we go to the residence?" CSW asked.

"If you could tell me what my agenda is, that would be useful."

Dorothy Harkins clutched the diary, which was, in truth, very lightly populated.

"The only two items are a video conference with President Vasiliev and the other leaders of the mega-countries and your speech to Angloland on January 1st."

"But who are my advisors and ministers?"

CSW replied, "Sir, this is, I suggest, is your main task. You will need to present your list of nominations to President Vasiliev and be prepared to justify the proposals. At the same time, I think it is critical that you know the ins and outs of the new ethos and the laws supporting it. To guide your ministers, you must be able to articulate the vision and its parameters."

Pensively, King Philip concurred.

"May we reconvene in thirty minutes time, please? If you have any ideas about nominations, I'd appreciate it if you brought them with you."

The meeting dissolved and the King retired to his rooms which, though not as palatial as Windsor Castle, were much warmer and more comfortable.

Twenty-nine minutes later, CSW and Dorothy Harkins were back in the Oval Office as Philip returned.

"I feel better, and Mustafa is happily doing whatever it is he does. What's first?"

CSW assumed responsibility for guiding the conversation.

"Sir, I believe all nominations for senior positions need to meet certain criteria. But first, we need to decide what the senior positions are and the broad remit."

"So, there is no template?"

"To a degree, we have one. There is no need to appoint anyone for defence, foreign affairs, or international relations. I think there needs to be a Prime Minister for each of the nations, and then people overseeing legislation, justice, education, internal security, employment, and culture. Other roles may well emerge, but this might be a decent starting point."

"I'm grateful for your thoughts. Let's proceed. What criteria do you think we should apply?"

Dorothy Harkins was making notes, but they all knew the conversation was being recorded anyway.

CSW made her recommendations.

"Firstly, loyalty. Secondly, a commitment to keep people safe. And thirdly, acceptance of you as the head of this government. Of course, they must all be experienced politicians and administrators."

The King agreed.

"So, Julia Jones takes the reins in the UK, and Padraig Kelly, the Taoiseach, in Ireland. That's easy."

"If I may, sir. Perhaps Julia Jones could be responsible for justice across our new lands, and Gemma Newman could take over in the UK. That way, you have someone you respect working very closely with you. Justice, and the application of our new laws, is the most important job."

"Great idea. I really like that. And Brian Quick remains in Canada?"

"Or perhaps he could take the lead on education?" CSW proffered. "His deputy is Sylvia Anderson, a very capable person."

"I've met her, at an official reception, but I have no real knowledge of her abilities. Do we have any more information about her, or indeed, others we might consider?"

CSW walked around the desk and placed her laptop in front of her new boss, the third in as many days. There were numerous tabs open, each of which was a file on the people CSW expected to discuss. This naturally guided the debate and restricted choice. She was aware the candidates had already been vetted by the Kremlin and deemed acceptable.

Within one hour, there were nominations in place for all the top roles. There was balanced representation from the United Kingdom, United States of America, Canada, and Ireland. As nations, it was the last of these which concerned Philip most. In the Republic of Ireland there was no support for the British monarchy. His own appointment would be deeply unpopular. He hated the thought that there might be a profound rebellion to stop it, which could turn violent and undermine his efforts to bring order and save lives. The outgoing Taoiseach would be fundamental to the smooth transition. That Padraig Kelly had been given a very big job might, only might, have a calming effect. Kelly's behaviour would be critical.

"What do we do to get these names agreed, and who tells them?" the King asked.

"Leave the confirmations to me," CSW was able to say with confidence, as she and Natalia Morazov had discussed them earlier, while the King was refreshing himself.

CSW continued, "Telling the appointees will be your first major task. There may be some reluctance. As well as reminding them of their duty, you may need to be clear regarding a direct connection between reluctance and becoming someone not deemed to be a friend of the Empire. There really is no alternative, but we do want people to be positive and committed."

"I understand, and I caught the implications for me as well. May we talk about my speech now, please?"

The King was unfailingly polite; it was his nature and his upbringing. Cheryl Simpson-Walters had become very keen for him to succeed, not least because it would reflect very well on her.

"There will be a final draft with you this evening. We're just tweaking it now that you are delivering it rather than a predecessor. If you would like to rest to offset the jetlag you are experiencing, I will bring it up to you in the residence."

"Why not? Thank you both for all your help. I must also ring my wife, for whom all of this will come as a surprise. I suspect she'll rather like being Queen of Angloland. She's always been particularly fond of Americans, maybe a little too much occasionally."

Chapter Fifty-Three

As she expected, Cheryl's phone rang ten minutes later. She almost answered with "Hello, Natalia," but that might not have been well received. If she was to progress, it was better not to take liberties.

"Hello Cheryl, this is Natalia. Thank you for so effortlessly getting our preferred people into the correct boxes. I have nearly all the proposals from all the leaders and will clear them with President Vasiliev shortly. The King will be able to make the calls later today."

After a few pleasantries, the call ended.

Natalia Morazov visited her husband's office as she made her way to see the President. Dmitriy was beginning to look haggard due to lack of sleep and the weight of responsibilities. Natalia, on the other hand, looked fresh and full of life.

"Darling, you're tired. Can you get home this evening?"

"I will try. However, there are a couple of minor glitches in the monitoring systems in Africana, unfortunately at a time when there's still trouble around the Democratic Republic of Congo. There is no threat to the Empire, as the tribes only want to kill each other. It's an early test for President Happy Imeh, the newly appointed President of Africana, but he needs our help through the technology. It will be sorted very quickly, but I can't go home until it is corrected."

Natalia knew this was typical of the man, dedicated to the task, but behind it all, also deeply concerned for the people losing their lives. It was all very unnecessary.

"I'm going to see the boss, with the lists of names for the top jobs in each of the mega-countries. We're on track."

"I never doubted it or you. I love you."

"I love you too," she replied, and she was gone. Never be late for President Vasiliev.

As Natalia walked into the President's outer office, his last meeting was finishing, and she walked straight in. Aleksandr Bychkov was also there.

For once, Natalia gave them a printed sheet containing all the nominations.

Vasiliev and Bychkov quietly read through them.

Bychkov asked, "No surprises?"

"None. Of course, there may be some people who decline the opportunity, and prefer the future of total obscurity cleaning streets."

Vasiliev gave his authorisation to proceed.

"Tell each of them to make this happen because this will be one of the criteria against which they will each be assessed. How is the King?"

"The reports are very favourable."

"Is this from your new best friend Cheryl?"

Ignoring the slight tease, "It is, and she is very competent."

"Excellent. I want him to succeed. Watch them well, please."

"The message is very clear. Leave it to me," said Natalia Morazov, well aware of the need to avoid errors.

Chapter Fifty-Four

On 30th December, Vasiliev's senior team convened in his office. They sat in a horseshoe shape behind the screen on which the faces of the various leaders of the new mega-countries were appearing. At exactly 9 p.m. Moscow time, Vasiliev switched on his camera.

"Gentlemen, thank you all for being punctual, although I'm not sure if anything could be more important than this session. For those of you outside of Angloland, allow me to inform you that the new leader is King Philip, until now Monarch of the United Kingdom and Head of the Commonwealth of Nations. This may prompt you to wonder, where is President Keaton? Well, he was removed very quickly as he resisted our takeover. I replaced him with former President Ronald Malone who, almost immediately, had Keaton murdered, and more disappointingly, killed his family. I want strong, even harsh actions but, and I cannot emphasise this enough, not petty retributions for imagined slights. Malone is now in Siberia, from where he may never emerge.

"Naturally, I had a replacement ready in the form of billionaire Bart Boulter. Again, almost immediately, Boulter began to plot to change what we want. Bart Boulter has departed from this world. I tell you all of this to help you understand my attitude towards any appointment. I will not accept disloyalty or independent thinking. You will not operate outside of the limits set by Russia. And, just in case you're wondering how I knew what was happening, we are listening and watching you all. This technology will also prove exceedingly helpful to you in keeping your areas of responsibility under control.

"Now, to more positive news. King Philip is here, and he is fully aligned with our actions. His priority is the same as mine, which is as few deaths and injuries as possible, with full acceptance of our rule. He, and you, now have the appointments your top teams agreed upon. Please ensure you report faithfully the message I have given to you today.

"Our commitment to our citizens is encapsulated as: *Safe, Clean and Useful*. To that end, your primary focus in the next few days is the eradication of criminality. Round up all known criminals, whether they have been convicted or not. Imprison them in your own country or arrange for the worst of them to be incarcerated in Siberia or the jungles of Africana or Asia. Any resistance should be met with terminal force. In the same spirit, anyone who does not surrender their arms in the amnesty by January 5th must be removed from society. This must be a key theme in your address to your respective nations. Safety is the number one concern, wherever people live.

"Over the coming days I will need you to provide plans to develop housing for everyone, and high-quality education for all young people and those needing to enter a new career, as we abolish many roles and create new ones focused on protecting the planet. Please make the crucial appointments to lead these themes. We must show a dynamic commitment to the positive aspects of the new order.

"However, I need you to have a strategy for dealing with people who can never be useful, the decrepit, the drug addicts, the insane, those with educational difficulties. This will include very basic accommodation and support, but it must also include ways to help them exit their turmoil. We will be doing them a favour by releasing them from an existence so difficult that we cannot imagine it.

"In a change to the immediate plan, your individual addresses to your mega-nations will follow another one from me on January 1st, then the power will be restored. It is at this juncture that is the most dangerous, as people will be able to communicate and possibly plan resistance. Television will be switched on, so make sure the networks are ready for this and are prepared to play enjoyable programmes, especially comedy. Get your sporting fixtures back on and your places of worship open. People need distraction and support. Find ways to provide it, appropriate to your people."

The President of the Russian Empire then read to his team the content of his speech to the people of the world, scheduled for forty-eight hours later. Whilst there were no surprises, the leaders were taken aback by the clarity with which Vasiliev intended to speak. Some of them even took notes, despite being told that a copy of the script was already in their personal inbox.

"Each of you has an advisor from my team, and they will help you set an ambitious agenda for embedding our collective approach. Does anyone have a question in this forum?"

A light lit up on next to the screen of Happy Imeh of Africana.

"Mr President, does it not seem anomalous that there is one King? Should we all have the title, rather than 'President'?"

"President Imeh, you are struggling to control the mobs in the DRC, and your question is about your personal job title. I am surprised."

Vasiliev nodded to Dmitriy Morazov, and the screen of Happy Imeh went blank.

"Gentlemen, you have just seen the removal of one of your number. Former President Imeh will now become a cellmate of Ronald Malone in Siberia. His replacement will be named within the next hour. Please do not fail me. Any other questions?"

Unsurprisingly, no one else had anything further to ask. Vasiliev's camera was turned off, though he was still able to watch his shocked subordinates, until, one by one, they too switched off their screens. "Well, I think that went well," Vasiliev concluded.

Part Three
Embedding - From January 1st

Chapter Fifty-Five

The world was watching for the second time in less than a week. President Vasiliev was to make a further announcement regarding the way the Russian Empire would rule. As before, there had been the same very brief warning: that at 9 p.m. Moscow time, he would speak to the people.

At exactly 8:59 p.m. in Russia, the power came on and television sets around the world came alive. Billions of eyes focussed on the screens, and the attention was intense. This would be a description of the way life was to be lived from that moment on.

Vasiliev was immaculately attired again. He personified power and authority.

"My people, thank you for joining me. A few days ago, I gave you knowledge of the Russian operation which has conquered the world, without the use of force. There has been no war, no battles, no bombing of civilian populations, and no crimes against humanity.

Of course, this does mean Russia and its people are now safe from the aggression of the western countries and organisations like NATO. There may have been ways to create a peaceful accord, but too many countries had too many politicians with too many agendas. I do not want you to blame Russia for this situation, because if anyone is to blame, it is those little people with big egos who had unachievable ambitions. All of this has its roots in the need to win elections. We are saving you from these fairly minor distractions. Macro-policy decisions will be taken by me and my team.

Unfortunately, for the last week you have been without power. This has meant a very difficult time, and there have been hardships, and some deaths. I am certain you haven't enjoyed it, and it is an indication of your future if people try to challenge our authority. Your nation's leader, with me, will describe the parameters within which we will live.

In a few minutes, you will hear from the man who will be the head of the mega-country of which you are a citizen. Over time, he and I will reveal more and more about the future and your part in it. But first, let me recap some of the announcements I made in the first address, because I know it would have been very difficult to absorb and remember it all, and then I will add to them.

Our overall themes are *Safe, Clean and Useful*. Everything we do, and ask you to do, will be set against those three simple words.

Our technology means we can monitor everything you do. There can be no criminality, no conspiracy, and no rebellion.

As I said last time, when we consider the best time to be alive, most people talk about the 1950s, although they love the advances in media, healthcare, communications, transport, and so many other aspects of life. We have brought you to a point at which we will have the best of both worlds.

Each of the mega-countries will have their laws and ethics described, but I remind you now: there will be no legalised homosexuality, no acceptance of transgender changes, no abortion except in very specific circumstances, no public demonstrations, no social media, and no instant credit to buy things.

Private companies will still exist to ensure a constant food supply and the basics of life. However, the profits will be reabsorbed for the benefit of the community. Professionals and executives will be rewarded with a salary two or three times the norm. Offshore bank accounts and other financial mechanisms will be irrelevant, as there will be no way of generating excess income. We will be citizens of the world, not cogs in a capitalist machine. This isn't communism; it is a third way of using all our talents. This also means a few powerful and unelected people in oil, fossil fuels, finance, and the media, for example, cannot dictate your way of life just because it suits them and allows them to make lots of money.

For the first time, you will be beholden only to society and to your fellow citizens, not to a boss who can sack you at any moment. Naturally, you will need to be assured that this will apply to everyone. And here is one of the things which may take you some time to get accustomed; we can monitor everything you do and say. This means we can eliminate crime, which could stop our balanced society from working. Initially, as people get used to all of this, the penalties will be severe, very much in keeping with the morality of yesteryear. The death penalty will exist everywhere, new prisons are being built in Siberia, and in the jungles of Africa, Asia, and South America. On some occasions, the immediate family of felons will also be punished.

Every society has rules and laws, and I have just explained the bases of ours. They are easy to understand and really do apply to every person equally.

You will be free to make suggestions regarding ways to improve society, but within the limits we decide.

You will be free to work and make a real contribution without the obscene practice of taxation penalising you for hard work.

We will guarantee employment, because the use of Artificial Intelligence will be banned in non-governmental business. There will be no online shopping, and retail will be through traditional shops. We will have a massive focus on infrastructure projects to make life efficient and to offset climate change. There will be an immense focus on keeping our environments clean and healthy. There will be no foreign travel unless authorised. This will mean that, in some countries, there will be fewer jobs in tourism, yet will mean others being created to compensate in different sectors and increased opportunities in local tourism, as people holiday in their own country. We will limit the use of technology in food production and restrict all germicides. The emphasis will be on vegetables and less on meat, which uses a wholly disproportionate amount of land to provide fodder for the animals.

There will be fewer jobs for bureaucrats, and they will be reallocated to useful jobs.

Work will be for six days per week, although which days may vary by nation due to religious convictions and traditions. Obviously, some jobs will require cover on a 24/7 basis, which is permitted, and shift patterns will be created accordingly.

You will be liberated from worrying about money, as income will be guaranteed and everyone will work, unless they are unfit. There will be no specific retirement age, and people will work until at least the age of seventy-five, as they will want to contribute. Pensions will be paid from that age, if appropriate.

Money which has been hoarded in secret bank accounts has been expunged, they no longer exist. All bank accounts have been capped at twice the annual salary. All debt has been erased, including student loans.

You can remain in your own home and keep your possessions, but there will be a low threshold allowed for inheritance. Properties will be converted and allocated to those in need.

Power, including electricity, will be free, but limited, so that people don't waste it.

You will be free from the worry of immigration, as there will be work and assured income across the globe. Jobs in your country will be for you and your family.

You will be free from being harassed by misfits on the street. Homelessness will not exist. Beggars and other parasites will be removed. Drug addicts will be taken into care. People suffering from mental strife will be absorbed by the state.

Without crime you will be free to go about your daily duties without threat.

Producing or watching pornography will be a crime.

Gambling will be a crime.

More of your time will be free, as trains and buses will run on time, and our systems will function efficiently.

You are free to love someone of the same gender.

You are free from guns, because we are all safe. There is an amnesty until January 5th by which time all firearms must be handed in. Anyone found in possession of a weapon after this date will be imprisoned. The argument that you need a gun to keep safe has been removed, as nobody will have one. Similarly, the argument that you need one to save you from the government has just been categorically shown to be facile. The government now holds total power.

You are free from worrying about the effects of climate change because there will be less movement of goods, less waste, reduced consumerism, and many jobs created to improve the state of the world. This is a cause we can all agree on.

Education will be provided free of charge. It will focus on themes which support society, to encourage people to contribute to its improvement, whether those relate to science, medicine, engineering, or the arts.

Medical treatment will be free, regardless of nation. This will mean a big training and recruitment campaign. Anyone qualified will be required to return to medicine.

Religion will be allowed, but persecution of others because of their religion or creed will absolutely not be. We have created the structures for peace, but it means peoples' behaviour must reflect that goal. We will make sure actions are in line with these.

People will be allowed to wear any clothes they want, as long as they are clean and doesn't obscure identification.

Freedom of expression through the arts is encouraged, but it must not conflict with the world's new values.

You are free to have a family, provided you are capable of caring for the children, and there are no defects in your DNA. In the future, we can only have people who will be useful. This will be achieved by our water having contraceptives in it, and only married couples designated as acceptable will be provided with the antidote.

We will have solidarity, in which everyone who is useful will be kept safe, in a world which is clean, with rewards that are universal.

To be young means you are free to look forward to a life of fulfilment and contribution.

There will be no social media, but we will support religion, television, and sport. We want people to be happy.

Television will resume immediately after the address from the leaders, as will power and telephone communications.

We will be stringently enforcing the laws. If anyone acts against them, they will feel the full force of the new State, which has full autonomy to use force and capital punishment. A softer penalty will be exile to Siberia for all those directly involved.

In the short term, you will see changes, but ultimately, you will realise the benefits which will come from our benevolence.

Every group has rules, and ours is no different. By monitoring everyone, we are making everyone free. We are all living by the same standards and laws.

I am giving you freedom. You are liberated. We have a government for the greater good, and it is predictable.

Finally, there will be a review in three years' time to assess our progress and consider any changes to enhance society even further.

Do your best, for yourself, your family, and society. This is not merely our duty, it is our honour.

SAFE, CLEAN AND USEFUL are our key drivers.

This speech will be available on the Government website to ensure everyone has the opportunity to read it carefully, and to keep people safe from making mistakes.

In a few minutes, your leader will appear.

Everything we do is for the greater good."

Vasiliev was switched off, and in every nation, people tried to take stock, and to decide what it all meant to them.

Chapter Fifty-Six

In the White House, King Philip was having his final conversation with Cheryl Simpson-Walters before his address to the people of Angloland.

"Cheryl, I am nervous. Of course, I've broadcast many times before, but never as the executive leader. Mine has been a ceremonial role, almost a sinecure. This really matters. What if it goes wrong and, rather than preventing bloodshed, my only true goal, I provoke it?"

"Your Majesty, you're prepared, you look great, and you believe this is the right course of action. Why would it go badly? Dorothy and I have heard you rehearse, and it's powerful and genuine."

"Thank you, Cheryl. How long to go?"

"Television connections will be restored again at your bidding, but as the people are already by their sets, let's catch them."

The King went around his desk and sat in front of the camera. His habit when nervous was to twiddle with his pen, which CSW had already observed, and there was nothing within reach for Philip to use as a distraction. He took a very deep breath and nodded to the producer. Above the camera lens, a red light came on. Simultaneously, CSW put up a thumb. Like about ten percent of men, Philip was colour-blind to red, and without CSW's signal, he might have sat looking silently at the camera.

"Good day to you. I use this phrase because across Angloland we have time zones spanning eleven hours, from London to Honolulu. Geographically, I suspect ours has the greatest span of the new mega-countries.

"As you are aware, until last week, I was the King of the United Kingdom. It never occurred to me that I would ever take on a political role. However, when President Vasiliev asked me, I felt it my duty to accept the position as Head of Angloland. My primary focus is keeping the people of Angloland safe, which is, as you have heard from the President, one of the three key principles of the new world order.

"Over the next few hours, I will be appointing the cabinet. There will be positions for justice, education, health, and a Prime Minister for the USA, Canada, Ireland, and the UK. Wherever possible, we will allow decisions to be made at a local level. These will need to be in strict accordance with the overall vision President Vasiliev has set out for us all.

"It is obvious that the last few days have been very difficult for everyone, some more than others. If you have lost a loved one, please accept my deepest sympathies. Our quest must be to minimise further losses in the short term and to build a new society as we move forward. I see this new society as being better, fairer, and with a broader sense of collective purpose.

"As we become accustomed to the revised laws, there will be some that people will not like. To give an inevitable example, many people in the USA will not want to comply with the amnesty and hand in their guns. The defence that it is a right under the Second Amendment 'to keep and bear arms' is no longer valid. The Law of the Russian Empire supersedes and overrides it. Please, and I really mean this, please hand in your guns, and any other weapons, to the police.

"Many people, especially younger ones, may feel disappointed at the loss of social media. Let's use this decision as one which encourages us to talk more and develop our relationships.

"All of this is going to take some getting used to, but think of the advantages:

A green and clean improved environment in which wildlife can flourish

Employment for everyone

No taxation

Free education

Free medical treatment

Free power such as electricity

No crime

"There are some changes which will feel unusual, but the benefits will far outweigh them. My most earnest plea to you is this: please do not react in a negative manner. This regime will not accept rebellion or collusion, and the penalties will be severe. As the President has said, there are new prisons being built, and punishments may even impact upon the family of the criminal.

"In a few minutes, all our utilities and services will be restored. Please, live a long and happy life."

The camera went off.

CSW was genuinely impressed.

"You were excellent, positive and sincere. I know you believe every word, even if some of the less appealing aspects wouldn't be your choice."

"True. But as I just said, the benefits will far exceed the downsides, unless some people attempt to resist. That must be our recurring message. Now, let's make some appointments. Julia Jones first."

Chapter Fifty-Seven

The Nolans in Strood were in shock.

Isabella recovered her composure first.

"Our King is now the head of our mega-country. I am astounded. It's good news, isn't it?"

Her son, Alex, didn't care about the King.

"It doesn't matter who is King or President or whatever, as Russia makes the rules now. Everything I heard seemed fine. Keep your nose clean and life will be okay."

Phil, Alex's father, was concerned.

"Are we really free? Will my job in IT still exist, or will I have to work in a fast-food joint?"

"Do you think they can really hear what we're saying or is it only over the phone?" asked Isabella.

Her husband sounded morose as he replied.

"I do and I'm taking no chances. If this is our fate, then I'm not going to say anything that might land me in trouble. Like the King said, there will be benefits, and we have to get used to it. You should ring your mother to see if she is okay and whether she slept through the King's speech."

"Gran always misses things as she dozes off constantly. Anyone who can fall asleep while holding a cup of tea can definitely sleep through a TV address. I bet it shocked her when it sloshed into her lap," Alex laughed.

It broke the ice of doom, and they moved off to contact mates and family.

In the town of Chickasaw in Oklahoma, there was a very disgruntled reaction to the news that there was to be a total ban of guns.

Herb Andrews had learned to shoot and hunt when he was eight years old and now, sixty years later, he wasn't about to give up his gun.

"No Russian or King of England is going to tell me what I can or can't do. They won't know I've kept my shooter, and if they come for me, they'll find out what men of Oklahoma are really about."

His wife, Dolly, wasn't as sure.

"What are you on about, you silly old fool? If they can shut down the whole world, do you seriously think you can fight them off on your own? If there is no crime and no government to resist, why do you even need a gun?"

"It's my right. That's it."

"Tomorrow you're taking that peashooter to the cop shop, and that is the end of it. Or else. And you know what I mean by that."

"We'll see."

"Yes, we will."

Their daughter, Dana, who was nineteen years old, stood in the doorway. In her arms was baby Cinnamon.

"God, can't you see this might be the best thing that has ever happened for us? Jed will have guaranteed work without enlisting in the army as gun-fodder. We'll have healthcare. Cinnamon and her brother will be able to go to school. What are we actually giving up?"

Herb was a proud and independent man.

"We've got to kowtow to the Russians. They are, and always will be, our enemies. Cut the crap. They want to win, and I ain't having it."

Dolly was the matriarch and her word was gospel.

"On Sunday, the pastor will tell us what God wants us to do. And that'll be that."

Across every country, every county, and every town in the world, debates were beginning. All of them, ultimately, irrelevant as there was no way to counter the Russian victory. For many, it was an attempt to assess how to adapt, and, just as crucially, how to avoid making a mistake that could carry dire consequences.

Chapter Fifty-Eight

Cheryl Simpson-Walters was in the room when the King made the call to Julia Jones. CSW had already spoken to Jones to arrange the time and to emphasise that she must be on her own for the conversation. Merely mentioning the fact that she was constantly monitored ensured the request would be met.

"Madam Prime Minister," the King began.

"Your Majesty, it's an honour to hear from you."

Julia Jones sounded calm, but she was in turmoil. The last few days had been exceedingly difficult, worrying about their safety, her career, and the situation for those closest to her. John Jones, her husband, had tried to placate her, but they all knew there was no way of influencing the outcome, and any words of comfort felt shallow. She did appreciate the support and was grateful. When the King's appointment was announced, they had allowed themselves to hope for some leniency from the worst possible scenarios.

"Tell me, how have the last few days been for you?"

Jones considered her reply carefully.

"Very difficult, Sir. I think it is the feeling of impotence. I imagine this has been the same for all of the people in every country. My concerns are for my staff and the citizens of the UK."

The King moved on quickly as he wanted to alleviate her worries.

"You heard my address, and albeit with reduced powers, there will be a Prime Minister of Great Britain."

Jones caught the nuance.

"Great Britain, not the United Kingdom?"

"Ha, well done. Northern Ireland will become integrated with Éire, so we have one Ireland. This resolves some issues but will create others as well. The big advantage is that some of the Irish people will be supportive of my position. We must find ways, both subtle and blatant, to bring peace and harmony."

"I will serve in any way you want me to, Sir."

"I am pleased to hear you say that, because I do have a position for you."

Inaudibly, Julia Jones gave a sigh of relief.

"It isn't as Prime Minister."

This time Jones' reaction, her show of disappointment, was obvious. But the King gave no indication of noticing it.

"I want to discuss you being a member of my cabinet, as Minister of Justice. What do you think?"

Jones was astonished. In thirty seconds, she had gone from worrying about her life to potentially being one of the most powerful people in Angloland.

"Sir, I said I would support you in any way you want, so this would be more than an honour. What do you see the role encompassing?"

"This is the tricky part. You will be responsible for security, courts, prisons, and punishments. This requires someone with the strength of character to ensure that very harsh penalties are carried out, but who can also find ways to ensure levels of compassion as well. To use a cliché: an iron fist in a velvet glove."

"I know President Vasiliev mentioned the death penalty. Does he mean to use it widely?"

"He does, if it is necessary. But the quicker we can bring about the compliant society he wants, the fewer deaths there will be. I would prefer the use of prisons in Siberia and the jungles, although they will be terrible. The President knows this is my opinion, but there will be harsh decisions to take until we get there. I would rather have someone who isn't bloodthirsty in the job, like you, but I do warn you, we will not be allowed to fail. Are you in?"

Jones knew there wasn't really a choice. If she refused, her 'card would be marked' and maybe another appointee might take lives just for the fun of it. It might be 'Hobson's Choice', yet it could be an invaluable chance.

"I am nervous, I will admit. We could be very successful, in the context of the situation we are in. Thank you for having confidence in me. May I ask about Gemma Newman's position? She has been an outstanding colleague."

"She will be Prime Minister of Great Britain, if she accepts the nomination. Please don't say anything to her, as I am about to ring her. Welcome on board."

The call ended before Jones could say goodbye.

CSW placed the call to Gemma Newman, and the King repeated the conversation. He also appointed the rest of the Cabinet. All the invitations were readily accepted, and the King promised to have a much longer conversation with them over the next day or so.

The King had left the most interesting appointment to last. The person suggested for the role of Prime Minister of the United States of America was James 'Griff' Griffin. Griffin was from Texas and had a very conservative background, a member of the religious Right. The general moral theme of the Russian script was very acceptable to him.

However, he had been a very outspoken critic of America's greatest foe, Russia, and particularly of Vasiliev.

"Mr Griffin, this is the King."

"Your Majesty, what an honour to speak to you." CSW had coached him regarding the proper way to address the monarch in an earlier call.

"Mr Griffin, you have been a senior senator for many years, but you haven't appeared to have ambitions for higher office."

"Sir, to serve has been my only desire. I have wanted to bring Christianity to politics, and that would never have got me elected to the highest role."

"Now that we are members of the Russian Empire, how will you deal with Vasiliev as your leader?"

"Sir, it is only known to a very small number of people, two of whom have died in the last few days, that I have been in personal conversation with President Vasiliev for years, and I have been pursuing an agenda which aligns with his."

This time it was the King who was taken aback.

"Why?"

"To use the Russian machine to undermine those soggy liberals and socialists. This wouldn't have been my preferred solution, but it's pretty good."

"Well, it certainly seems you are an ideal fit for the President's view of leadership in America. Will you accept the position of Prime Minister of the United States of America, the first person to serve in this role?"

"Thank you, I will. Titles don't concern me; doing God's work is what matters."

"Prime Minister Griffin, I would appreciate it if you would come to the White House later today for a more detailed conversation."

As the call ended, Philip turned to CSW.

"Wow, we have got a live one. Now I think we have someone we'll need to watch, and he will soon want my job, to do even more of God's work. As you're aware, I'm a person of faith, yet I suspect my views are a little adrift from the zealot Mr Griffin."

Chapter Fifty-Nine

It had been three hours since President Vasiliev had finished his speech. He knew the leaders of the mega-countries had made their inputs and that the power had been switched back on. Natalia Morazov had arrived at his office to give him some feedback about the initial reactions.

"What is happening?"

Natalia was quite relaxed and assured, not least because she knew her boss was not one to shoot the messenger.

"Bursts of gunfire in very many places, some casualties, and continued feuds between tribes and gangs. Local forces have dealt with them pretty effectively. Our troops are in key locations and there is no sign of insurrection against our regime. Although, again, I would say it is too early for there to be any coordinated resistance."

"Has your husband identified any technical problems?"

"On the contrary, the surveillance equipment is working very well. Local leaders are having criminals taken into custody at an exceedingly fast rate. Lots of crying about rights, fairness of the situation, and protesting their innocence. I suspect some of it is true, but for the greater good, we move on."

"What about in the highly religious regions?"

Natalia looked at the handwritten notes she had made as she collated the inputs from around the globe.

"At this moment, there are no more disturbances than other places. However, I imagine these will be the worst spots over the next few days."

"What about my new best friend, the King?" Vasiliev asked.

"Do you know, I think this is your most inspired appointment, even if it was due to the circumstances which forced it. CSW is most impressed, and his lack of ego, or at least ambition, gives a sense of certainty that is contagious. The USA will give him some problems due to the collective feeling of their own importance. Naturally, there will be individuals everywhere who want a different type of freedom to the one you are prescribing."

Vasiliev nodded.

"Do you know, I think a few Robin Hood characters might be useful to us. Skirting around the edges, making no real impact, but fulfilling the fantasies of the people still living their mundane but safe lives."

Natalia was a little taken aback.

"Are you saying that, in various countries, we should allow dissent?"

"Be careful with your interpretation of my thoughts. No, but we must focus on the big issues, and the odd person operating outside the system isn't going to hurt us. However, if they attract others in any numbers, they will become visible, and a priority. My question is, how would we convey this to our people? It's counterintuitive."

"I will talk to Cheryl Simpson-Walters. Perhaps it would appeal to the King's whimsical side."

Vasiliev was pleased but cautioned Natalia,

"We aren't looking to create the situation, just to use the occasional example, to use tales of escape to satisfy the yearnings of the captives."

"You are remarkable, Sir. I'm not sure anyone else would have considered this."

"Put yourself in their shoes, too scared to rebel themselves, but living vicariously through the more daring. Then imagine the effect of the rebel being expunged. The hope extinguished. The fire in their bellies doused. We are playing a long game if we want a peaceful, even harmonious society."

Chapter Sixty

As ever, Huang Peng, the President of the Chinese Empire was discussing the situation with his closest allies: Xiu Feng Wang, the Deputy President; Duan Bai Bolin, the Minister of Health; and Chang Wei Lei, the Minister for Coordination.

Chang was updating the group regarding the status of the newly absorbed nations of their Empire.

"I've asked the Ministry of Defence to send 100,000 troops to Japan. It isn't going smoothly."

Huang interjected coldly.

"Send 200,000, and the navy, to show real strength. Then have bombers fly over the worst spots and make them suffer. This must be squashed in the next day. Tell the head of the Armed Forces to report to me by midday tomorrow, and that I demand this is over."

Chang and Duan had heard rumours of Huang's brutality, and even witnessed some of its effects, but this was the first time they had been in the room when his ire was unleashed. It was a chastening experience. At the same time, it was a message from which they would adapt their own behaviour and style. Targets had to be met, who knew what might happen otherwise.

As quickly as Huang had switched into monster mode, he returned to the image of an equitable, benevolent leader.

"What news from inside the Kremlin?"

Xiu glanced at his colleagues. They had looked so surprised when they first became aware of the embedded agent. This time, however, they were alert and interested.

"Things are going well for Vasiliev. Naturally, there are local issues, and these may translate into larger problems as communication is now possible again. The key for us is the relative stability and the acceptance that we are not a threat. To reinforce this view, I suggest we move more troops away from the Russian border."

The President agreed.

"These are forces which may be needed in Japan, and to quell other pockets of dissent. Chang Wei Lei, please continue with your update."

"Mr President, thank you. The review of local laws is nearly complete. We will then overlay the relevant statutes from China and begin communicating them. There is great similarity across most of the other nations, but Japan, Taiwan, and South Korea are more distinct. I propose we secure the easy wins first, in Vietnam and its neighbouring states, and Mongolia."

"As ever North Korea is complicated. The quickest way forward would be to remove the leader which would lead to a relaxation of the restrictions its people are enduring."

Huang was listening intently.

"I've been thinking something very similar. Let's get Paik Han-jae to Beijing as we have discussed and install his replacement whilst he is here. Combine North and South Korea into a single entity, making Yun Dong-woo as the regional leader. The North Koreans will accept him, except perhaps Paik's closest allies and family. Make sure Paik brings a large entourage, as his status would dictate. None of them can ever return home."

Chang understood and it would happen. He wasn't going to fail after viewing Huang in full flow earlier.

Chapter Sixty-One

The studios of *Common Sense News* were based in Maida Vale in London. *Common Sense News* was always known as CSN, and had only been created three years earlier, as a vehicle to promote conservative values. It had been secretly funded by Bart Boulter, the man who would later become, albeit very briefly, President of Angloland.

One of the station's star *News Presenters* was Andrea Evans. On this occasion, she was interviewing Raymond Burke, the Leader of the Nostalgia Party. CSN only featured guests whose politics matched its own. Interviewees were never given a hard time, so the conservatives were lining up to appear. However, the most frequent visitor to the studio was Burke. He had once considered changing his surname but had been advised it would open him to more ridicule.

"Raymond, how are you feeling about becoming part of the Russian Empire?"

"Well Andrea, what's not to like? I know we're now an element of a much bigger entity, which may seem at odds with some of my previous statements. My issues have always been the way liberals have damaged our country. Now I am fully aligned."

"Which aspects do you particularly like?"

"It is all we have wanted, Christian values, hard on criminals, no immigration, British jobs for British people, wasters removed from society. It's all good."

"Have you spoken to President Vasiliev?"

"Not since he conquered the world. But he's well aware of my views, and those of all right-thinking people."

"What else would you like President Vasiliev, or our King, to dictate?"

"I just hope this marks the end of politically correct nonsense, and we get back to proper relationships. In the longer term I would encourage them to take two further huge steps. Firstly, now that there is guaranteed work everywhere, there are no reasons for immigrants to be here. There should be a process to repatriate them to their homelands. Secondly, I remember very fondly coming home to find my mother cooking our tea. The house was spotless, our clothes washed, dried, and ironed. We should pay women to stay at home, to fulfil their true career as housewife and mother."

Andrea Evans was taken aback. This was a statement which might impact her on two levels: as a woman, and as someone with a secret lover who was originally from Jamaica.

"How close are we to wanting a world in which women return to being second-class citizens, as servants rather than partners?"

Burke backtracked a little.

"Far from seeing them as lesser, this acknowledges that women have a vital role men simply cannot perform, and they will be respected for it. Talented women like you, Andrea, will be free to pursue what you are great at."

Evans was not placated.

"What about freedom of speech? What about justice?"

"Clearly, anyone can say anything so long as it's not against the Empire or the President. There are no restrictions on that. And given we have peace and full employment, what is there to criticise?"

"And justice?"

"Look, we all know criminals are always going to be criminals. If someone's locked up for something they didn't do, chances are they haven't been caught for something they did. The risk of error is minimal; the State can monitor every call and conversation. We need to accept that life has changed."

Evans accepted she needed to move the interview on.

"We will have contraception in our water supply, with only approved women receiving the antidote. Who will decide and what will be the criteria?"

"Of course, I am making assumptions but family defects, criminal records, age, marital status, and whether they're good citizens would be on my list."

"Do you have concerns about men working until they are seventy-five years of age?"

"Not in the slightest. We all need to be useful, or why are we here? Most men are still fit at seventy and yet retire. They then wonder what to do. Let them carry on for a few more years. All of this, surely, must appeal to your viewers, as it is, the essence of common sense."

"Doubtless, Raymond Burke, we'll speak again soon as we learn more about the changes to laws and standards. Thank you."

Chapter Sixty-Two

In Washington DC, the King was meeting for the first time with the new Prime Minister of the United States of America. Griff Griffin arrived in a huff and out of puff. Already running late, security at the entrance to the White House had refused to let him in, as he had no ID. Cheryl Simpson-Walters was called and had to vouch for him. Griffin had actually uttered the words, *"Do you know who I am?"*

As he burst into the outer office, he glared at Dorothy Harkins.

"Are you going to get in my way? Because believe me, I am in the mood to deal with any petty bureaucrats."

"I'll let His Majesty know you have finally deigned to be here."

Griffin's face became the colour of a prune.

"I will have the King deal with you."

As Griffin turned, he found the King standing in the doorway.

"And you should believe me when I say that Mrs Harkins will be here long after you, especially based on your current behaviour."

"King, I'm sorry, but this isn't a good day."

"Firstly, you address me as *Your Majesty* at first, then after that in any interaction, it is 'Sir'. I am surprised to hear that it is a bad day for you when you have been appointed Prime Minister of his country."

"That's not what I meant, but why am I not President of the USA?"

"It is the consistent approach in all nations. The role of President has been replaced with that of Prime Minister."

"Will I be residing in the White House, a place is for Americans, not the British? Remember 1776 when we whipped your collective arses?"

The King didn't smile.

"I assume you're attempting to be humorous."

"No. This is ours."

"You are now a citizen of Angloland. Further, I would advise you to be careful about making objections regarding status. I could let you know of a few examples of people who have misunderstood their position and now are either in the ground, or in Siberia. Do you wish to continue debating this?"

Griffin shook his head. At that moment, the phone on the King's desk rang. Philip knew it must be important, Dorothy would never have put the call through otherwise.

Answering it, the King listened, then looked at Griffin.

"It's for you."

Griffin frowned.

"Who is this?" he demanded.

"Mr Griffin, this is Natalia Morazov."

"Never heard of you."

"Mr Griffin, your appointment as Prime Minister is entirely dependent on this conversation. His Majesty has nominated you, and President Vasiliev is minded to accept it. However, the behaviour that you have displayed in the last five minutes has put that in doubt. Every word you speak or write from now onwards is monitored. King Philip is one of the President's most trusted allies, so do as he says, and do not contest every word. Is this clear?"

Griffin was about to argue when CSW walked in.

"Stop talking, Mr Griffin, or you will be very sorry."

Griffin remained argumentative.

"Or what? What will *you*, a bureaucrat, do?"

In his ear there was a buzzing, and he remembered Natalia was still on the line.

"Mr Griffin, you now have exactly five minutes to decide whether to be a team player, or whether to die."

The King spoke again.

"Griff, this is the most significant moment in your life. You must accept you are now part of something far bigger than anything your imagination could have created."

From the outer office came the unmistakable sound of approaching soldiers.

"Be Prime Minister, recognising the limitations, or meet your maker. Your choice."

Griffin bowed his head.

"Your Majesty, I am your humble servant."

"Excellent. Cheryl, please stand down the guard.

"Griff, you've just observed the power of the State. Natalia Morazov is one of the most significant figures in the world, even though you had never heard of her. I, too, am her most humble servant."

Griffin looked down at the phone still in his hand, a hand which was trembling from the fright he had experienced.

"Natalia, please accept my apologies. I will learn quickly."

"Prime Minister, congratulations on your appointment. I believe the bases by which we wish to live will be in alignment with your own. I look forward to seeing you apply them vigorously."

The call was terminated without the need for pleasantries.

Cheryl Simpson-Walters walked across to Griffin and shook Griffin's hand.

"Learn quickly where the real power lies, Mr Prime Minister. And then take clear and decisive action to bring about, to deliver the results President Vasiliev demands."

The newly ordained Prime Minister nodded. It had been the most sobering few minutes of his life, and the bluster had expired.

Chapter Sixty-Three

In the Starbucks in Strood, in the UK, Alex Nolan was talking very quietly to his mate, Jamie Goodwin.

"So, what do you think?"

Jamie was sceptical.

"It may sound fine for us, if we do as we're told, but what is implied by the word 'useful'? What will happen if we become useless? We may be safe, but are we really free? All of the President's fine words about freedom seemed to mean we aren't free."

Alex was confused, but he was often confused.

"What do you want to be free to do?"

"The beauty of freedom is that we can make the choice when opportunity occurs, or circumstances require it. To be honest, I am very uncomfortable with this new government."

Nolan blanched.

"Be careful, you know they are listening. What will you do?"

"I don't know, but I'm thinking about it."

At the same time that Nolan and Goodwin were having their chat, Herb Andrews was making his own decision.

"I'm going into the hills for a while."

Dolly, his wife of twenty-seven years, was appalled.

"You are walking out on us because there is no reason to own a gun."

"That's not it and you know it. I will not live under the foot of a Russian master."

"So, there is every likelihood you can never return. What happens if you fall ill? What about us?"

"I'm fit, and living off the land is the healthiest existence. You can come with me if you want."

"Why would I come? We're now safe from crime. We have guaranteed work and will pay no taxes. How many times have you moaned about paying taxes for the liberals and faggots to squander?"

"It's my right to have a gun."

"It was your right. Now it's a crime and this lot will not mess about. You could be killed."

"Better dead than a Commie."

"Let's understand exactly what you're saying: your gun is more important to you than your wife and family."

"You don't understand."

"If you leave, you can never come back home."

Andrews had always been an obstinate man, and having his wife argue with him was too much for his Alpha Male ego.

"My bag is packed. See you."

He was gone. Dolly slammed the door behind him, not knowing if she would ever see Herb again, and at that moment, not caring.

Herb Andrews had chosen a path with no obvious end point. He trudged into the woods situated at the back of his house. In an hour he had reached the summit of a fairly steep hill. As he looked out over the sweeping plains of his state, Oklahoma, he had never been more in love with his country and his family. The irony wasn't lost on him, yet he pivoted and went further away from civilisation.

Chapter Sixty-Four

President Vasiliev pulled together his original team for an update.

"Dmitriy, forgive me, but the technical issues are the ones which worry me most because I don't understand them well enough. Where are we? Are there any issues?"

"Thank you, Mr President. We are highly confident that everything is working well. There are many people to train to use the monitoring equipment and, crucially, to send out the message that we are listening and watching. In total, there are 2000 trainers spread out in each corner of the world. The kit is very easy to use, and each trainer can bring 100 people up to speed every day. In a week we have nearly one and a half million 'spies'. The general population will be told through the state-controlled media about the proliferation of agents. Just knowing this will keep most people in check."

"Dmitriy, this is incredible. It is I who must thank you, this is excellent. What is our target?"

"Eventually, there will be sixty million, which is about one spy per one hundred people. There will need to be an acceleration of the production of the kit, the handheld listening devices."

"Does a problem exist?"

"The usual delays due to logistical complications."

Vasiliev considered Dmitriy's points.

"Tell the manufacturer the full sixty million will be ready by the end of the month. Failure isn't a healthy option for the manager or anyone slowing the processes. My second nagging fear is China. Comrade Bychkov, what intelligence?"

"I am delighted to report that China has moved battalions back from our borders. They are mainly being used to suppress the populations of Japan, Taiwan, and Korea, at least in the area which was known as South Korea. I spoke to Deputy President Xiu this morning. He is confident that full control will be asserted in the next twenty-four hours.

"We are discussing the inscrutable Chinese, but there is no reason to doubt they are pleased with the current status and will not breach our joint boundaries."

Vasiliev took a moment to absorb Bychkov's feedback.

"This is a huge relief. My relationship with President Huang is very good, and I know he is very grateful for Japan being included in our deal."

The group discussed the movements of armed forces and the ongoing resistance.

Boris Gusev was very clear. "There are various tribal conflicts, but my biggest concern is for the Middle East. Israel and the Arab countries seem to be cascading into attempts at mutual genocide. We can stop them fighting within days, as they can only use mechanical weapons, however, there cannot be peace. It is religious fundamentalism."

Vasiliev paused the meeting.

"Before we look at other topics, what can we do to stop this? Or do we just let them fight it out?"

It was Sokolov who spoke first.

"I think it sends the wrong message to allow it to escalate. Our first commitment is 'Safe' and this clearly isn't. We can leave a peace force there. We can take as many arms off them as we can find, but these are not solutions. None of the countries in that area can easily be self-sustaining. Therefore, building a wall isn't enough of an answer. There needs to be provision of supplies to keep people healthy and fed. Should we be radical and make a dramatic change? What about moving all the Jews to another land, one which is totally theirs and where there aren't Islamists for neighbours?"

The meeting was genuinely surprised. Vasiliev wanted to know more, so Sokolov continued.

"The lands of Israel have a historical and religious potency for people of the Jewish faith, and especially Jerusalem. But they are a smaller group and less disparately dispersed. We could create a similarly sized area for them elsewhere. My personal suggestion is in the American Midwest. Many Israelis speak English."

Bychkov perked up.

"Would we create the new infrastructure?"

"We need to think it through, but yes, a great deal of it. The relocation would ensure safety, it would be clean and fresh, and King Philip could, with a little creativity, find useful work for them. Let me be honest, this would be strongly resisted because of Israel's deeply embedded connections to their homeland."

The President was sufficiently interested to order a quick review of the implications and ramifications.

"Let me have something by this time next week, please. Natalia, how are the leaders of our mega-countries performing?"

"Mr President, the answer is generally well. If you will excuse the expression, what the fuck is wrong with Americans? I am spending more time monitoring Griffin than all the others put together."

"Should I talk to him?"

"Not yet, Sir. The King is doing a good job, in his own style. His aim is to get Griffin, and everyone else, on board with the overall thinking and approach. He keeps saying, 'one volunteer is worth ten pressed men'."

"Fair enough, but don't let him prevaricate. I will intercede if I feel it is necessary. Is anyone else a problem?"

Natalia shook her head and, given nobody had a desire to be there any longer than necessary as they were all very busy, the meeting finished.

Chapter Sixty-Five

On January 6th, Prime Minister Griffin of the USA was being interviewed by Grace Williams on Coyote News.

"Mr Prime Minister, how does it feel to be in the top job?"

"Well, Gracie, it feels good, but remember, above me is the King and above him is the President of the Russian Empire. But I can tell you we are all on the same page. To have waited for democracy to reach this point would have meant I was an old man, or perhaps I should say an even older man."

Williams was polite and smiled at this very small attempt at humour.

"How are you squaring the loss of voting with your views of American independence?"

"The key factor is the state of society. Following the will of God is the most important thing. True power will rest in the hands of the people who preach the Word. Think of the good that full employment will bring. Most people want to work and feel part of something. Anyone who chooses to ignore the opportunities of employment or, and I emphasise this, skives when at work will find there are severe consequences."

Williams delved deeper.

"What about people with disabilities who can't work at one hundred per cent efficiency?"

"Simple: either they receive less, or their family will look after them with no extra income for them. The society I remember, and want, relied on self-sufficiency. Families looked after their own. Of course, in the longer term this will not be a conundrum, as there will only be authorised procreation, which will eliminate non-productive citizens. Until then it isn't reasonable for others to have to deal with another family's cripples."

"Would God want us to behave like this?"

"He surely does. The Lord Almighty wants us to seek perfection. We are able to read this in the Scriptures. Now, I wouldn't have imposed all of the Laws but, if you look at the bigger picture, we are closer to Nirvana."

"So, which Laws wouldn't you have?"

"We should all have guns. Guns prevent crime, and we all know that criminals will be dealt with harshly, but that is after the event. Too late! I will argue for the restitution of arms for all our people."

Williams acknowledged this point enthusiastically.

"I agree, and I hope you are successful. What about abortion being banned and transgender freaks being eliminated?"

"I am pro-life, and I will kill anyone who goes against this. Freaks of every kind need to come into line or be outcasts. Normal people will thrive."

"Becoming rich will be impossible. How can we motivate people to work if they cannot make more money than their friends?"

Griffin paused for a moment, his brow furrowed, his grey hair glistening with perspiration. Arguing for Vasiliev's new world was taxing, as he hated a lot of it. However, Natalia Morazov had been very clear about the consequences of failure.

"Money isn't everything. Jealousy will diminish, and the currency of success will be the way we all contribute to our nation. I have always said greed is good and we may need to revisit this, but for now we must hunger for a better life."

"Will you miss voting?"

"Liberals and Socialists can never come to power, so absolutely not."

"Thank you, Prime Minister."

Chapter Sixty-Six

In Moscow, the general feeling amongst the public was one of jubilation. Russia had won, was safe, and had a President who ruled the world. After the hardships imposed by the West on Russia, through sanctions and threats of nuclear war, this was liberation.

Crowds had assembled outside of the Kremlin, even though temperatures were below zero degrees Celsius. In previous times, all of ten days ago, any mass gathering would have been broken up. This was different, and there was universal acclaim for President Vasiliev. The weather wasn't going to improve, salaries weren't going to increase greatly, and extravagant welfare wasn't about to become widespread, but there was a new feeling. As one member of the public put it: "Russians are safe, and people in the West can now suffer a little bit like we have."

Vasiliev had implied that citizens of the Russian Empire would be treated better than others, but they didn't know what that meant yet. But, perhaps strangely, that didn't matter. They could relate to the strapline 'Safe, Clean and Useful'. These were their aspirations, particularly as there had never been any expectation of becoming rich.

One question which was being asked was what was to happen to the oligarchs who had plundered Russia after the Soviet Union broke up. There was intense dislike of these money-grabbers, and it was felt that there must be action against them. In his ornate office, President Vasiliev had been made aware of the growing impetus amongst the people for retribution. He wondered if this was also directed at him, as he had become rich and gained power through the friendship of this small group of billionaires.

The door opened and Natalia Morazov entered, thanks to Vasiliev pressing a buzzer under his desk connected to his secretary's phone. Nobody else knew that he also kept a revolver attached to the underside of the desk, just in case of an emergency.

"Natalia. How is my favourite co-conspirator?"

Morazov blushed. She was always mindful not to indicate to the President that this was about anything other than matters of state. The rumours about Vasiliev's conquests preceded him.

"Mr President, I am well, thank you. And you?"

"I am. Do you know, nobody ever asks me if I am well. It is as if it would be too impertinent to be so personal. However, our small team is so close, I am glad you ask. I like you all, and it pleases me more than I can say that you and Dmitriy are such a happy couple."

"Thank you, Sir. I bring an update."

"Excellent. Progress?"

"Everywhere. At home you will have heard the people of Moscow, but the same sentiments are being expressed across the whole of Russia."

"Natalia, I am well aware of the distaste there is for my former, let me call them travelling companions, the oligarchs. What are my options?"

"Sokolov, Gusev, and Deputy President Bychkov would be better advisors than me, but my view is that politically you are unshakeable, and if bank accounts have been expunged there is nothing else to do. It might help if the general public were told about it, although it may be wise not to let it be known they all still live in luxury."

"Indeed, thanks, interesting thoughts. What about Africana?"

"There are still issues around communications. Notwithstanding, the feedback is generally very positive. If people are given jobs and can therefore remain with their families, the restrictions are okay, even if not liked. As long as there is no favouritism in the allocation of positions it will be accepted. It is a very large area, so sweeping statements are fraught, but if our recently appointed President Ekoku can stop the warfare and pay people fairly, Africana can be the least of the worries."

"Great. What about bridging the Atlantic Ocean in Angloland?"

"Grumbling rather than outright dissent. Britain is stunned, Ireland doesn't want a King but at least it is united, Canada is too cold to make a fuss, and the USA is fiercely independent. Prime Minister Griffin is making the right noises, but he needs to be watched. Griffin doesn't seem to recognise he cannot be President of the 'Greatest Country in the World'. However, the King has made a big impact with his sanity and wisdom. There will be pockets of resistance, but short of coordinated violence it is more a refusal to willingly accept defeat."

"Where next?"

"Because it is quiet, we haven't discussed Europe very much. I suspect it is a combination of denial and concern about a Muslim leader. They want to see what happens. Again, it is winter, which is helpful, as is the multitude of languages. If there is a pushback it will come from within specific nations, rather than widely across the continent. Scandinavia has had a very supportive welfare system, and I think the Laws of the 1950s will be a psychological shock."

Vasiliev was very well aware of the generosity displayed in Scandinavia, albeit they had paid high levels of taxation.

"We must be consistent. Make sure there is no slacking in the application of all aspects of the Law. Thank you, Natalia. I now must call the President of South America."

Chapter Sixty-Seven

The King had his Cabinet with him. There were two reasons: it was their first meeting to set strategy and, linked with that, there was a directive due from Russia concerning the economy and employment.

"As I welcome you all, and thank you for coming at such short notice, may I wish us all great success. This is the most dramatic, even traumatic, time in the history of the world. I know that, privately, we may regard some of the laws we have to apply as going against our natural principles. However, apply them we will. We will seek to minimise deaths and use our best efforts to create a society of which we can be proud."

The Education Minister from Ireland, Padraig Kelly, felt he should be the first to respond.

"Your Majesty, thank you for hosting us and for your welcome. I suspect we are all still trying to assimilate the directives and information that are overwhelming us. I would support your positioning statement, as I believe we have to be pragmatic. I have heard the very clear messages about dissent and will focus all my efforts on developing the very best situation for our people, including in my own country of Ireland."

"I appreciate your words, Padraig. What has been the reaction to the unification of Ireland?" asked the King.

"May I ask Sinead O'Meara to answer, as I have relinquished my duties to her?"

The King laughed.

"My apologies. You were Taoiseach for so long, it's a habit to break."

Sinead O'Meara took over.

"Sir, and I say this without any clever subtext, we would say re-unification. This means the vast majority of the people are enthusiastically in favour. Naturally, the one group who may be upset are the Unionists in Ulster. However, given there is no longer a United Kingdom to be a part of, it seems irrelevant. The issue now is religion. I have made it extremely clear, as has President Vasiliev, that there will be no violence based on differing faiths. Catholics, Protestants, Muslims, Sikhs and every other religion will live peacefully alongside one another. The weapons amnesty has massively helped this."

"This is all very good. What about the situation in Canada?"

Brian Quick looked up from his papers, a short, stocky man with the face of someone who had enjoyed more than a few physical confrontations. Yet, he was, at his core, a man of peace.

"Sir, Canadians are waiting to see how this unfolds. There is disquiet regarding some of the social laws being imposed. Ours has been a very liberal country and dislikes the 1950s approach. That being said, there is no rebellion or even a hint of unrest. I am grateful that, as I take up the position of Minister for the Environment in your Cabinet, you have allowed me to nominate my successor as Prime Minister of Canada. It will be the previous Finance Minister, Geraldine Quick who, as we all know, just happens to be my wife."

The room laughed, but everyone knew she was a highly capable operator. Over the years there had been a great deal of debate around whether it was Brian or Geraldine who was the more effective. This appointment was not nepotism, just logic. The married couple looked at one another and briefly smiled across the table. They preferred not to sit next to each other, as being opposite meant they could see one another, and nobody could accuse them of whispering and covert politicking.

The King moved on.

"Prime Minister Griffin. What is your overview of the USA?"

"Sir, less balanced. In the Deep South, the principles are loved, but the loss of guns is total anathema. There is still local trouble, but it will be stamped out. There will be groups who also think it is a green light for racism. The Ku Klux Klan had re-emerged. Believe me when I say, it has disappeared again and will not pop up. In the former liberal states, there will be intellectual resistance, but there are no vehicles to express their disdain, and it will be suppressed."

As ever, the King was impeccably dressed, his valet performing at the top of his game. Whatever the situation, the Monarch would be appropriately attired. Had Mustafa held the similar position in 1649, King Charles I would have been executed in his very best clothes.

"Finally, Great Britain. Ms Newman, how are things being taken?"

"Sir, again thank you for your confidence in me. I would reflect very similar views to those from Canada. I am certain the appearance of troops from the Russian Empire would be a provocation, but as long as our guys are patrolling, there shouldn't be too much trouble."

"Excellent," His Majesty stated. "I see your assistant at the door, CSW, presumably with the President's next policy proclamation."

Cheryl Simpson-Walters strode towards the door to take the paper from Kerry Smith, her Executive Aide. Taking it from her, she hurried back to the Cabinet table.

"Read it to us, please, Cheryl."

"It is addressed to the Presidents and the King, with the heading *The Economy and Employment*. The text reads:

Gentlemen,

Firstly, let me applaud your efforts in bringing order to our world. Clearly there will be pockets of resistance, but with your total control of communications media and armaments, I know this will be a short-lived situation. Please do not fail.

We have described many of the principles by which we will live, including promises of full employment and an eradication of the old capitalist economy. Allow me to headline some further points for you to overlay onto your respective national approaches:

- *There will be no need for financial services, as there are no shares, no investment banks, no mechanisms for making a profit based on the efforts of working people. The only banks will be for simple transactions and for keeping people's money safe. Banks will not apply interest rates, and there will be no loans. The maximum anyone can keep in their account will be 10000 roubles*

- *Property which forms the main family home will not be taken from people, but they must maintain it and keep it in good order.*

- *Cash will be the medium of transactions.*

- *Private companies will continue to operate, and the current management will remain in place. Some of these managers may feel it is unfair that their wealth has been diminished and may not want to work for the greater good. I want them to be there and to do a good job. But if they equivocate, remove them. Rather than earn twice the salary rate, they will have no income for six months. Then they will be placed in menial jobs.*

- *The base salary rate will be 300 roubles per week. Please encourage people not to attempt a conversion into their traditional currency, as this is effectively a totally new one.*

- *There will be no inflation, so people can be confident their salary will provide for them.*

- *There will be three levels of salary, and ninety-five per cent of citizens will earn the base rate. Managers and highly skilled specialists will earn twice the base rate, and high-level executives will earn three times the base rate. Your administrations will decide which jobs meet these levels. Let me be very clear: I will be beyond annoyed if I find there is any bribery, corruption or favouritism involved. It will mean death. We are creating a fairer society, not an immoral one.*

- *All capable people will have a job. If need be, just create them, but in the long term, implement new projects in rail, roads, housebuilding and other infrastructure areas. Employ people in retail and supply chains. Ensure the towns and cities are clean, children have great teacher-to-pupil ratios, police forces are manned and have full support staff, and that local tourism has plenty of guides and hospitality staff. There can be adequately populated railway and bus stations. In short, think broadly, within the boundaries of a society which doesn't want pestering call centres, home deliveries except for the very few people who genuinely cannot get to the shops and have nobody to help them, or the complications of self-service in shops.*

- *If we are honest, the problem is reduced because not everyone is employable. Those people will either be looked after by their family or taken into very, very basic state accommodation.*

- *Everyone who can work will do so until they are seventy-five years old.*

- *The working week will be fifty hours and will require shift work in some circumstances.*

- *In all of your thinking and the creative development of the economy, apply our themes: Safe, Clean and Useful. There are many clues implied in those three simple words. If society is seen to be fair, the problems you are facing in small pockets will go away, and gradually, people will want to work and to make a contribution. We can give them real purpose.*

Signed,

Vasiliev

CSW put down the paper and took an extremely deep breath. Around the room, the Cabinet members were looking at each other. The implications, particularly relating to people unable to work, began to sink into their collective consciousness, although not all of them were appalled.

"Prime Minister Griffin, you seem to want to express your first impressions," the King said pointedly.

"I do. This will make us great again. Real work, for real men, and some women. I think we need to focus on each household having at least one earner, and initially that will be the husband. I know Vasiliev couldn't describe every area, but I think agriculture will be a big area for the growth of work."

"I agree about agriculture, but I am less committed to men being the workers instead of women," King Philip opined.

The Environment Minister, Portia Green, spoke next.

"Sir, in both the short and long term, I firmly believe the Green Economy will require many more workers and, as a bonus, save the planet from the previous excesses of our capitalist economy. There will be numerous jobs in animal care and husbandry, in protecting our seas and rivers, in carbon capture, and in the exceedingly clever technological advances we need."

"As you know, this is an area of great interest to me, almost an obsession, I admit," Philip added in support.

"It's your theme, Frank, as Employment Minister."

Frank O'Farrell had been Business Minister in Canada and had always been passionate about skills and people development. A dapper man who combined an inability to stand fools with a most generous disposition. He never meant harm, but his tongue could be cutting when those in front of him displayed stupidity. His promotion to the Cabinet of Angloland had come as a surprise. Now in position, he was determined to make the people his priority. This had been a very attractive quality to the King.

"Your Majesty,"

King Philip stopped him.

"Ladies and Gentlemen, we live in a totally different world today. Outside of this room, we must display our authority by using proper titles. However, I think in the Cabinet and in our conversations, we can drop some of the formality. Please call me Philip, but, and I emphasise this, never call me Phil."

The feeling in the room changed in an instant. It was Julia Jones who reacted.

"Philip, and believe me, that feels weird to call you that after the years I have had the honour of your acquaintance, thank you for this. I think it does embody the change. I will endeavour to limit my deference whilst in here!"

There was a general murmuring of agreement. Even Griff Griffin understood the significance of the King's statement.

"Anyway, Frank, discuss employment," Philip continued.

"Thank you. My sense is that many people, especially amongst the young working class, have felt disenfranchised, precluded from the world of work. High tech has left them behind. Much of the technological advancement has been brilliant, but not for certain sections of society. This gives us a chance to re-write the employment agenda.

"I appreciate all the suggestions, which will be implemented, as will a massive retraining programme. As an aside, the first focus will be Health and Safety, as I imagine bankers working on the railways might not spot all of the possible dangers, for example.

"This is a priority, because without work we may find growing dissatisfaction and social unrest. Truthfully, our biggest logistical issues will be in the businesses as they take on new staff and substitute them into areas which have been driven by technology. Of course, we need some aids. Imagine trying to create train timetables by hand, but the rail operators will be given more than adequate staff to man stations and trains. It's a balance. There will be issues of uniforms and kit, a bit like when war broke out and we weren't fully prepared. Motivated people will accept the situation for a while, but we must move quickly.

"I am establishing a working group for each sector. Please send your thoughts, requests and issues to the relevant one, or through my office, as we iron out the metaphorical wrinkles."

Philip responded.

"Frank, I like that. But, and it is a big but, the devil will be in the detail. People who resist must be dealt with promptly. The message has to be understood and the implications clear. Shall we move on to the subject of those who are not designated as 'useful'? Does useful mean incapable, or partly incapable, or limited, or infirm, or what?"

O'Farrell replied, but not with great clarity.

"I think we need to consider this as it develops. Perhaps, in the first instance, we take the view that the person must be able to work the full fifty hours and perform the duties to a large degree. Later, when we know if there is a need for more labour, we can reconsider who is eligible to work. I will look to the Health Minister for guidance regarding destinations for the less able who aren't going to be looked after by their family."

The King was very pleased with the progress.

"Finally, for your information, I will be meeting my nomination for Minister for Health very shortly.

"I will submit all our ideas and actions for review through President Vasiliev's office. Hopefully, some good ideas will come in the other direction. Thanks for your time. And I know you will want to get back to your individual countries. Before you do, I believe each of you has been allocated a slot for a one-to-one meeting with me. I look forward to discussing your portfolio later."

Chapter Sixty-Eight

Herb Andrews had reached the Bromide Hill Trail near Sulfur, a town in the state of Oklahoma. It had been given the name for the obvious reason that the smell of sulfur (sulphur) pervaded the whole area.

It was a place Herb knew very well. He had been walking the hills all his life. As far as Herb was concerned, this was the world. He had been to Texas a few times to visit relatives, and once a year he went to Oklahoma City. Herb had no idea why folks wanted to live surrounded by concrete and metal. That wasn't the way God had planned for man to live; the outdoors was the real world, and it was certainly his.

The track meandered, unlike most of the roads which went in a straight line, irrespective of the topography. Herb was not scared of the creatures with which he was cohabiting the hills, but he was wary. There were rattlesnakes, copperheads, spiders, coyotes, and his friend Mike had once glimpsed a cougar. There were scores of other animals to avoid. He wasn't the brightest man, but he had amused himself by creating an acronym for the things to worry about in Oklahoma: STAGE. These initials stood for snakes, tornados, arachnids, guns, and earthquakes. Maybe it wasn't the easiest place to live, not even the prettiest, but he absolutely loved it.

It had been two days since Herb had left his home, with no plan and no ambition. He was lost in his own world. It was a major surprise when a voice spoke.

"Herb, it's me, Sheriff Wayne. Please don't move too quickly as I can see you're carrying."

"Hi, Michael. How did you find me? More importantly, why were you looking?"

"Herb, the new regime wants to know where everyone is. You left home and took your phone. Easy to pinpoint. Why are you out here?"

"If you're now part of it, you want my gun."

"So what? You don't need it."

"That's what Dolly said, but I need it to hunt."

"Herb, it's a new way of life. People are being sent to prisons in the jungle, not to learn a lesson, but to die. If you give me your gun now, I'll take you home."

Even at this point, Herb Andrews was unsure. This was his freedom.

"Will I still be able to walk the hills?"

"If you let us know your whereabouts."

"But what if I meet a rattler? Or something bigger?"

"You'll just have to avoid them. Come on, get in the car."

It was with reluctance, but Andrews did go with the Sheriff. As they drove, Sheriff Wayne told Herb about a poker game he and a few friends were having on Sundays.

"We call it the Escape."

"From women?"

"From whatever you need to escape from."

"I'm not a gambler."

Wayne laughed out loud.

"You are. Look at the last few days. Every second was a gamble. And you may like to hear about the things the others are looking to escape."

Herb looked at the Sheriff, whose gaze was fixed on the road.

"Are you hoping to escape?"

"Maybe one day, if I sorted it right."

"I may come over this week."

"Do not tell anyone the name we have. They may make assumptions, and remember, randomly walking into the hills can only ever be for a very short time."

Chapter Sixty-Nine

There was a real ale micropub in Strood called the *10.50 from Victoria*. It opened for limited hours because that was the owner's preference, children weren't allowed, and most people walked there because of the strength of the beer and the ever increasingly harsh drink-drive laws. Inside, there were seats, but even with the floor covered with standing patrons, only about thirty people could get in. However, there was a garden, with some of the seats under cover and a few huts, like the ones found at the seaside near the edge of the beach.

For Alex Nolan and Jamie Goodwin, there was the double-edged sword of great beer, brews which changed almost daily, and a very quiet place to talk. Over the last few days, Jamie's dislike of the new rules had begun to influence Alex's thinking. Alex had been almost shocked when his father asked if he could join them on the Thursday night.

Phil Nolan liked a drink, but it was the first time he had come out with Alex and a mate. As it was January, they all wore thick jackets and gloves. Phil, who was bald, also wore a woollen hat.

Five minutes were spent discussing the chances of promotion to the next division in the Football League for Gillingham Football Club. They were all regular attenders at the Priestfield Stadium, having season tickets for seats under cover behind the goal.

Phil leant forward and very quietly asked the question he had turned up to pose.

"So, what are you pair of prats thinking of doing?"

Neither Alex nor Jamie feigned indignation.

"Why do you ask, Dad?"

"You're spending more time together and speaking in hushed tones, which is not the norm."

"We truthfully have no idea, but we do dislike the new ways so much. There are inhuman laws and severe limitations on our freedoms."

"Freedom to do what, or from what?"

Jamie joined in.

"We're not sure, and the reality may not be too bad. Alternatively, it might be worse. If it's really bad, what could we do? We aren't going to be rash, but we would like to have an outline of something to do."

"That is good news. I was scared you would do something silly. Believe me, I'm starting to worry about the future, but let's see how it goes. My round."

"I haven't got much money, so you're buying all night," his son determined.

"Of course you haven't. It's a good job this pub closes at nine o'clock."

Chapter Seventy

President Vladimir Vasiliev was conducting a series of interviews with the leaders of the main religions. For some faiths, this was difficult, as they were split numerous times, such as Shia and Sunni Muslims, and there were leaders in many countries. However, he was making the effort to bring them onside with a carrot-and-stick approach. A religion could perpetuate and congregate, but it must be loyal to the Russian Empire.

For Muslims, the biggest issue was the desire to apply Sharia Law, which held many similar values to those being implemented by Vasiliev. The President was clear: only Russian Law would be used. The Imams were encouraged to emphasise the overlaps and, if they wished, they could claim it was their influence which had ensured they were set for the whole world. It was also made very obvious that they would be held personally accountable if there was widescale rebellion.

There was a greater schism with the Roman Catholic Church. In the Vatican, there was major disquiet about any single person seeming to act like God. The Pope had been attempting to talk to Vasiliev since his first address. Finally, he had a scheduled conversation.

"Your Holiness, thank you for taking my call," Vasiliev began, as usual starting as if he sought a relationship of equals.

"Mr President, it is good of you to return my requests."

"Your Holiness, it is my pleasure. I am certain that you will understand the demands on my time as we bring order to a chaotic world. I assure you this is one of my first calls to dignitaries outside of the political circles, and a most important one."

"Mr President, I have three concerns. Firstly, the right to worship; secondly, the sanctity of life; and finally, that the Holy Roman Catholic Church maintains its treasures of historical and theological value."

"You are encouraged to worship, so long as no other religion's similar rights are impinged. I want everyone to survive and thrive, albeit there is no longer a route to extreme and vulgar wealth. Your third request is trickier. However, if I can see total obedience to the secular laws, most of which match with your morality, then you may retain and preserve the heritage of the world. Please believe me when I say that if the Catholic Church resists in any way, I will remove everything, even moving you from the Vatican. I want fulsome support and strict guidance from your priests. They can be too independently minded, which must be suppressed. The lives of thousands of people, and the retention of your wealth, are in your hands. I think I am clear."

"You are, Mr President. I just ask that you give me time to get the message across. We have our messengers of God's Word in every country, speaking nearly every language. This will not be easy."

"Your Holiness, it will be easier than watching your precious artefacts being taken away. I am sorry, but you have no extra time. I suggest, very strongly, that you begin communicating urgently and expressing the need for complete acceptance."

The phone call ended without the niceties which the Pope generally expected.

Pope Leonardo looked to his right, where his most senior Cardinals were listening. Six elderly men, with an average age of seventy-seven. Devout and less worldly-wise than the typical senior manager, they were all in shock. Nobody spoke to the Pope in that manner. People asked him to do things, no one had the right to tell him what to do, and this was a threat to, in effect, finish off the Church by stripping it of all its physical attributes.

"My friends, please inform our representatives far and wide that the laws of the Russian Empire are to be obeyed, in word and in the spirit in which they are made. Our one billion followers can pray without concern, but the price is acquiescence. We have existed for two thousand years and, if we take a pragmatic approach, we will outlive this regime and any that may follow."

The Cardinals nodded and left. It had been the correct decision to let them hear President Vasiliev's comments. They were as shocked as the Pope was, and were now as committed to the requirements, to maintain their positions.

Chapter Seventy-One

King Philip was with Cheryl Simpson-Walters.

"Philip, is the President personally addressing the citizens to explain the employment situation?"

"No. Therefore, I have decided that the respective Prime Ministers will lead on the announcements. If they do it consecutively, Frank O'Farrell can join them to give it underpinning strength."

"What will be the next subject?"

"The latest information is that it's going to be health. For many of our people, a state-run health service is the norm. But, as we know, this isn't the case for the USA and Canada. This is one of the big 'wins' for people in those countries. Whether they will admit it or not, this will be a major boon for many people who cannot afford health insurance. My biggest concern is the possible reaction of the medical professions. Doctors, in particular, are used to making a very good living by hiking the prices of treatments, and pharmaceutical companies have always made a killing, which isn't meant to be a joke."

"Maybe it is fortunate that your next meeting is with Doctor Joanne Fraser."

"Is she here?"

"She will be, I expect. Shall I ask her in? Do you want me to stay for the meeting?"

"Yes, and yes please."

Joanne Fraser was a striking beauty, 5 feet 10 inches tall, although she was bored of telling people that equated to 178 centimetres when they asked what that meant, with raven-coloured hair and blue eyes.

Holding both a medical doctorate and a PhD in Sociology attested to her intelligence. The combination of her attributes scared most men off, and the few who remained interested couldn't meet her high expectations for a real relationship. Or they were married, in life's profoundest irony.

Dr Fraser glided into the room. The King had seen her on TV, but he was amazed at her presence. Somehow, without making a discernible effort, Doctor Fraser automatically became the centre of attention.

"Doctor Fraser, welcome."

"Thank you, Your Majesty."

"May I call you Joanne?"

Naturally, she blushed and acquiesced.

The King continued, "My new rule is that in meetings here and in one-to-ones, my closest people may call me Philip, but never Phil."

They both smiled, although Joanne Fraser was taken aback by this assumed elevation.

"Thank you, Sir."

"Let me get straight to the point. You are very highly regarded across the medical profession, particularly in the USA. Your background has given you an overview of both the medical and pharmaceutical industries. Additionally, and I apologise for making this a factor, you are excellent with the media."

"You're very kind. How can I help you?"

"Doctor Fraser, Joanne, you are my nominee to be Minister for Health in Angloland."

Fraser literally sat down in shock. It was very fortunate she had been standing in front of a chair, and whilst that could have had a comic effect, it would have mortified her. As it was, she was embarrassed to have sat without being invited to do so.

"I am very sorry. I didn't mean to sit."

"On the contrary, I'm sorry as I ought to have asked you to take a seat first. What are your first thoughts?"

Joanne Fraser just sat there, stunned.

"I'm sorry, but this is not something I could have imagined. What is the scope of the job?"

Philip looked to CSW.

Cheryl Simpson-Walters had a grasp of every aspect of the government of Angloland, as far as it had been outlined by Russia.

"Joanne, to a large degree, we can describe it for ourselves. Of course, it covers the nations which have been brought together to form Angloland. There are different structures in each which need to be harmonised, although President Vasiliev has decreed that all healthcare will be free. The caveat to that is that over-seventy-fives will only receive palliative care."

CSW took a breath, while the King observed Fraser. She was engrossed. He had no doubts she would take the position.

"There will be numerous policies to decide and issues to address, such as some of your colleagues being unenthusiastic about working for little money compared with their current typical salary."

King Philip interjected.

"Joanne, you will have heard President Vasiliev be very clear about people who refuse to work. They will receive no money, and given that savings have been slashed, that would make life very difficult for them.

I know this is very much a stick rather than a carrot, but it's absolutely the reality. Perhaps one of our major tasks is to positively motivate these professionals. It may not be the universal truth, but I assume most of our clinicians wanted to do well for society when they chose the medical profession. Let's show them the ways they can make a positive difference."

"That's very helpful, but I'm not sure I can impose the stringent penalties. It isn't me."

"Steel yourself, Doctor. A few people with big egos being taken down a few pegs is nothing compared with the good you can do, especially for the poorest in society."

Joanne Fraser didn't look certain, but the role appealed to her massively.

CSW saw her indecision.

"There will be unlimited funds for research. All relevant university departments will be under your broad oversight, as well as all pharmaceutical companies. Remember, no companies can make big profits to distribute as dividends and bonuses. It will all be ploughed back into research."

Everything changed at that instant for Joanne Fraser.

"Philip, I don't know if you're aware, but it's heavily rumoured that the pharmaceutical companies have been operating a cartel. Most importantly, they have kept secret some breakthroughs in order that doctors must prescribe the same drugs for their patients over many years, when, in fact, there are cures which would cost a fraction of the price and eradicate the suffering."

The King went white.

"Is this true?"

"It is believed to be the case. I imagine President Vasiliev would like these cures to be available worldwide, and affordable."

CSW was equally excited.

"Joanne, we need to appoint your team with top people. This is the single issue which could make the new world order harmonious and peaceful."

Joanne grimaced.

"No pressure there, then!"

The King looked out at the garden of the White House and considered the last ten minutes and the implications of the discussion.

"I wonder what else has been suppressed by the self-appointed global elites. I assume you are accepting the offered role."

"I certainly do. Nobody could deny the chance to save so many lives across the globe. It is also one of those rare situations in which we will have a fair idea of the impact, as we compare death rates in the future."

"In which case, please also investigate with urgency whether there are any effective anti-ageing medications being withheld, so that both death rates and average lifespan will be the measures."

Without any further conversation, the meeting broke up.

Chapter Seventy-Two

Twenty-four hours later, President Vasiliev was meeting Natalia Morazov. She had become his daily advisor and confidante. This was not favouritism, merely reflected the fact that the roles of the other key players were taking them into tangential issues.

Natalia's regular and frequent calls with Cheryl Simpson-Walters had given her, and indeed Vasiliev, great confidence in King Philip and his team. Today's conversation was profound. CSW had brought Natalia up to speed with the appointment of Joanne Fraser, and in particular her bombshells relating to pharmaceutical companies holding back cures for cancers and many other breakthroughs.

As Natalia briefed Vasiliev, his face expressed numerous emotions, as it ranged from anger to hope, to confusion, and to amazement.

"Natalia, what do we think the situation is with our Russian scientists and chemists?"

"Mr President, I have no awareness of any issues, but if there aren't, why were we so far behind the Americans?"

"I smell corruption. Please invite my security services to investigate and report to me by the weekend."

"Of course. Have you thought about the value this has for your Presidency, and for humanity?"

"As soon as we have facts from Angloland, we will spread the benefits everywhere. At the same time, we will make examples of the executives who hid their discoveries, just to make bigger profits and to pay themselves bigger bonuses."

Power Denied

"Very good. I will keep close to CSW. She is fulfilling our expectations of her potential. As is the King, and now, in Doctor Fraser, we may have a third strong leader in that country."

"Tell me about the Middle East."

"My most earnest plea is to move the people of Israel as soon as possible. Even if he wants to prevent genocide, President Shirvani of Greater Iran is struggling to maintain any level of order."

"Create a conference call with the King, Bychkov, Gusev, and Sokolov, please. This must be today."

The conference call was held four hours later.

Deputy President Bychkov confirmed that Natalia Morazov's fears were very real.

"Mr President, we have already deployed fifty thousand troops from Africana and Angloland to keep the peace around Israel, as well as our own forces. At the same time, over one thousand people from the Arab areas have been arrested and dealt with harshly. But they keep coming."

"Your Majesty, you have been made aware of the idea to transplant the Jewish people to a new homeland in the USA."

"Mr President, my people are now calling me Philip, but never Phil."

Again, this did raise a small titter, even amongst the serious people in the room. The King went on,

"I do know, and we have been considering it. There is no getting around the conclusion: there will be mass disruption both in Israel and in any new location. We have looked for an area which is relatively sparsely populated and concluded that the State of Oklahoma meets the criteria. If the current residents want to remain, they can, or we will offer them generous relocation grants. The cities of Oklahoma City, Tulsa, and Enid will be expanded to accommodate the people from Israel and provide services such as schools and medical centres. Nobody will be happy, but fewer will die."

"A very practical solution, Philip. Thank you. What are the timescales?"

"There are nearly eight million Jews in Israel, approximately twice the number of residents in Oklahoma today. This is a minimum one-year project to achieve even the basics."

"Twelve months it is. A solid deadline, which must be met."

"Yes, Mr President."

"Thanks, Phil."

This time they all did laugh, even the King.

Chapter Seventy-Three

The Chinese President was discussing the situation in the Russian Empire with his Deputy, Xiu Feng Wang.

"Mr President, our agent in the room, in the Kremlin has provided us with some incredible news. Firstly, they believe American drugs companies have been keeping secret that they have found cures for cancers and many other illnesses, and they have suppressed the news for commercial gain. Secondly, they are planning to create a new Israel in the middle of America."

"What they do about Israel is their business, but that will occupy a lot of time and effort."

"It will happen in just one year."

President Huang was equally amazed and dubious.

The Deputy President went on,

"King Philip is making a very strong impression, and Vasiliev trusts him. The King is apolitical and totally focussed on the wellbeing of his people. It's a model worth recognising and considering for future appointments, whether in situ or as alternatives from within the nations. You know what they say: 'The last people you should give power to are politicians.' We need leaders who think about the big picture, rather than self-aggrandisement."

Huang considered the thoughts carefully.

"I like it. Clearly, the King is displaying loyalty to Vasiliev because it is the optimum approach for the wellbeing of his citizens. We all have egos, but for some people, those are best stroked by recognising their achievements, in this case, a better society for the whole population. Do many of these people exist?"

"The short answer is not many. But perhaps the longer answer is, they must do. It's just a matter of how do we find them? In the civil service? In pressure groups? In business?"

"Let's look diligently, and urgently."

Chapter Seventy-Four

Jamie Goodwin arrived at the *10.50 from Victoria* with someone Alex Nolan didn't know. Immediately, Alex felt uncomfortable, as these were times in which trust was at its lowest level. Already people were already wondering whether their closest friends, even family, were going to reveal to the authorities any indiscretion or mistake.

"Alex, this is Robert Harper. Robert, this is Alex Nolan, who I have talked about as a frustrated citizen."

The three of them were sitting at an outside table. It wasn't raining, and they were confident they couldn't be overheard.

"Let me get the beers," Robert said, and moved off to get them.

"Who is this?"

Alex was looking annoyed and uncomfortable. Despite the near-zero temperatures, he was hot and bothered.

"Keep calm, Alex. This is Robert Harper, a lecturer at the University of Medway. There is no resistance movement, but more and more people are feeling that the Russian regime isn't doing us any favours. We are heading for a very sterilised existence, with little scope for different thinking, and no space for dissent. We're just having a chat about any ways we can influence the future, which is a long way from trying to resist the authorities."

Alex scowled and said nothing until his new acquaintance returned with the ales. After the inevitable pleasantries, Jamie brought the conversation to its purpose.

"I suppose this is just an initial get-together to consider the words of Vasiliev and King Philip, how they will affect us and, therefore, whether there are alternatives without breaching any laws. Nobody wants to go to jail, here or in the jungles, so this is an open conversation about the implications of the pronouncements."

Having made that overall positioning statement, Jamie was hopeful that if they were being monitored, there would be no comeback on them. They were merely good citizens discussing the ramifications and potential benefits of the Russian Empire's governance of the world.

Robert Harper picked up from Jamie.

"That's an excellent positioning introduction. Alex, I'm well aware that there's no way of reversing the Russian takeover, indeed, why would we want to? The President's description of the ways we are freer in many ways makes a lot of sense. We are gaining in several respects, but my question is: what are we losing, and does it matter?"

These were the very questions Alex Nolan had been thinking about without being able to articulate them. His concerns that they may be overheard were lost in the focus he was now giving to Harper's words, which continued,

"I downloaded the text of the President's speech off the Government's website. It's one of the few sites still accessible, which I suppose is the first issue. We can only research in places designated by the authorities. For an academic like me, that makes lateral thinking and problem-solving incredibly difficult. If we assume libraries will be opened, the impact is to make research as effective as it was in the 1950s, which is the expressed preferred period by Vasiliev. However, the rate of progress in all fields, including medicine, has increased exponentially thanks to computers and access to all knowledge."

Jamie Goodwin asked, "Playing devil's advocate, if there is research and progress emanating from 'the top', does it matter?"

"Of course, it's a reasonable question, if we're happy that Vasiliev and his associates do have our best interests front and centre of their concerns, and, this is crucial, can a few Russian-controlled people achieve as much as millions of academics and engineers could, if they were allowed? It restricts development to the elite's favourites."

Alex was becoming agitated and burst in, "That is crazy, just using simple maths. It also assumes that all advancements will be spread evenly, and Russians won't get the advantages and the rest of us are left to fester."

"Correct. But I have taken the conversation into specifics, when there are broader principles to consider first. Society is being sanitised, encapsulated in the three words: safe, clean and useful. The basics of life will be guaranteed for most people."

Alex jumped in, "But not everybody?"

"No. People who aren't considered useful won't be given the same considerations. Remember, the over seventy-fives won't receive medical treatment. A larger group will be those who cannot work, for whatever reason. Vasiliev said they won't be paid, and their family will have to absorb the costs of keeping them. My expectations are of something akin to the workhouses which were eradicated in the nineteenth century. They provided work for the desperately poor, and very basic sustenance and care for the infirm. There will be a lower caste.

"It's only fair to acknowledge that as I make my comments about the contrasts between the new and old ways in Britain, in other parts of the world, many people will be lifted out of poverty, and that is good news.

"Whilst there are commitments to better health and cleaner environments, they come at costs. If we don't comply with the letter of all laws, we'll be dealt with harshly. And crucially, our families may suffer because of our errors. There may be punishments we cannot imagine. The death penalty will be used and possibly used widely. This particularly concerns me, because some petty officials might use the law to settle old grudges. Will the application of the law be transparent?"

"Trumped-up charges could lead to you being hanged, is that what you mean?" Alex asked.

"I do. However, I suspect that sort of behaviour would ultimately lead to the demise of those vindictive individuals, but that would be too late for the innocents wrongly executed, or for the families trying to survive in the snake-infested jungles of the Democratic Republic of Congo. Let's move on. For better or for worse, we only have relative freedom of speech. Now our every action and word will be monitored. This will mean the end of crime, at least to a large degree, but do we know what will be deemed to be a crime in the future? As laws change, could our previously acceptable comments be used against us? Do we even know the laws today? I am very confident that dissidents will be found to be guilty of something, if that suits those in power.

"Some people won't be able to live as they do today. 1950's morality means no open homosexuality and no legal abortion, for example. But what about segregation and other discrimination? Will some groups be treated badly because of skin colour or religious beliefs? These aren't examples of freedom, unless it's the freedom to discriminate and abuse.

"Naturally, everyone will be pleased to have guaranteed employment, but will the work be stimulating? Will there be chances for advancement? What are the penalties for being unable to work? We will be free from taxation, but for many people, their salary will be much, much lower than before. Work will be for six days each week.

We won't be free to choose a different working week. Any savings will be removed, though the horrid issue of interest rates being imposed to boost bank profits will also disappear. We won't be able to pass on very much inheritance to our families, but they will be guaranteed employment."

"We won't be able to travel to other countries. Is that restriction a form of imprisonment? We will have to go out to shop, but is everyone physically capable?

"We cannot choose who governs us. Now, I accept that nowhere has been truly democratic up to now. In the political parties, just a few people have picked the candidates, and once elected, they could do whatever they wanted for the next few years. The King and the House of Lords were never subject to the electorate. Yet somehow, we felt like we were part of the process.

"We'll be able to love who we want, so long as they are acceptable to society. We can have a family. But this is not a universal option, because the State will deem who is and who isn't eligible to procreate. And medical care will be available, but not to everyone.

"President Vasiliev is right. We are free, within the bounds of his parameters. We are free to live a safe life, but within a sanitised style and approach. We are free, if we meet the criteria being set for us. God forgive those who miss the acceptable standards.

"So, each of us will react differently. We each have priorities. Our lives have minimum levels beyond which we cannot fall, but every day is going to be the same. Don't imagine that our entertainment is going to be varied, or critical in any way of the regime.

"And linked to the censorship, which will certainly be applied, there is surveillance of everyone, not just political activists. It's the way they can eradicate crime and, at the same time, ensure loyalty and commitment to the new world order.

"Do we want to be safe but bored, clean but sanitised, and useful, if we are capable? It's a world in which the devil will take the hindmost. We'll only want people dedicated to purifying the system, and we'll applaud the demise and the punishments for those who go beyond the limits of behaviour described by the all-powerful."

Alex and Jamie sat there, stunned. Robert had told them nothing they didn't already know but laying it out that crisply was sobering. Jamie went to fetch the next round of drinks. When he returned, the other two were discussing football.

"Sorry to interrupt! Perhaps we should talk about the rest of our lives, and not the big issues of West Ham United's form," he said sarcastically.

"We were waiting for you," Alex said. He continued, "Do we actually have any choices?"

"There are no really obvious options," was Harper's reply. "If we want to resist in any practical way, we will very quickly be identified and sent to jail, here, or in Siberia, or in the jungle. Those are appalling possibilities. One thought is to leave the grid, to opt out and to go and live in the wilds somewhere. Truthfully, we could be making our own decisions, but it would be from a menu that's also very restricted. We could say we're ignoring Moscow, and at the same time picking an existence without proper housing, heating or prepared food. We would have to scavenge, we couldn't have a phone, we wouldn't have money, and we wouldn't have access to doctors or dentists. How much do we value independence?"

"What if we try it? What if we go off into the woods? I think my dad would drop off food every so often. If we went in early April, we would have warmer weather for six months. Then we either have readied ourselves for winter, or we come home," mused Alex Nolan.

Jamie Goodwin wasn't sure. "If we come back in, won't the authorities ask why we haven't been useful for half of a year?"

"Initially, you were the one feeling rebellious, and now the roles have changed. I think my dad being interested in what we do has influenced me. I want to try it in the woods. We have a couple of months to plan it. We may also know more about the new laws by then."

Robert Harper agreed. "Let's discuss this a lot more and start to plan. Until we walk off into the distance, we can still change our minds. Don't discuss this with anyone. Alex, get the next beer to seal our potential agreement."

Chapter Seventy-Five

"Mr Prime Minister of the United States of America. How does that sound?" asked Grace Williams on her TV show.

"Gracie, I'll be honest, it sounds strange, just because that isn't a title we have ever had in this country. I am getting used to it and, as we both know, it's achievements and not titles that matter."

"Griff, that's great. What have you achieved in your first month in office?"

"Foundations, Gracie, foundations. We have our monitoring equipment in place, and we've trained the staff to use it. We have arrested thousands of potential rebels, homosexuals, and skivers. Most have been warned and sent home, but they now know that we know about them. Next time, it's the Amazon jungle and its deadly snakes for them. We have identified millions of jobs and begun assigning people to them. Everyone is receiving their wage, and nobody is paying taxes. The King is overseeing a compassionate approach, which marries with President Vasiliev's desire for a society which is safe and clean, and in which everyone is useful."

"But Griff, you and I go way back, isn't this communism against which we have been fighting?"

"We have known each other a long time, but no, you are wrong. This is a society based on Christian principles and morality. Everyone will be looked after, and everyone will make a contribution. We must have a simple system for now, a system which is understood universally. Look, the foundations are there: 1950s morality, no abortions, no homosexuality, no sex changes, men being given jobs first, traditional family roles, and Bible-based ethics."

"I accept that, but everyone getting the same pay?"

"For now. It's honestly the only way we can get all the things we want. We have a country in which no one can challenge us, but in return, they must be treated fairly. The President will be making more announcements in the very near future."

"Well, we surely look forward to hearing more. But for now, let me congratulate you on the ways you've made America the great place we all remember."

Chapter Seventy-Six

In the Kremlin, Vasiliev was meeting his inner circle.

"Natalia, an update, please."

"Mr President, gentlemen. Three weeks ago, the King brought us some incredible news. His new Minister for Health, Dr Joanne Fraser, had revealed that Big Pharma, the drug companies, had been keeping to themselves the knowledge of major breakthroughs in curing diseases, including some cancers. They did this to maximise profits, whilst accepting it meant thousands of deaths of totally innocent people.

"Since then, I have been working with Dr Fraser and Cheryl Simpson-Walters to establish the veracity of the claims. They are true."

There was an audible gasp from the other people present.

Natalia went on, "The Board members of these companies have been arrested, as have their families, due to their complicity and the fact that they benefitted from this heinous behaviour. Naturally, we're investigating more deeply, as many others must have been involved. President Vasiliev also asked for a review of our own pharmaceutical companies to see why we were so far behind. I regret to tell you that some of our most senior scientists were also involved. Their plan was to escape to America and live a luxurious life. They no longer have a life. Their families have been spared because they hadn't enjoyed a better life."

Aleksandr Bychkov asked, "Is there an estimate of the number of lives which could have been extended?"

Vasiliev replied, "Not really, but it's in the millions. The question now is, how do we apply these new cures?"

Mikhail Sokolov wanted to be cautious.

"Mr President, like everyone else here, I want it rolled out as quickly as possible. My only thoughts are we don't want to create discord that would need managing. And that you should take the credit."

"Thank you, Comrade. Giving me recognition isn't as important as sending a message: that the capitalists failed you, and the new order is making the world a better place to live, by an order of magnitude many times greater. Do I make a major announcement, or do the Presidents of the mega-countries? Do we combine it with other news which will not be well received?"

Dmitriy Morazov joined in the discussion.

"Mr President, based on the technical work we've been doing, I believe this is opportune. Given we have decided to keep extensive data on every individual, this is a chance to say we are looking after your health, but this means we must hold lots of information. I know we can do whatever we want, but let's make it as acceptable as possible. Let's reduce any resistance."

"Dmitriy, you are your wife's husband, I love you both. This is the way to go. Natalia, write the script. Now, where are we facing problems?"

The next hour was spent discussing the places of resistance and unrest. While Vasiliev kept pressing his team, and through them, the respective Presidents, he was very pleased with the relatively limited disquiet. He had anticipated a great deal more than had occurred. There had been a rapid acceptance of the new status quo. The application of a carrot-and-stick approach, and at times, stick-and-stick, was producing results.

The meeting concluded with a decision to brief the Presidents and the King the next day. Good news for them all, except for Natalia, who had to draft the speech before then.

Chapter Seventy-Seven

At 5 p.m. local time in Washington D.C., the King met with his Cabinet. The Prime Ministers of Canada, Ireland and Great Britain joined the meeting virtually. It was good fortune that the other Cabinet members were in 'D.C.'

"Ladies and Gentlemen, I have just been on a call with President Vasiliev. He has informed the leaders of the mega-countries of his next address to the people of the world. It will be at 9 p.m. Moscow time today, which is 1 p.m. here and 10 a.m. on the East Coast of the USA, and 6 p.m. in Great Britain and Ireland. Times that work quite well for us, though I suspect not so for Australasia and the Pacific Islands."

People nodded, especially those attending online, who felt it necessary to ensure their colleagues knew they were being attentive.

The King went on, "Dr Joanne Fraser has done some amazing work uncovering unacceptable behaviour in pharmaceutical companies, which means millions of people have died or suffered greatly because of the corporate thirst for more profits, dividends, and bonuses. It seems capitalism may have had the resources to look after everyone but couldn't satisfy the intense craving of the very wealthy to be even wealthier. The investigations are ongoing and will be for a while. However, numerous senior executives have lost their jobs and lives, and for some, their liberty. Sadly, some of the families are now inhabiting prison cells in the Amazon. When President Vasiliev makes his address tomorrow, he will use these people as examples to ensure there is no further behaviour like it. Thank you, Joanne. Due to your personal diligence and, let me say, courage, many more millions of good people will now be cured of life-threatening diseases."

Fraser was embarrassed when her colleagues banged the tables to express their admiration. The King was the most enthusiastic in his congratulations, then brought the meeting back to order.

"By tomorrow the world will know of these discoveries. At the same time, the President will describe how the data of all citizens will be retained. Some of it may cause a degree of discomfort because it will be wide-ranging, not just information regarding their health. Any thoughts or comments?"

This news was very much in line with the preferred modus operandi of the USA Prime Minister.

"Philip, this gives us even more control. I know this isn't an acceptable thought in some parts of society, but because we see the whole picture, we can make better decisions than they ever could. Am I correct that the information will also let us make better decisions regarding which people should be allowed to have children?"

"President Vasiliev didn't make that specific connection. It seems likely."

"I'm delighted. We'll need fewer people in the future as numerous sectors like finance and government become irrelevant. The next generation needs to be fit, healthy and bright. Less deadwood is vital."

The King wasn't overly impressed by this outburst. Whilst the rules had been made for good reasons within the logic of the Kremlin, his primary focus remained the wellbeing of the people of Angloland.

"Well, we only have to wait a few hours to hear from the President.

"Joanne, how are the medical profession preparing for the rollout of these newly discovered drugs?"

Joanne Fraser had the intense attention of her audience.

"There are two factors: production of the drugs and their administration. With regard to production, we have sent details to the other mega-countries. Each of us will manufacture our own. Naturally, there are no longer any issues of patent. We've already produced thirty per cent of the predicted requirement, and the rest will be available within three months. In itself, production is less of an issue. The training of the clinicians is more problematic. However, there is tremendous enthusiasm from the people 'in the know'. Our plan will mean patients in a critical state will be treated first, and all sufferers will be attended to within a year."

"I know it isn't directly in my sphere, but this can only improve the reaction of people to the new laws and reduce the problems of the Justice Ministry," said Julie Jones.

Philip was in agreement.

"I think this is the key subject which will permeate throughout the functions of our government. Thank you, everybody. On a personal note, my wife, Queen Priscilla, is holding a very informal dinner this evening for those of us in Washington. This is the first time she has travelled here since my appointment. A word of warning, because as you know, I twitch if my name is abridged; that is nothing compared with the reaction from her if you call her Cilla. For those of you elsewhere, she has promised there will be other occasions to meet in the near future."

Chapter Seventy-Eight

All over the world, people listened or watched as President Vasiliev made his latest address.

"Ladies and gentlemen,

Thank you for joining me again for my third address to the world.

You will be aware of the numerous improvements we have already made in just a few weeks. Thousands of criminals have been taken off the streets, some of them permanently. Because they have supported and benefitted from their crimes, the families of some criminals have also been sent to prison.

In some parts of the globe, there have been attempts to settle old scores. Again, these people have been dealt with thoroughly. The Russian Empire will not accept bad behaviour, and by now that message will be getting through everywhere. In the future, some of the survivors from the prisons in the jungles and Siberia may return to their previous homes, although their property has been reassigned. They will tell you stories of extreme temperatures and many dangers. Please do not let this be you. I must assure you we will not be relaxing our laws or approach in the near future. To that end, we have now trained and equipped thousands of security personnel, living in the communities, and we will monitor your every action. Because we have set targets for the number of convictions, you can assume they will be diligently approaching their role.

It is a matter of some satisfaction for me that we haven't needed to again use the sanction which would mean all power being switched off in a particular mega-country. People are becoming accustomed to our new style of governance and their individual responsibilities. So, for that, I thank you.

More jobs have been created, and this will continue. Please don't make the mistake of thinking a particular job isn't for you. Instead, consider your contribution to our new order. Many of these jobs will be in green industries, and we will update you soon about the excellent work being undertaken to stop climate change.

Let me now tell you about some astonishing progress we can reveal. The King of Angloland and his team have discovered that pharmaceutical companies have kept secret new drugs which would cure some cancers and many other diseases. This was done in the name of capitalism, the quest for vast profits, at the expense of you and me.

Inevitably, this heinous behaviour has resulted in the demise of the senior executives and the removal from society of their families. This encapsulates part of the reasoning for our actions. Previously, I admitted to you that our primary focus was to protect ourselves in Russia, but in doing so, we want to create something better than we had. We are working on behalf of everyone, irrespective of rank or status.

These cures and health-improvement drugs will be produced and made available, free of charge, to everyone. I have previously said that people over the age of seventy-five will not receive medical treatment. However, they will be eligible for these drugs because of the illegal decisions previously made to withhold them. It isn't possible to express the level of anger I feel about this, and nobody should suffer due to the actions of a small number of parasites.

This has led us to decide to design and implement a new personal data collection process. To deliver a comprehensive medical regime, we will be asking you for some detail. I know the medical professional teams already hold some of it, but this will mean full care being universally available, thanks to your full disclosure.

You will be pleased to know we are going to ask questions around several topics in this document. This means we won't need to trouble you numerous times to complete tedious paperwork. Again, I understand some of you will be inclined to resist this. It is for the greater good, as we can assign resources appropriately, and it is compulsory.

To reassure you, let me tell you the types of things which will be included:

- Where you live and who lives with you. This will ensure relevant payments are made and, in the event of a medical emergency or epidemic, we can narrow down potential recipients.
- Your medical history, as you know it.
- Family information for genetic investigation. We will be taking blood samples to create a universal database. This will significantly boost medical research.
- Your work history. We need to know about your work environments.
- Similarly, we will be taking fingerprints to assist with the elimination from suspicion of innocent people when there is very occasional crime. Likewise, we will need examples of your handwriting.
- Your sexual history and the names of partners, including people of the same sex.
- Your skills and qualifications.
- Memberships of clubs, political parties, and social groups. What skills have you gained through involvement?

- Your volunteering history.

- Your criminal record, even down to fines for speeding and littering, for example.

- Historical records of taxation, credit scores, and purchasing history.

- Property records.

I am certain you will be delighted with this update, especially the progress in healthcare, and will want to support your local community, as well as being part of the fairest society ever created."

As the programme finished, there were literally cheers spread across societies everywhere: *"Cures for cancer!"*

Vasiliev and his team hadn't known about these drugs when they began to plan world domination many months before, but by chance, they had been given the tool to potentially achieve the successful integration of their view of the manner the world should be run.

Chapter Seventy-Nine

"Let's test the friendship of President Vasiliev, shall we," opened President Huang to his closest team. "Will he give us the new drugs? Now that he has gone public, I can be very direct and ask for the formulae."

Xiu Feng Wang, Deputy President, Duan Bai Bolin, the Minister for Defence, and Chang Wei Lei, the Minister for Coordination, were with President Huang Peng.

"Minister Duan, you are new to your function. Why don't we have these drugs already?"

"Mr President, it is clear we were making progress towards this. The Americans were more advanced and there are no excuses. As yet, we don't know what the key factors were, so struggle to analyse our failure."

"Thank you and, as I said, you are new to the role, and no blame can be attached personally. If Vasiliev lets us have the information, we must make it accessible very quickly. We do not want our people feeling we have let them down. Please let me have a plan to implement it as quickly as possible. This is the priority and use your full authority to make it happen."

"Thank you, Mr President, and I hear the implications in your voice. No individual will delay this. No ego from our scientists will hinder the introduction of new life-extending pharmaceuticals."

Xiu Feng Wang joined in. "I hear Vasiliev combined the good news of these life-saving drugs with some further restrictions on the people. Despite the negative implications of the latter, he has been received as a hero. It is a breakthrough moment. Watching from afar, we have observed some interesting lessons, even if some of his success has been good luck."

Huang offered, "As Napoleon said, he wanted lucky generals. May his good fortune run out soon. You imply a number of thoughts, and I want us to use the news of our health advances to soften the resistance we are experiencing in certain quarters, notably Japan and Taiwan. This will be a factor in your planning, Chang Wei Lei."

"Yes, Mr President. The value of this is undeniable. What will happen if Vasiliev refuses to give us his secrets?"

"One way or another, he will."

Chapter Eighty

The Three Kentish Men, as people in their part of the County of Kent are known, had convened just minutes after the end of Vasiliev's address to the world.

Alex Nolan was bursting to speak.

"That was incredible. People have been patting each other on the back, shaking hands, laughing and cheering. Russia has been in power for under two months and there is a cure for cancer. Have we misjudged them?"

"Russia and Vasiliev have done nothing. However, the bastards who ran the big drugs companies have literally made profits out of the suffering of millions of people and their families. I do give him credit for making them available for everyone, irrespective of their nationality and age. But did you listen to the second part of the statement? We are all going to be made to hand over all our personal details. He listed many and I am certain when we see the form there will be a lot more. We will not be able to fart without permission," opined Robert Harper.

Jamie Goodwin reacted, "But you agree about the cures being fantastic news?"

"Of course I do. My point is we should have had access many years ago, but the arch-capitalists screwed us. I do not advocate the death penalty being used at any time, yet there is an emotional reaction for me which says they deserved it. We also heard that the families of these executives have been imprisoned. Presumably, they are thought to be complicit."

Jamie was considering those points.

"Do you think those executives were all men? I imagine they were, and it just feels like machismo run wild."

Robert wasn't so sure.

"Women can be as hard-nosed as men. This was all about money and making lots of it. There was more money in prescribing drugs that mitigated symptoms over many years than there was in curing an illness in just weeks or months.

"How do you feel about telling the authorities extensive details of your life? You heard him demand information about sexuality, numbers and names of partners, political affiliations, Trade Union memberships and much more, as they eradicate what they might call fringe behaviours. Russia wants compliance, loyalty, and obedience. We might give them clues about us or people we know. You can be assured there will be cross-checking. If you don't tell all, unintentionally others might do."

"How do you mean?" asked Alex.

"Suppose one of the questions is, *Are you a member of a political party?* You say no, but someone else who has admitted to being a 'Green' is then asked to name other people involved and, innocently and being a good citizen, they mention you. You are twice damned, once for being a left-wing supporter and a second time for not admitting it. Imagine the same for every issue, including sexual partners."

"Well, that is one very short list," said a disconsolate Jamie.

Robert went on, "I expect that payments for employment will go into bank accounts which the authorities can access. They will know on what you're spending your money. You may be subject to checks to see if you are living at the address on your form. We heard about the monitoring and the equipment. Yes, it was said to scare us, but for sure it is true. Will they be able to check up on everyone? I don't know, but I do know they will be making examples of people."

They sat in silence for a few minutes and swallowed mouthfuls of beer.

Alex looked sombre. He had been coming to terms with the idea of *heading for the hills*, as the three of them were calling it.

"This is so intrusive. How could we possibly escape? What pressure is it putting on our families? If my dad says I live with them, I say I live with them, and then I am constantly absent, what will be the ramifications?"

"I still want to go," said Jamie Goodwin.

Alex Nolan accepted Jamie's desire.

"I absolutely get it. But let me ask a different question, not why do you want to leave, but what is success? Will it be worth it if you live *off the grid* for six months or twelve months? Is it a victory if you stay alive?"

"I hate the feeling of helplessness, of impotence. At least I will be making a statement."

"If we could work towards changing the Government, I would be all in. This lot has us tightly controlled. We will be safe, even safer now cancers can be cured. The environment will be clean and healthier. We can be useful, so fully employed. Which throws up another question: if we disappear and our fathers fall ill, how will we be able to look after them?"

Robert had been watching the back and forth.

"Are we better off seeing the ways this pans out? Then looking for holes to go through and protests to make? There must be many thousands of people having this debate for themselves. How can we find them, or would that be exceedingly dangerous?"

Alex went to replenish the glasses as they tried to absorb the reality and its implications.

Chapter Eighty-One

Chickasaw in Oklahoma, USA, was populated by people who were both pleased and confused in equal measure. The news about cancer was very welcome. The typical diet in Oklahoma was full of red meat, and there had been growing confirmation that there was a direct link to certain cancers. It had reached an epidemic scale. The people were unsure about the effects of giving personal information to the new government.

"On balance, I think this is a better position than we have been in. Clearly, our government, and President Keaton, had been in cahoots with the drug companies. I bet he was taking backhanders," thought Dolly Andrews out loud.

"I bet you're right about that pussy Keaton. But I have got to tell you, I'm not handing over my personal details to anyone," said her husband, Herb.

"Don't be daft. In the end, we will all hand over our data. They won't do anything with it, they never do."

Dolly and Herb looked at one another. They had never been people who discussed politics or concepts like freedom. Now it was all they thought about, and the impact on their children. Herb got up from the table, brushing the crumbs from his lap.

"Anyhow, I have a meeting this evening."

"Do not get involved with anything silly," his wife pleaded.

"Don't fret. The sheriff will be there. It is nothing to concern yourself about. A game of cards and one beer, or maybe two."

Sheriff Michael Wayne had called together a few close friends, including his brother Hank and Herb Andrews.

"Gentlemen, it's great to see you all. In a few minutes we'll play a few hands of poker and have a beer or two. Firstly, I want to give you all an insight into the way things are being told to us in Law Enforcement.

"The messages are very, very clear that the new laws are to be strictly applied. If they aren't it is the police who will be in trouble, and I'm not going to let that happen. In this county we already have a monitor attached to my team. Her name is Holly Marchant, and she is a true believer, a zealot. She has extensive intrusive equipment and access to all our records.

"Let me tell you, her remit is very wide. For example, I'm informed that the Prime Minister of the USA, Griff Griffin, has directed the monitors to seek out adulterers as well as gays. It is believed he also wants to revive old laws which restrict the ways in which people have sex. He is especially against sex outside of marriage. Now, I know some of us have close friends we're not married to, so I encourage you to either distance yourself or be very careful."

Hank Wayne was shuffling in his seat, something which was noticed by all of them. There was a certain lady named Gloria Frost, who was anything but frosty around Hank. Fortunately, Gloria's husband didn't care about her additional relationship. The concern now was, would the Prime Minister be as relaxed?

The Sheriff went on, "I am also aware there are people in this town who believe they can exist in the wild. In the short term, this may be true. In the longer term you will have to come back in and face the consequences, which may be severe."

This time Herb moved around in his chair, but he wasn't alone. Two or three of the others also seemed to be affected by the Sheriff's words.

The Sheriff concluded, "I understand the frustrations with the system being imposed on us, and previously I may have had thoughts of flight. But seeing things from the inside, I'm going to follow the rules. This also means I'm going to do my duty. Remember, I know the hills as well as any of you. If I'm given information by Holly Marchant, I will deal with it. Now, let's play some cards."

Later, Herb spoke quietly to one or two others and agreed to meet for a coffee during the next week.

Chapter Eighty-Two

Grace Williams was enjoying the profile her show was getting due to the frequent interviews with the Prime Minister of the USA. It had quickly become apparent that government policy was being announced on the TV.

"Mr Prime Minister, thank you for coming on the show again. You must be delighted by the way things are going."

"Gracie, I am. Thank you for having me on the show again."

"It is truly a pleasure to have you on my little show. What do you wish to discuss today?"

Griffin sat upright in his chair, trying to optimise the perspective of his height. He claimed to be five feet six inches tall, but this was, as an aide ironically put it, 'a stretch'.

"I think everyone will agree that, under my leadership, society has improved. Crime is almost non-existent, there is order, new jobs, full employment, no taxation, and so much more. Now, as you know, I am rolling out the cures to numerous diseases, including cancer."

"Which is, of course, great. Forgive me, but shouldn't the credit for the widespread use of new pharmaceuticals go to Doctor Joanne Fraser, a real American hero?"

"Doctor Fraser has done a good job, but she is just a medic. The real complexity arrives on the desk of powerful politicians. So, I am humbled by the people's congratulations I have been receiving."

"It is all fantastic news, and I am sure you have played a part, but I want to recognise the bravery of the woman who exposed the greatest deceit in history, Joanne Fraser."

Griff Griffin spluttered at the temerity of a mere TV host, and a woman at that, challenging him.

"Ms Williams, if you continue to correct me, I will make announcements elsewhere. However, I am here, and there are important issues to present. The laws I am going to reveal relate, at this point, to the USA alone. Even within Angloland, the individual nations can apply new restrictions, as long as they fall within the overall mission of the Russian Empire and the phenomenal leadership of President Vasiliev."

"So let me understand. This announcement hasn't been cleared with Moscow? What about with the King?"

"The King, or Philip, as I like to call him, has appointed me as Supremo of the USA, and I do not need to seek his approval."

To be questioned was thoroughly annoying Griffin. The viewing public could see for themselves his physical reaction. Few of them were feeling any sympathy, as it was the King and Joanne Fraser who were seen as the heroes.

"So, what are these new, albeit unapproved, laws?"

"As everyone has accepted, we must have a society in which there is structure and obedience. Therefore, as we are also an enlightened nation, I can confirm that everyone is entitled to opinions, just not allowed to express them. We all have thoughts and dreams, but these must not confuse the natural order. People's minds will be active, and that is great. The issue arises when they try to spread their ideas."

Grace Williams' mouth opened and closed like a catfish.

"Do you mean in a public forum, or even at home?"

"Anywhere. And remember, we are monitoring, and monitoring very efficiently."

"This would also mean I can only have government appointees or authorised people on my show, and that I cannot challenge them."

"That's right. I suggest you stick to film stars and sportspeople."

"Is there anything else?"

"Yes. At the end of each month, people will receive a list of their breaches of the laws through the post. It will include fines to be paid. Any lawbreaking of a significant level will be dealt with immediately through the courts. A principle of the courts will be to accept the evidence of the police or other relevant authorities without challenge.

"In the first month, the fines will not need to be paid, as everyone becomes accustomed to the laws and regulations which have to be obeyed."

"Let me get this straight. We may not know of a law, yet we will be penalised anyway?"

"You've got it. Very quickly people will come to terms with the manner in which we want to move things forward."

"This is a great deal to take on board. Please tell me there is no more."

"Just one more thing. I have decided that my office will make any additional laws, without the need for oversight by any legislature."

"Mr Prime Minister, this sounds like a coup. I understand we will not have any voting rights, but surely there has to be some checks and balances?"

"Not at all. Vasiliev has set the foundations, and we will operate within them, but that is all."

"As we finish, may I just ask about the roles of women? On a couple of occasions, you have implied that women need to be subservient. I will give you an example from today's discussion. Joanne

Fraser has done all the work, and you are taking the credit. It is like the days when women couldn't win a Nobel Prize, their male supervisor was given the award. Is that your approach?"

"Grace, I think you need to suppress your hostility. I am Prime Minister and should be treated with respect. You are failing in this, and I will tell you, women will resume their natural role as home builders and supporters of their husband."

"Does the King agree? Because he seems to be far more attuned to the realities of the world of work. Will Gemma Newman be imposing these principles over Great Britain?"

"She is a weak woman. That, madam, is your final disrespectful dig at me. I will be in contact. This interview is over."

Griff Griffin pulled off the microphone, threw it on the chair, and stormed out.

Chapter Eighty-Three

In London, Raymond Burke, the Leader of the Nostalgia Party, was watching the conversation between Griff Griffin and Grace Williams. He turned to his friend and the Chairman of his Party, Dick Dickenson.

"What are your thoughts, Dick?"

"Griffin is our role model. His approach is the one we need. Gemma Newman is a wet, as are most women. Too much sympathy and empathy when we need to be strong leaders. Grace Williams showed us who she really is. You must get onto TV and push for the UK to take a similar stance."

"Would it be sensible to wait and see how the King and President Vasiliev react?"

"You heard Griffin, the President sets the parameters, and the national governments set laws within them. Why wait?"

"My relationship with Vasiliev has endured for years, on the quiet, but I know he would hang me in a minute if it suited him."

"So, use this moment in time to set the agenda. With Griffin implementing Christian values, you have nothing to lose."

"Do you mean *we* have nothing to lose, or are you hanging *me* out there?"

Dickenson blushed.

"No, not at all. But you are the face of commonsense politics."

Andrea Evans was sitting behind the desk at *Common Sense News*. Since the banning of social media and the continued release of information regarding the new order through news channels, shows like Andrea's had raised their viewing numbers by millions.

"Mr Burke, welcome back to the show."

"Thank you, Andrea. I hope we can be of one accord today after the disagreements we had last time. I know you saw yesterday's interview with Prime Minister Griffin in the States, and the way he dismissed Grace Williams and made her role redundant. I am sure this won't happen to us."

"Well, there wasn't even an attempt to bring subtlety to your threats. Am I right to assume you are expecting to lead the government of the UK in the near future?"

"Gemma Newman is a well-meaning person, but she isn't what is needed today. I am confident that President Vasiliev will intercede and put a strong leader in place very soon."

"Isn't that the decision of the King?" Andrea queried.

"Technically, yes. However, the President is the authority."

"So, is this interview your way of attempting a peaceful coup?"

"Absolutely not. Yet the people want me, the President wants me, and, as they say, the rest is history."

"Notwithstanding, you are looking to the future and creating something to your advantage. You are clearly stating you are more important than our boss, the King, aren't you?"

"Not at all. The King will be making the appointment of me as Prime Minister, if he reads the room correctly. And then the UK will move forward at pace."

"Give me some examples of your policies."

"I would repeat verbatim Griff Griffin's pronouncements about morality and the enactments of new laws, and the bypassing of any checks and balances. This is a time for action."

None of this was a surprise to Andrea Evans, although the brazen bid for power was too blatant.

"You will recognise that the role of women in our new order is a key subject. What would you impose?"

"Even after Griff's warning to Grace Williams in Washington, you still feel emboldened to readdress this. I made it clear last time we met that strength, both physical and of character, is crucial. It is about key skills, and therefore, women will support men to be successful. They will create the time and the home environment which will enable men to relax and recuperate."

"Subservience?"

"No, appropriate use of talents."

"Mr Burke, there are many millions of women viewing this. How do you think they are going to react to your ideas?"

"Frankly, Andrea, I don't care, and the sooner you are back in the home doing your proper womanly job, rather than pretending to understand politics, the better."

The last word the viewers heard was, "You…" as the screen blanked out. Most people guessed the rest of the sentence was not complimentary to Raymond Burke.

Chapter Eighty-Four

Cheryl Simpson-Walters entered the Oval Office at pace. This was the closest she had ever come to displaying signs of panic.

"Philip, Natalia Morazov is on the phone, and she says it is urgent."

The King shrugged and apologised to the ten people in his meeting regarding climate-friendly agriculture. They all took the hint and filed out of the room. The King waited until the door fully closed, then picked up the phone.

"Natalia, how are you?"

"Philip, I am well, thanks. And yourself?"

"Very good, thank you. How can I help you?"

"President Vasiliev has been reading transcripts of the TV interviews given by Prime Minister Griffin and Raymond Burke."

"I saw the Griffin one, and I too have read about the Burke 'conversation', if that is what it was."

"The President has asked for your thoughts."

"I disliked them both, but Burke in particular lived up to his name."

"Broadly the thoughts of the President. He thinks having contrasting models is good and interesting but loathes the crass politics of Burke. It is true Burke has been a useful puppet, but he is no longer needed. The President wants to see the outcomes which will emerge from the different regimes. Therefore, he would appreciate your support of Griffin until we can see the results. What you do to Burke is entirely up to you, but the President doesn't want to see him on TV ever again."

"Messages understood. The Nostalgia Party has run its course and doesn't need a leader. I am uncomfortable about Griffin's ideas, and I will not let him install himself as a dictator."

"We agree to a large degree. However, let's measure the effectiveness of the USA version of the new order and compare it with the rest of Angloland. On a personal note, I am very concerned that dismissing the talents of women purely based on their gender seems counterproductive. But I would say that, wouldn't I?" she concluded, and rang off.

CSW was sat across the desk from the King.

"They both make my skin crawl."

The King paused for a moment to consider his options.

"Cheryl, please place a call to Prime Minister Griffin. Then, in no particular order, I want to speak to Gemma Newman to reassure her, Raymond Burke to redeploy him, and Grace Williams and Andrea Evans. Given there are no opposition parties, it is important our people can see a demonstration of the power of logic by being questioned by the media."

"Where is Burke being redeployed to?"

"I think an aftersales job at a refuse disposal company. Please arrange for the management to be expecting him on Monday morning."

CSW picked up the phone and asked to be connected to Griff Griffin. Of course, the King could only hear her end of the conversation.

"I know who you are. The former executive officer of the Prime Minister of the USA, unless he comes on the call now."

The King looked quizzical.

"Griffin isn't taking any calls, but she has gone to interrupt him."

There was a noise from the other end of the call and CSW listened.

"Thank you for trying. On Monday, you will be in a call centre. Goodbye."

The King had his mouth open.

"The Prime Minister is in 'repose'. Presumably that means he is making up with Grace Williams in a physical manner."

The King's mouth dropped open even further. He had never been a man of the world.

"Ring her number."

This time the call was direct to Grace Williams' own phone. She made the mistake of answering.

"Miss Williams, I believe you are with the Prime Minister. Would you mind getting from beneath him and telling him to call the King immediately."

CSW put the phone down, and within thirty seconds the King's phone on his desk rang, as Dorothy Harkins put the call through.

"Prime Minister, I have just been talking to the Kremlin. Let me list my concerns:

You preach morality but behave immorally. You act without any level of discussion. You see yourself as a dictator. You are nakedly ambitious. You appear to be so stupid as to think the USA can act in isolation."

There was incoherent spluttering from the other end of the line.

"Please do not interrupt, this isn't a dialogue. You remain in post. You will not associate privately with Ms Williams. You will reconsider the extremes of your policies regarding women's subservience. Finally, do not try to contact your political soulmates in the UK. The UK will operate differently, in order for us to assess the effectiveness of alternative approaches.

"You will understand I don't like you, but personal feelings are irrelevant. Please pass the phone to Ms Williams."

There was a delay, with furtive whispering in the background.

"Your Majesty," opened Grace Williams.

"Ms Williams, I shall be brief. Your affair, or however you would describe it, is over. You are to be allowed to continue to present your TV show, and you will be seen to hold politicians, including Griffin, to account. Now, walk away from the bedroom, and remember, I am listening."

The King cut off the call.

"Cheryl, place a 24-hour per day surveillance team on both of them. Please get hold of Burke."

As CSW was making the call, the King found himself physically twitching. He despised some of the people with their hands on the 'levers of power'.

Cheryl nodded and the King picked up his phone.

"Burke, this is the King."

"Your Majesty," came the weak-sounding reply of the bully facing a stronger opponent.

"The Nostalgia Party is disbanded, and you and Dickenson will be working in a proper job on Monday. Any questions? No? Good. Goodbye."

CSW was chuckling.

"Too harsh?"

"No, perfect."

"Also place surveillance on this guy. I suspect he will prove to be a complete fool. Would you mind talking to Andrea Evans, reassuring her and asking her to do a good job for society?"

"An absolute pleasure," she concluded.

Chapter Eighty-Five

President Vasiliev, Deputy President Bychkov, and the Morazovs were meeting in the President's office. It was the end of another draining day, and nobody was delighted to be there.

"Let's make this quick. Natalia, give us some numbers."

"Gentlemen, the number of people who have met their death due to resisting us after we conquered the world was a relatively low 105,000 until a week ago. Since the announcement of the cures for cancer, there have been hardly any. To be explicit, it is 105. If you consider the number of gangland murders which would have occurred in this period, Russia has, in fact, saved many, many lives."

Bychkov, whilst knowing the answer, turned to Natalia and asked, "Have people emotionally traded democracy for improved healthcare?"

"They have, comrade. Of course, in many parts of the world this is all liberating, as there is no democracy, and they are giving up nothing. Poverty and early deaths are being replaced with stability, great healthcare and guaranteed incomes. What's not to like for billions of people?"

Vasiliev took up the discussion.

"Let's be honest, we have been incredibly lucky with the Americans finding the cures, and then immediately sharing the drugs with us. This has given us cover for the less pleasing impositions. What will we announce next to take advantage of the situation?"

Natalia flicked her papers over to the relevant page.

"Mr President, it seems to me that there is a similar theme regarding Climate Change. Evidence is emerging that the fossil fuel companies, particularly in the Middle East and the Americas, have again suppressed knowledge of the impact of fossil fuels and ways to offset them. It is just like the pharmaceutical companies' behaviour."

Bychkov spluttered but said, "We need to be very careful because it has suited us to promote oil and gas use."

President Vasiliev nodded.

"Comrade, we will just point our stubby fingers towards our previous enemies. At one level, that will help them, as it is clear we are trying to operate openly. Again, the King will be seen as the 'Honest Broker'. We can make this into a very positive statement of intent for the good of humanity. My follow-up question is, is there another topic we could bury in with this positive one?"

Aleksandr Bychkov was at heart a climate change denier but had recently been concerned about the number and ferocity of storms.

"If we are truly going to address this, let's go all in. For example, we have severely limited travel for security reasons, now let us ban food transportation by air, and by any transport over five hundred miles. Of course, this will mean less choice, but it will encourage local farming, the food should be fresher, and it cuts adverse pollution."

Vasiliev was all for it.

"As it should be, but we will hear cries of despair from anyone denied strawberries."

Dmitriy Morazov loved strawberries.

"Will these restrictions apply to Russia?"

"Not at all. As President, I am obliged to ensure the best the world can offer is available to the Russian Empire."

Vasiliev laughed, and the other three joined in willingly.

Chapter Eighty-Six

Herb Andrews threw down the letter which he had received that morning.

"They're telling me that the Jews of Israel are being moved to Oklahoma. They are just up and dumping them on top of us."

His wife, Dolly, was stunned.

"What will happen to us?"

"It says here we can accept the situation and remain here. Those are fine words, but will there be enough doctors and shops, and everything we need, when the population of Oklahoma multiplies? Our alternative is relocation to Wyoming, for heaven's sake. Wyoming! We can make separate arrangements of our own, but who will buy our house?

I am telling you, it's time to walk off into the hills."

Herb and Dolly's daughter, Diane, was listening.

"If I hadn't got my daughter, Cinnamon, I'd be coming with you."

"Calm down, both of you. Am I the only voice of reason? What will really be different? We can assume that the people moving in will be as nice as anyone else and, I suspect, they, and therefore we, will be treated very well. We may get services we couldn't have previously dreamt of."

"It's not that I am a racist, it's just that they will all know each other, and we'll be outcasts in our own homes," Herb replied.

"You really think that six or seven million people will all know everyone else?"

"Obviously not, if you put it like that, but they will have shared customs. What will happen to ours, like our churches?"

"Tell me when you last went to church?"

"Not recently, I admit. Sundays are a busy time for me."

"Yes, for fishing and drinking beer," said his wife, as she tried to finish the discussion, but Herb wanted to say more.

"We only have six months to decide. That's not fair."

Dolly was exasperated by the conversation.

"Do you think the people from Israel want to move to Oklahoma, the home of snakes, spiders, earthquakes and tornadoes?"

"Well, I love it, and I want them to keep away."

"Go tell the King that, you moron."

Chapter Eighty-Seven

"Has our agent sent more news?" asked President Huang Peng.

"There are important new insights," replied Xiu Feng Wang, the Deputy President. "American capitalist companies have been suppressing knowledge of great importance for beating climate change, to boost their profits and personal bonuses. This time the oil-rich Middle Eastern countries are also complicit."

"What is Vasilev going to do about it?"

"Tomorrow is the three-month anniversary of Russia's conquest and, to mark the occasion, Vasilev will address the world again to show what a great and benevolent leader he is."

Huang took a moment before speaking again.

"If we are honest, he is doing a good job of holding his dominion together. He has been very fortunate to be given the ill-health cures, but he has managed it well. Our problems still fester. How many dissidents have we killed?"

Xiu looked at his notes.

"Nearly half a million, Mr President."

"Which is five times the Russian body count. We have given the Chinese Empire the same health benefits, as Vasiliev did give them to us. Why are we having problems?"

"I suspect the decision to prioritise Chinese nationals was the issue, or at least, making it plain that everyone else is secondary was the catalyst."

"I will consider who to blame for that and exactly what it will mean for their career."

Chapter Eighty-Eight

The King was holding an Angloland Cabinet Meeting in Washington. All his Cabinet colleagues were in Washington DC.

"Ladies and gentlemen, welcome. This evening, President Vasiliev will make another statement to the world. I am aware that this will focus on the green commitments he has made."

"Tosh and hooey," muttered Griff Griffin.

"You have a comment to make, Prime Minister?" the King enquired.

"Not at all, Philip."

"It's just that you seem to know the content of President Vasiliev's speech."

"I don't."

"Come, you have had a thought, and I wouldn't want you to waste it."

Griffin's skin turned a nice shade of puce, somewhere between scarlet and purple. He wasn't so unaware that the barb from the King was missed.

"Philip, I had the privilege of working with many executives of oil companies over the years, and a finer bunch of people you will never meet."

King Philip was exasperated by Griffin.

"Were any of these fine people ever contributors to you?"

Griffin's heart rate hit danger level.

"That's not relevant. You are biased, a well-known tree-hugger."

Had it been possible, the other members of the Cabinet would have made themselves invisible. For every one of them, this was one of the most embarrassing performances by a subordinate they had ever seen. Griffin's face had achieved a blotchy plum colour, and yet he hadn't realised it was time to shut up.

"The USA will not adopt any practices which limit the use of fossil fuels. Period."

Philip was in complete control of himself.

"I am sure you have read extensively on the subject. Which experts, who haven't been funded by the oil and gas industries, are you referencing when denying any effects on the climate? Please do tell us."

Griffin had now lost it.

"You think you are so clever, don't you?"

The King sat back and gently nodded his head. If anyone had known him long enough, they would have recognised the danger signs.

"Intelligence is a relative concept. To be honest, in this conversation, I feel like a genius."

"Are you calling me stupid?" blurted Griffin.

"Perhaps 'under-informed' would be a kinder view. To address your absolute statement about applying climate-improving strategies, I would advise you to wait until you have heard from President Vasiliev before making such bold statements of your own."

Philip turned to the rest of the team and smiled. Everyone, including Griffin himself, knew how badly he was now perceived by them all. He was isolated and, therefore, dangerous. The King didn't appear to notice or, perhaps, he was happy with the outcome.

"Prime Minister Griffin, how are the preparations going to accommodate the Jews from Israel in Oklahoma?"

"We have written to the current residents of that State informing them of the possibility and giving them the option of moving to Wyoming."

The King raised just one eyebrow.

"Possibility? You don't think it will happen? You don't think the Jews are facing extermination in Israel?"

"It will settle down and the plans will change," Griffin opined.

"I rarely swear, and never in front of ladies, but I am this close to expressing myself in the most base of terms. You are denying a direct order from Vasilev himself."

"The President and I are very close. He would tell me directly if that was his wish."

"You are rejecting my authority and the directive from the Moscow. How're you going to operate if you're proposing to be that independent?"

In the corner of the room, just behind the seat occupied by Griffin, there was a screen. As the King finished his last question, the face of President Vasiliev appeared. The people looking in that direction were startled. Griffin was aware of a change in body language but assumed it was related to the debate he was having with King Philip. He was, therefore, so shocked by Vasiliev's voice that he literally slipped down his chair, which was unfortunate as it made it seem that he was trying to hide.

"Good morning, everyone. Let me say how lovely it is to see you all and to compliment King Philip and his team for the excellent progress being made. I think Angloland is the exemplar. Having said that, it does concern me there is some outright dissent in the room.

"Perhaps it has escaped some of you that I am all-seeing, or at least, all-hearing. Prime Minister Griffin, you are only in post because I saved you. I wanted to contrast your approach with the style of others. Would you mind telling me the nature of your message to Grace Williams which you sent to her yesterday, please?"

Griffin said nothing.

"A few moments ago, you lost an argument with the King in which you came across as stupid. Having been told to terminate the relationship you have with Ms Williams, it is truly utter stupidity to try to continue and to not imagine you were being watched. Thankfully, Ms Williams ignored you.

"There is now a total breach of trust and confidence in you. Let's put it crudely, your cock rules your brain, which is not acceptable at any level, let alone for the Prime Minister. By now, my security forces are at the Oval Office door. You will be pleased to know I will want your replacement to have a similar approach, but it will not be you. Your next job is as a labourer on a house-building site in Oklahoma. There you will realise I was very serious about relocating an oppressed people to a form of freedom. My final point to you is that I will continue to monitor your behaviour."

James 'Griff' Griffin stood up and, with as much dignity as he could muster, walked out of the Cabinet Office towards a life with little prestige and a lot of physical work, in a hostile climate. He would never see the irony of it.

"Philip, please continue your meeting. I would appreciate your nomination to replace Griffin by the end of the day, please."

The screen went blank. Nobody assumed that President Vasiliev wasn't observing.

King Philip resumed.

"Unfortunate, but a lesson for us all. No one can behave in ways which conflict with our overall strategy."

Chapter Eighty-Nine

The Nolans of Strood were sitting in their lounge when the doorbell rang.

Not untypically, when the bell rang, everyone looked at one another, as if someone had x-ray vision or instinctively knew who was at the door. Quizzical looks ensued.

The bell rang again. This time, Alex made the effort to move across the room to see who was there. It was a middle-aged man whom most people would describe as average. Brown hair, average height, typical build, bland face.

"Alex Nolan?"

"Yes, how can I help?"

"My name is Gordon Godfrey. May I come in, please?" Even Godfrey's voice was non-descript, with no discernible accent, and he spoke in a low volume.

"I'm sorry we are just having a family afternoon and don't want to be interrupted."

Taking his ID from his pocket, Godfrey showed it to Alex Nolan.

"I'm from the Department of Internal Security, and I suggest you *do* want me to come in."

Nolan stepped back and allowed the visitor to enter.

"Good afternoon, Mr and Mrs Nolan. I hope not to disturb you for long. However, it has come to my notice that you have been considering taking some level of action which might be deemed to be unpatriotic. A Mr Robert Harper has been assisting us and, as a condition of his release from custody, has been naming his friends.

"Since then, we have been monitoring your every move and utterance. Now, it appears to me you are not really a proper threat to the order of the nation but, and I emphasise this, you must cease to give any thought to protest or to attempting to live off-the-grid. Is this clear?"

A very shaken Phil Nolan, Alex's father, was the first to speak.

"I assure you we aren't thinking of doing anything."

Gordon Godfrey was disappointed.

"Please do not mess around. We've been listening to you. You *have* given it real consideration, so don't lie to me. I'm prepared to let this go as a warning. However, you will now understand that I will know it if you fart upwind and cause someone discomfort. Is this clear?"

They all nodded.

Godfrey wished them well and left. When asked later, none of them could really describe Gordon Godfrey, a civil servant.

"Now will you listen to me?" asked Isabella Nolan.

Alex scurried off to talk to Jamie Goodwin.

Goodwin answered on the first ring.

"Have you been visited by a Mr Godfrey?"

Goodwin took a moment before speaking.

"I have, and I think we should always be careful what we say from now on. Suffice to say I am pleased with the new Government's healthcare initiatives. This means I am very happy to live a quiet life."

Nolan laughed.

"At least try to speak naturally. If I was listening to you, I'd assume you don't mean what you're saying."

"Believe me I am very serious. I may be emphasising my words, but they are the words which will direct my life from here on."

"Fair enough, and I agree with you. I'm loath to speak in front of my refrigerator."

Jamie Goodwin was aghast.

"Do you really not realise that anything which has a level of Artificial Intelligence can be a two-way process? They are listening."

"Here's to a very sterile life."

"Beer?"

"See you there."

Chapter Ninety

President Vasiliev was in a one-to-one meeting with Natalia Morazov. They had tweaked his address for later in the day and Vasiliev was pleased with her draft.

"Just one more thing, Natalia. We previously discussed potential low-level Robin Hoods becoming local heroes. Has this happened?"

"It hasn't. The truth is that the security forces are too efficient for it to happen. People know there are few chances to break away, and even if they do, the authorities will catch them very quickly."

"That is a shame in one way. In another way, I am pleased we have total domination, but…" his voice trailed off.

"Leave it with me, Sir, and I will consult some colleagues. The King will have some ideas, and such a thing will appeal to his suppressed rebellious side."

"Not many. We don't want to encourage people to think there is an alternative to our society," Vasiliev finished.

"One more thing, Sir. Have you seen the reports of Chinese forces on the move?"

"Yes, Bychkov made me aware, so I have spoken to President Huang. He is very reassuring. They are still enduring unrest, especially in Taiwan and South Korea. The Chinese forces are moving to centres from which they can deploy anywhere very quickly."

Natalia thanked her boss and left to put the final touches to the room from which the Worldwide Address would be made.

Chapter Ninety-One

Natalia Morazov went directly to her office and rang King Philip, or at least she rang her friend Cheryl Simpson-Walters, whom she knew would be with, or near, her boss.

"Good morning, Cheryl. Are you with the King?"

"I am. Do you want to speak to him? We are in a brief recess between meetings, so there is nobody else here."

"Brilliant. Use the speakerphone, so you are both in the chat."

"Good morning, Natalia," said Philip, entering the conversation. "How can we help?"

"Firstly, as you know, the President was pleased with your nomination of Yvonne Long to be Prime Minister of the United States. Her record as a hardline Republican and Southern Baptist means she has the right profile."

The King replied, "I have given her a clear remit, to create contrasts in approach to governing the country compared to the others. But at the same time, I have made it very clear the reasons there has been so much turnover of leaders in the USA. She gets it. She isn't ambitious for herself and has a very stable relationship."

"That is exactly as we want it. Now let me set you thinking about another small problem. Vladimir Vasiliev is delighted that our security forces have been so efficient and doesn't want wholesale resistance. However, it seems too good to be true. Surely, there are some independent spirits out there trying to live outside of the system. It would be good if there were a very small number of rebels through whom the general population could feel free, vicariously."

The King considered the concept Natalia had proffered.

"That is an interesting proposition. I can see the value, and if it gets out of hand, we could very quickly terminate his or her time in the wild, thereby sending out a serious message."

Natalia was very impressed that the King had grasped the notion so quickly.

"How could we facilitate such an idea?"

CSW was keen to join in.

"I saw a report yesterday which indicated some disquiet in certain areas. Let me make some calls. Obviously, we don't want it to appear sanctioned, but we could look the other way for a while."

Philip hadn't seen that paper but was on board.

"Specifically, where might this be?"

"Not surprisingly, in Oklahoma, where there is nervousness about six million Israelis being inserted into the State. Leave it with me."

Natalia Morazov disconnected.

CSW rang a number to ask for the details of a particular sheriff near Chickasaw, Oklahoma, who had been referenced in the report she had mentioned to Natalia and Philip.

"Do you want to listen?" CSW asked Philip. When he nodded his desire to do so, she called. At the second ring, Sheriff Wayne answered.

"Good day, Sheriff. This is Cheryl Simpson-Walters here. Do you know who I am?"

There was a long pause and CSW could hear the change in the breathing patterns of the person on the other end of the line. Finally, he replied.

"I do. You are now a very well-known person in this country. Should I be concerned that you have rung me?"

"Not at all. I need you to help me by thinking of someone who might meet the criteria for a little issue I'm working on. Let me explain. Your name was in a report which spoke to the rumblings from people in Oklahoma, spooked by the imminent influx of new people, and that you have personally sat on people thinking of absconding. I want you to avoid stopping a very small number from living 'freely'. Don't encourage anyone but be somewhere else when they flee. Do you understand?"

"I do, and I even think I know who it will be. May I ask why this should happen?"

"Forgive me, but this needs to be our secret, just you, me, and I imagine you'll be amazed to hear, the King, who is also on this call."

"Good morning, Sheriff," the King said.

This time, the Sheriff did pass out.

Chapter Ninety-Two

After the drama of the last speech by President Vasiliev, nobody wanted to miss the next one. There were billions of people crowded around radios and televisions.

As ever, Vasiliev was immaculately attired and completely composed, a man in control of both himself and his circumstances.

"Good day to you, wherever you are.

Thank you for joining me, especially if the timing of this programme is difficult for you. Over the past four months, there has been tremendous progress. There is stability, there is employment, there is greater and better healthcare, more young people are going to school, and the foundations upon which we live are clearer and more in line with most people's values.

The last time I spoke to you, I was able to reveal the inequities of the capitalist system by showing that pharmaceutical companies had deliberately kept from you cures for many serious medical conditions. They did this for personal gain, and for money funnelled into their secret bank accounts. In effect, this was paid for by the deaths and ill health of millions of you. They have now paid the price for these abhorrent acts.

It is a totally legitimate question to ask: what else has been hidden from us?

Well, if your wellbeing is a concern today, we must also be thinking of tomorrow. Our planet is dying and dying at an accelerating pace. The fossil fuel companies have known for decades that their products were the problem, yet they said nothing. Today, I can reveal that they also knew how to solve these difficulties but, as those solutions were expensive and would again affect dividends and bonuses, they used every means available to keep them secret. Those executives, and, in some cases, their families, have now been dealt with by us. Some are dead.

As we combine new solutions with the disciplines that we must all follow, we will gradually turn back the effects of climate change and restore the natural world.

You will be keen to hear the types of behaviours we will all be adopting. Today, I can only give you examples, as these will be developed over the coming months.

We will need to make sacrifices, such as only being able to buy food that is very locally sourced. Food will no longer be transported by planes and ships. As an aside, this will help build the local economies.

There will be very little overseas travel. Your country is your country.

There will be fewer motor vehicles, and they will all be electrically powered. This will be created from sustainable sources. This may mean there being more pylons near you.

Mines are to be closed. Alternative employment will be available for the affected people.

The use of plastics will be minimised, which will improve our health both directly and indirectly. No longer will the food we eat be contaminated by microplastic beads.

Water will be cleansed. The current management teams will be required to deliver decent quality water, or they will face the consequences.

I am sure you are seeing the emerging themes. As I said, there will be sacrifices to be made but imagine a world in which wildlife can make a comeback, and the seas become purified. We will be converting ships to collect the vast amounts of polluting rubbish in our oceans.

We are extending and improving the performance of the railways for both local and national journeys. Again, this is creating worthwhile jobs.

As well as the railways, new employment is developing in agriculture, infrastructure, housebuilding, personal care, retail, warehousing, logistics, aftersales, green industries, and indeed, in so many other sectors.

All I ask of you is a personal commitment. Society is protecting and providing for you, and you will play your part in its delivery.

Occasionally, because of the location of jobs, a small number of people will need to relocate. The State will make those decisions and there will no longer be migration, including illegal migration. Attempting to live in another country without permission will be deemed to be treason, which, at its harshest, could mean the death penalty.

Given that most people want to be with their families, and that we are creating jobs everywhere, there is no need for migration, so please do not attempt it.

You may be interested to know that there is almost no resistance to our new order. I am not naïve, there are people who prefer the old ways, but they are very few. Change has had to happen, and it has generally been welcomed.

Thank you for your time, and I hope you thrive."

Chapter Ninety-Three

The Nolan family heard the broadcast in their home. The lights had been dimmed by Isabella Nolan. When she was asked why she had done it, her reply was that *'they'* were watching. That they were potentially actually only listening did not matter to her.

"It's just in case."

"In case of what?"

"Oh, just in case."

This time, there was no shock as the style of President Vasiliev was now something they recognised, and there were no announcements that affected them directly.

Phil Nolan broke the ice.

"Nothing to worry about. I wasn't thinking of emigrating to Africa. In fact, I think the way things are panning out are quite good."

His wife, Isabella, was relieved.

"At least you've stopped thinking about doing something stupid. What are your thoughts, Alex?"

Her son had been scared by Godfrey's visit.

"I am aiming to be the most compliant citizen in England, and I think we have seen that being well-behaved in their terms is all that matters."

"But what a boring life we are going to lead," Phil said.

"Safe and bland," his son agreed.

Herb Andrews was having a beer with Sheriff Wayne and a few others. It was Wayne who took Herb aside.

"Are you still considering alternative living?"

Herb looked at his friend quizzically.

"I'm not sure I should answer that."

"Fair enough, so I won't press you. Suffice to say, none of my people will be covering the road out of town towards the hills next Sunday."

The Sheriff just walked off, leaving Herb to wonder what that was about.

By the time he reached home, albeit having drunk more beer than his doctor would have recommended, Herb had decided: he was going. The big question was whether to tell Dolly, his wife, or to just disappear. On balance, he thought, I'll just get up, pretend to be going fishing. Perhaps a note left in the linen cupboard would be reasonable.

Now he needed to make some surreptitious preparations. Food, guns, clothes, blankets, tent, torch, batteries, glasses, medication, fishing equipment, lighter, pan, and the list went on.

How to carry it all? Or should he just rough it without the tent and many of the items?

How to hide it all until Sunday?

He was totally convinced it was the only option, as the communists were not going to be benevolent forever.

Chapter Ninety-Four

President Huang and his closest associates had listened to the latest address by Vasiliev together.

"Thoughts?"

"The Russians have been lucky with the good news that they have been able to spread. Having said that, they do appear to have a tight grip on a very large number of countries and people," commented Chang Wei Lei, the Minister for Coordination.

Xiu Feng Wang, the Deputy President, was very pleased to confirm that the appearance of control was accurate.

"Remember, we hear from our agent in the Kremlin. The Russian Empire has expanded its dominion, and the people are behaving extraordinarily well."

President Huang Peng asked, "Before we consider our plans, let me enquire, what is Russia's biggest challenge at the moment?"

Xiu answered.

"The mass movement of the Jewish population from Israel to the USA, specifically to Oklahoma."

"How far have they got?"

"Announcements have been made, security is keeping the antisemites from massacring the Jews, and infrastructure is being built to receive them. They wanted it done in a year, but the skills are unavailable locally. Tradesmen and project management are being moved in. The intelligence suggests it will take two years. Vasiliev has every confidence in King Philip."

Huang mused, "Should we delay our plans until all of this is completed?"

"That is the billion-yuan question. I think we can take over and leave most of the people in their roles, especially King Philip," opined Chang Wei Lei. "And if we wait, might the Russians' technology advance further? This is our moment."

"Chang, are we certain our technology will work?"

"Certain. And as I say this, I recognise the price of failure."

Huang was very pleased with the confidence being shown.

"Shall we say two months from today? Duan, are you sure our troops will be in place?"

"Mr President, over half of them have already been moved to locations from which they can reach their designated destinations within twenty-four hours. The Russians are aware of the movements so far and are fully conversant with the difficulties we are having with Taiwan and South Korea. They are unworried."

Huang then surprised his colleagues.

"Therefore, we must not completely suppress the rebels until after our plan has been actioned. Otherwise, there would be no reason for moving armed forces around the world."

"That is obvious, now that you say it," agreed Xiu.

Chapter Ninety-Five

A month later, Sheriff Wayne and one of his deputies set out to find Herb Andrews.

Herb had heard the drone buzzing overhead and knew what it meant. He was both worried and relieved in equal measure. The reality of the situation was that he couldn't continue to avoid the authorities, so he was pleased when he saw it was his friend Michael Wayne.

"Herb, I know you are nearby. Please just walk out, showing me that you don't have anything in your hands."

Andrews stood up and shouted.

"Michael, I am here, and I don't want to give you any idea I am going to resist."

Wayne was amazed at how close they were to each other, but Herb Andrews had been hunting in the hills for many years.

"Herb, I am going to ask my deputy to pick up all of your kit. Why don't we have a chat?"

The now former fugitive walked slowly over to his friend.

"That wasn't fun. Being a hunter is exhilarating; being the hunted is horrendous. Perhaps I am going to give it up. It doesn't feel fair. I thought you might find me quicker."

"Do you know how famous you are?"

"What do you mean? I haven't spoken a word to anyone since I came out here."

"Everyone in the USA knows of your escape. The problems are now twofold: if I can find a solution to your problem, can Dolly keep her big mouth shut? And I need to be seen to be dealing harshly with you."

"Dolly I can deal with, and I hope you know she wasn't aware I was coming out here."

"Oh, we know she didn't know. She has been quoted in every newspaper in the country and on every TV channel."

"Why?"

Wayne chuckled.

"You are seen as a modern-day hero. You have fought a bear, for example. Did you fight a bear?"

"God, no!"

"The second issue is you ought to be sent to prison in the jungle. However, I know some very well-placed people who would accept it if you and your family were rehoused in California. How does that sound?"

"Unbelievable. How did you swing it?"

"You can never know. When we get back to town, I am going to put you in a cell, as we must be seen to be acting in line with the Kremlin's orders. Tonight, I will move you. Tomorrow, I will tell the media that you have been sent to prison in the Amazon jungle. You will not be able to take much with you, but my influential friends have set up your new home and a new job. I am sorry, but you are no longer Herb Andrews but Henry Anderson. Papers will be provided. Questions?"

"Do I have a choice?"

"Not unless you fancy Brazil's worst jail. Here comes my deputy, who knows nothing of this. I will talk to Dolly."

Two hours later, with Herb in a cell in the local police station, Wayne visited Dolly Andrews and her daughter.

"Dolly, we have captured Herb."

"What is going to happen to him? I have been so worried, but I think I am even more concerned now."

"By rights, he should go to jail in the jungle. However, if you want it, you can have a new life with a new identity in California. One of the problems, Dolly, is you talk too much. I need to know that you will never reveal your true identity. Is that possible? And do not protest, because you are a gossip whose tongue is constantly flapping."

Dolly Andrews was going to argue, but her daughter put her hand on her mother's arm and confirmed that she was the least discreet person in the State.

Still flustered, Dolly said she would try to keep the secret.

"That really is not good enough. I cannot emphasise this enough. If your cover is blown, you will all go to prison, and it is very likely you will never see Herb again."

Gradually, the gravity of Wayne's words sank into Dolly's consciousness.

"I will be silent. When would we move?"

"Tonight. Pack nothing except medication and the most personal items. Everything else will be there for you when you arrive in California."

"What about me and my daughter?" asked Diane Heaton.

"Your choice, but it is the two of you, no husband or lover."

"Let's do it, Mum," urged Diane, knowing it would solve another problem at the same time in her own life and relationships.

"Let's. It could be the very best thing that has ever happened to us. A new start. Michael, do you know if Herb did fight a bear?"

Chapter Ninety-Six

Accompanied only by their interpreters, Presidents Vasiliev and Huang were on a conference call.

Vasiliev opened.

"My friend, I hope you are well. How are the troubles in Taiwan and South Korea going?"

"Firstly, I would like to stress how grateful I am for your support for the Chinese Empire and for sharing the scientific breakthroughs. Our forces are gaining control. I want to have harmony, so I am trying to avoid even more bloodshed if possible."

"A sensible approach, but I would advise you to take any action you feel is necessary to retain power. You cannot be seen to be weak."

"I am considering my next move. How long has it been since you took control of the whole of the world, excepting the Chinese Empire, of course?"

"It will be six months next week."

"And what do you think is the biggest learning point?"

"I will be frank with you, my friend. We have been incredibly lucky to find the cancer cures and the like. However, again almost by chance, we have appointed some great people. The most obvious is King Philip to lead Angloland, but there are others as well."

"Why is Philip so successful?"

"A number of factors, such as he isn't ambitious for himself, he has made good appointments, albeit the arrogance of some American politicians and businesspeople has surprised us, and he is very intelligent."

"Fascinating. Of course, we only see information in the public domain, so this is useful for me. I need to think about my future nominations for senior roles, bearing this advice in mind."

Vasiliev continued, "One area where we can really cooperate is climate change. If either of us isn't committed, it will undermine the efforts of the other. Now that we have eliminated the need to make great profits without considering the long-term effects, we can create a much better physical world. In the same way that China has always thought in a timeframe of a hundred years or more, the whole world can plan for the future."

Huang smiled broadly and in a collegiate manner.

"I couldn't agree more. What are you proposing?"

"I thought a conference for all of our national leaders so that they can see our mutual convictions."

"When?"

"I suggest in three months' time, to allow us to orchestrate it properly."

"Our people can coordinate."

Vasiliev had one more thought to pass on to Huang.

"Our psychologists had predicted, and I had been doubtful, that once the new order had settled, the people who had been resisting because they liked the status quo are now the most fervent defenders of the change; it is their new status quo. It doesn't take people long to adapt or, perhaps another way to see it, it is their alternative security blanket."

Huang was intrigued.

"Even when there has been violent resistance?"

"We have been lucky that there hasn't been as much resistance as there has been factional disorder, so I am not sure I can comment on that sort of situation. Maybe, for you, it will occur when order is restored, and the people see this is the way to lead safe lives."

"I must look into this with our scientists but, my friend, I really appreciate all of the thoughts you have shared today."

Chapter Ninety-Seven

The announcement from the Government in The New York Times was brief.

After a very short hunt for the recalcitrant Herb Andrews in Oklahoma State, he was captured yesterday. He was in a very bad condition after four weeks in the wilderness.

Mr Andrews was executed last night, and his family have been incarcerated for a number of years, depending upon their behavioural transformation. A court will decide at its convenience.

There was no glory in Andrews' flight, and the messages are very clear.

As fast as news of Herb Andrews' adventure crossed the world, the fatal end zoomed around the globe many times faster. People were devastated; he wasn't Robin Hood, he didn't carry out heroic acts for the good of other citizens, but he was a figure of hope.

In England, The Times carried the story on its front page. Ordinarily, Isabella Nolan would not buy The Times; she was a Daily Mail reader. Today, she felt compelled to purchase a copy. Isabella read it on the bus as she travelled from Maidstone to her home. It was amazing the way bus regularity and punctuality had improved. Was that better management and systems or was it fear of failure? she wondered.

Arriving home, Isabella found Phil, Alex, and Jamie Goodwin at the kitchen table. They had heard the news regarding Herb Andrews on the television and were glum.

"Do you see what would have happened if you had pursued your brainless scheme to escape?" she asked, almost rhetorically. The Times split into many separate sheets as she threw it from the doorway towards her family.

"Not only would you be dead, but I would be both in mourning and in prison."

Her husband, Phil, just shook his head.

"You are right. This might be life with fewer surprises, but it is life. We are safer and we may live longer. But even if we don't actually live longer, it will feel like it."

Alex Nolan and Jamie Goodwin sat quietly, wondering if they had a future.

But then, Gillingham were at home to Crewe Alexandra the following day. There was always the Hammers to look forward to seeing next week. Maybe they would win a game one day!

Chapter Ninety-Eight

In Beijing, the Chinese Government inner circle was in session.

"Chang Wei Lei, tell me the date we should activate our system and take over the Russian Empire, and control the whole world? By the way, as an aside, I love saying that. At all times we have been looking to protect the Chinese Empire and to fulfil our vision for the world but knowing we can install our culture over the other six billion people is very pleasing."

"Mr President, I could press the button now. We will maintain power for the Chinese Empire but again close down everywhere else. Perhaps the ultimate determinant is the deployment of the armed forces. May I defer to the Minister of Defence, Duan Bai Bolin?"

Duan Bai Bolin looked up from his papers.

"Mr President, as you know, by subterfuge we have been moving our people into place. There are eight thousand planes and four hundred ships ready to deploy the army to the key points. They will move at the same instant that the power is cut off elsewhere."

Huang was aware of the progress but was very satisfied to hear the words spoken out loud.

"Do you know, I actually like Vladimir Vasiliev. It is a shame he must be eliminated. Xiu Feng Wang, are the plans in place?"

"As you know, our agent, who is in the room, will deal with him, although it almost doesn't matter, as our blackout makes him and everyone else totally impotent."

Huang wanted to move forward quickly.

"So, when do we go?"

Xiu was ready.

"At your command, Mr President. May I suggest one week from today, to allow full communications. Taking our lead from Russia, we should do it at 10 p.m. Beijing time, which is the optimum moment for greatest effect."

"Agreed. One week from today is C-Day. C for China's."

Chapter Ninety-Nine

Sokolov was concerned. He looked to Vasiliev.

"Do you trust the Chinese?"

"Huang is like a brother to me. The way we have given him Japan and the cures for cancers means he is beholden to us. We have now agreed to work together on the biggest and most important challenge of them all, climate change."

"There is just something that is niggling me. Perhaps it is the troop movements, although I know there is a rationale. There is a whiff of deceit."

"Old friend, remember we could, if we wanted, just black out the Chinese Empire, but why would we do that?"

"I am sure you are right. Moving on, how are Natalia and Dmitriy doing?"

"Do you know, in our business the most fragile facet is trust. These two young people have delivered everything for me. They are such a devoted couple as well. I feel like I am their favourite uncle."

Sokolov continued.

"I only ask because I hear rumours of disquiet amongst certain sections of the Politburo, that they are treated too well by you."

"They have nothing to fear. They are different to many of our colleagues, in that they deliver on their commitments, and frequently a lot more. Crucially, they deliver for the good of Russia and not for their own advancement. I love them both."

"Mr President, I cannot tell you how pleased I am that you feel this way. We have both seen gossip become a self-fulfilling prophecy, indeed, the purveyors of rumour know it can be highly effective."

"Trust me, Comrade Sokolov, they, and you, have nothing to worry about."

Chapter One Hundred

"What I need is a break, Cheryl," King Philip said.

It was a beautiful summer's day in Washington DC.

"I haven't been in Great Britain since this all began. How quickly could we pack up and go?"

Cheryl Simpson-Walters knew the King's diary without referring to it.

"Over the next week you are receiving a number of dignitaries from around the world, but as technology is so wonderful, after that you could do your business from anywhere, until a month's time, when you are to visit Moscow for the Leaders' Summit."

"Brilliant. The Queen and I will fly in one week. Please ensure that the staff in Buckingham Palace are aware we are coming, to ensure all is in good order."

"Philip! You could arrive there unannounced this morning and find everything in perfect functioning order."

The King was very well attuned to the ways of his British staff and knew CSW was correct.

"Moving on, what has happened to Herb Andrews and his family?"

"Fully settled into their new life in California. There is so much movement that their arrival was barely noticed."

"Next, on to the key issue for us, where are we with the transfer of Israeli Jews to Oklahoma?"

"The Prime Minister of the USA will be here to update you tomorrow. It does appear that she has accepted her predecessor made mistakes and is focussed on the job. My sense is that it is happening, but it is a two-year project."

The King knew CSW was correct again.

Philip went into a fully reflective mood.

"Whilst I am very aware that our words are monitored, I would like to tell you how I feel about the way the world has changed. Please be assured I do not need you to respond. If there are any comebacks, they should all rest with me. They are my thoughts, and mine alone."

"Philip, I am quite clear about my personal perspectives and very happy to share them too."

"Thank you, Cheryl. Your support for the Queen and myself is most keenly appreciated. Let's be frank, when the lights went out last Christmas, most of us thought it was a disaster, and it was extremely uncomfortable. People did die, perhaps unnecessarily, and others are now suffering in prison for crimes which, in other circumstances, would merely be expressions of free speech. Few people in the West would have been fans of President Vasiliev.

"And yet… there is less crime, there are new cures for life-ending diseases have been released, war is eradicated despite a few skirmishes here and there, there is guaranteed employment and no taxes.

"My relationship with the President seems to be equitable, and I strongly believe that we have saved thousands, maybe even millions, of lives by me being personally involved.

"I am missing Britain, despite the luxury in which I live in Washington DC. I have become a politician without it ever being a thought, let alone it be an ambition.

"I have learned a great deal, especially about the psychology of the masses. I might have guessed that people will give up anything if the fear is large enough. We can see from the way the vast majority of the people in 2020 obeyed the lockdown rules during the Covid pandemic to know their natural reaction was to forego freedoms to prevent more deaths. This was also a lesson that politicians can be dangerous, whereas scientists were bringing facts to the table and were lifesavers. Perhaps that is the basis of our success, and why the people who, six months ago, were scared are now big fans of the new status quo. It is truly fascinating to observe."

"Philip, please do not underestimate your influence in the calm and rational approaches we have adopted. You have been a giant amongst men, a leader, not a manipulator; a pragmatist, not a schemer. The world has seen it, and the people who matter appreciate it. None of us can rebel, but I do believe we have earned the right to express an honest opinion. We can and will do a great deal more to improve society and the manner in which people go about their daily lives. Most importantly, they are alive."

"I suppose my questions to myself are, what will happen next? What is the ultimate future? What can change and how do we make any changes? The typical days of the citizenry are ordered and safe. How can any individual genuinely achieve happiness and, to use the jargon, self-actualise? And all of this when there is scepticism about people's motives and possibly too quick to punish lateral thinking."

CSW had, without realising it, sat down in front of the King. It seemed to happen a lot when there were deep-thinking discussions. Clearly, thinking was exhausting.

"I know you are not challenging the situation. Does mankind need to be intellectually stimulated, or are most of us followers rather than initiators?"

"We must return to this over the next few weeks. We must have ideas to proffer which balance keeping people thoughtful without becoming rebellious. Who would have thought I would be a friend of Vladimir Vasiliev?"

Chapter One Hundred & One

The weather in Beijing was unseasonably and unreasonably hot. Across the city, people and animals were seeking any respite from the direct glare of the sun. Even for those used to hot summers, this was extreme. Thanks to the careful release of information from the State, there were very few who weren't clear that this was due to man-made climate change, and especially that it was due to the behaviours of the capitalists in the West. Thank heavens for the enlightened leadership of China's Communist Government.

The head of the Chinese Government was on a video call to the top fifty or so members of the Party hierarchy. President Huang Peng was outwardly calm, but he had never felt more nervous. If this went badly, he wasn't just out of power; his enemies within the Party would see him die. The same fate would await his colleagues and their families. On the other hand, if he succeeded in one day's time, he could expunge all threats to his position of total dominance. He knew now how President Vasiliev had felt six months ago. Now Vasiliev was certain he was one hundred per cent safe, a lesson he, Huang Peng must learn immediately and pre-empt any challenge. Vasiliev had been a friend and a fool in equal measure.

"My friends, thank you for coming on this call. As you know, on 25th December last year as described by the West, Russia took over the world. Graciously, President Vasiliev ceded a number of territories to the Chinese Empire, including Japan and Taiwan. Even more generously, Vasiliev allowed us access to the now known cures for many serious diseases.

You may not be aware that at that time China was very close to having the same technology that Russia used to conquer the world. Russia was a matter of weeks behind China. As it happens, I think Russia has done all of the dirty work, bringing order to a much larger area of the world.

I spoke to Vladimir Vasiliev only last week, and again he was gracious enough to give me some very helpful insights into controlling large populations. You know we have had trouble in various places within the Chinese Empire, and we will be applying some of his learning. There will either be acceptance of Chinese control, or we will impose very harsh terms on the local populations.

Let me move on, because this isn't a lesson based on hindsight. Today is truly the next momentous day in the history of the world. For millennia, this date will be written about by academics and historians. Today, the Chinese Empire assumes responsibility for ruling the whole world."

The expressions on the faces of the men, and again it was all men, changed. They ranged from disbelief to euphoria. Behind the smiles and laughter, for some of Huang's 'colleagues' there was an almost immediate calculation of the implications, especially if it all went badly wrong.

"In one hour's time, the world beyond the Chinese Empire will be plunged into blackness, in just the same way that it was last December. The difference this time is that we will be in control, and Russia will be subsumed by us.

Our troops are in place, and over the next three days will move into strategic positions. The Russian leadership will be expunged, and we will impose our rule literally everywhere.

You may feel slightly disappointed that you are only hearing about this now, and please accept my apologies. You will know that only by keeping knowledge of our plans to the smallest possible group have we been able to keep this a secret. We know Vasiliev has no idea of this because we have an agent in the room."

At that moment, there was a spontaneous outbreak of applause and table-thumping which lasted for more than two minutes and only stopped when Huang put up his hands in acknowledgement of the acclaim being heaped upon him.

"There will be a tremendous amount of work to do as we apply our principles and laws. Everyone on this call will have increased roles. This is the moment the Chinese Empire has been working towards for centuries.

Over the next few hours, you will be given a great deal more information and updates, because the button is pressed in less than one hour's time. It is now!"

Chapter One Hundred & Two

King Philip fastened his seat belt as they prepared for take-off in Air Force One. Alongside him, Queen Priscilla and Cheryl Simpson-Walter also buckled up. Each of them had a three-seater sofa which reclined. It was the ultimate in comfort. The King insisted on basic safety measures, as all flights were subject to turbulence and other natural forces.

Philip was still in a reflective mood.

"I really am looking forward to seeing England again. Are you excited, Priscilla?"

"To finally see my children and grandchildren? I must say that I am. Duty is all fine and good, but our lives have taken us in directions I could not have imagined."

"Well, in four hours we will be in London. I understand the whole family is joining us for dinner. Prior to that we can have an hour with the youngsters before the nannies prepare them for bed."

Queen Priscilla had a contented look on her face. CSW was almost jealous of the intimacy the royal couple showed each other. She also felt like an intruder in their togetherness.

"Cheryl, how are you?" asked the Queen.

"Very good, thank you. I hope being in America hasn't been too taxing, but please believe me, the impact the two of you have made is incalculable. So many lives saved, so much good done."

Over the intercom, the captain's voice interrupted the dignitaries.

"Your Majesty, we are taking off now, with your permission."

The King pressed the connecting button.

"Please proceed, Captain."

Take-off was at 8.15 p.m. Moscow time, midday in Washington DC.

Chapter One Hundred & Three

Mikhail Sokolov had been in Ankara, meeting with Mehmet Akbas, President of Europe. Boris Gusev was in Tehran, meeting Ayatollah Ahmad Shirvani, Supreme Leader of Greater Iran.

Almost simultaneously, both Russian power brokers received urgent summonses to return to Moscow. Their abrupt departures unsettled their hosts, but within an hour each man was airborne, with arrival in the capital projected for 10 p.m. Moscow time.

This was unprecedented. Adding to their unease was the enforced silence between them; strict confidentiality meant they could not discuss the matter until they were face-to-face.

The aircraft carrying Sokolov and Gusev were well-appointed, though far from the opulence of Air Force One.

Sokolov, the deeper thinker of the two, sat staring ahead, mind churning over possible scenarios. Was President Vasiliev ill? Was there a major uprising, perhaps in Africa? Or, unthinkably, was China preparing to flex its muscles? Whatever the cause, he needed to anticipate the consequences and consider pre-emptive measures.

His first instinct would be to urge Gusev to place all forces on high alert. That would be his strongest recommendation the moment they met, unless, of course, the President had already acted.

And if the President had to be replaced temporarily? Bychkov was next in line, but what support would he need? Who would become Deputy President? Could there be plotting within the Politburo? Who would dare, and would they have the necessary backing from many people?

Sokolov realised he had a hundred questions but didn't even know what the emergency was. With nothing to do until they landed, he leaned back, forcing himself to rest before the storm broke.

Boris Gusev, by contrast, took a more phlegmatic view. The lack of information was frustrating, but he channelled his energy into poring over paper charts detailing troop positions and proposed movements.

He intended to be fully prepared for any discussion with the President. His working assumption was that it concerned the suppression of a major rebellion or escalating tribal conflict, most likely in Africa.

The best thing I can do, he thought, is have a sleep, so I am primed for any circumstance.

As an old soldier, Boris Gusev could sleep anywhere and could always drop off in an instant. He closed his eyes and he let himself drift quickly into a dreamless Neverland.

Chapter One Hundred & Four

With Sokolov and Gusev in transit, President Vasiliev was only able to summon Aleksandr Bychkov, Dmitriy Morazov, and Dmitriy's wife, Natalia.

Natalia was the last to arrive. She had been in conversation with several African Presidents when her phone buzzed. The message was brief, even curt:

Come now. Use the rear private entrance to save time with security. Something is happening in China.

Natalia Morazov dropped off the calls without explanation and ran.

Using Vasiliev's private door helped as there were no checks through which to pass, and she burst into the room at 8.50 p.m., Moscow time.

President Vasiliev turned to see his favourite aide enter.

"Natalia, join us, and thank you for coming so quickly."

Natalia nodded to Bychkov, then let her gaze linger warmly on her husband.

"What is happening?" she asked.

Vasiliev looked drawn, worry etched deep into his features.

"To be honest between us, we don't yet know. I wish Sokolov and Gusev were here, but they are where they are. China's forces are moving, and Huang hasn't returned my call. I am fobbed off with excuses. Normally Huang would rush to take my call because he knows I could black out the Chinese Empire entirely. Couldn't I, Dmitriy?"

"You could, with just two days' notice, Mr President."

"Dmitriy, please move quickly to prepare us to take over China. Aleksandr, what is your opinion?"

Bychkov looked as if he had aged ten years in a day. It had been his task to bring the President the first troubling reports, always a delicate balance. Speculation was one thing: deep-seated fears another. Knowing when to escalate was tricky. But two hours earlier, he had laid out the facts, and together they had considered the implications. It was then that the Morazovs had been summoned.

"What else should we do?" Vasiliev asked.

At that moment, the world fell into darkness. All power was lost.

Without hesitation, Natalia slipped on night-vision glasses concealed in her jacket pocket. They cut through the pitch-black room with ease. To her right sat Aleksandr Bychkov; ahead of her, President Vasiliev; to her left, Dmitriy.

"What has happened?" demanded Bychkov, until now considered the world's greatest spy.

Natalia, now holding her pistol fitted with a silencer, turned and, without a word, shot Bychkov once in the head.

The President jolted in shock.

"What was that? It sounded like a shot."

"Mr President, you are one of my absolute heroes, but ultimately, you have been weak. The Chinese Empire has learned its lessons and will now rule the whole world. Please… forgive me."

President Vasiliev died without ever truly understanding what had just happened.

Natalia turned to her husband. "Dmitriy, you are truly the love of my life. But there are greater matters at stake than personal feelings. Please forgive me. I will suffer for this moment forever."

Even though he was sitting in pitch darkness, Dmitriy Morazov closed his eyes. Life had just lost its purpose. He didn't hear the gun fire or anything else, ever again.

In the final irony, his blood was the same colour as his socks.

www.ingramcontent.com/pod-product-compliance
Lightning Source LLC
Chambersburg PA
CBHW052009070526
44584CB00016B/1680